PROCEDURE IN THE
CANADIAN HOUSE OF COMMONS

CANADIAN GOVERNMENT SERIES

General Editors

R. MacG. DAWSON, 1946–58

J. A. CORRY, 1958–61

C. B. MACPHERSON, 1961–

Procedure in the Canadian House of Commons

W. F. Dawson

UNIVERSITY OF
TORONTO PRESS

TO THE MEMORY
OF MY FATHER

DURING THE LAST FEW YEARS more public attention than usual has been focused on the procedure of the House of Commons. It is odd, therefore, that no study has yet been made of the rules and practice by which the House governs itself. There are handbooks for the member of Parliament, but virtually no attention has been paid to the question of how the rules of the House have developed since Confederation. As a result, the material available for research is scarce, and there is little to help the student outside of the official records of the House.

Three authors must, however, be mentioned, as their names have become synonymous with Canadian parliamentary procedure. They are Alpheus Todd, Sir John Bourinot, and Arthur Beauchesne. In 1840, Alpheus Todd, at that time Assistant Librarian of the Legislative Assembly of Upper Canada, published his book *The Practice and Privileges of the Two Houses of Parliament*. It was a study of British parliamentary government and was prepared for the guidance of the Assembly of Upper Canada. Forty-four years later Sir John Bourinot, who became one of the early clerks of the House, published the first edition of his work on procedure. This volume was a sharp change from Todd's. It was a work on current Canadian procedure designed to help Speaker, Clerk, and member in discussions on points of order. Obviously Bourinot's work fulfilled its purpose, for it went to four editions. Nevertheless, as a source of ready reference for members of the House, it was too cumbersome, and in 1922 Arthur Beauchesne, later Clerk of the House, produced a small compilation of the standing orders of the day and a collection of citations from various authorities designed to facilitate their interpretation. This book, entitled *Rules and Forms of the House of Commons of Canada*, has also gone into its fourth edition, has grown in size, but has changed little in content and not at all in its form.

Beyond these three standard works Canada has produced little of significance on procedure. Texts on government discuss it only very briefly, with occasional inaccuracies quite understandable in view of the complicated nature of the subject. A literature on the workings of

Parliament which contains only two items—Gemmill on parliamentary divorce and Alfred Todd on private bill procedure—can hardly be called extensive, but with the publication of Norman Ward's *The Public Purse* a notable stride forward has been taken.

This book proposes to take another step in the same direction. It is emphatically not meant to be a day-to-day reference book to be consulted by a member when he wishes to raise a point of order, or by the procedural expert in the House when he takes issue with his fellows on a minute point. But if the book is not meant to be so immediately and severely practical as that, it is quite definitely intended to be useful in a less direct way and in a larger sense. An attempt has been made here to survey the whole field of Canadian procedure historically and analytically, to establish what the procedure of the House was in 1867 and to trace its slow development—its evolvement through principles, traditions, rulings, and precedents—to the present time. A particular interest has been taken in depicting how the House operates in practice as compared with how it is believed to operate in theory. Certain weaknesses in the procedure of the House have revealed themselves, and suggestions have been made for possible remedies. Quite aside from these explicit recommendations, it is hoped that a concentrated examination of this kind will provide a new perspective on procedure both to those who are caught up in the day-to-day functioning of the House and to those, both in the House and outside it, who are concerned about larger, more distant implications.

It is necessary to go beyond the quibbling over detail that goes on in the House and realize what procedure means to the whole parliamentary system. It is conventional to refer to our great traditions inherited from Great Britain and assume that these will protect the Government from obstruction and the Opposition from being trampled by a majority. Experience has shown that tradition is not enough, either in Great Britain or in Canada. We have the tradition of centuries as a foundation on which to build. We have also added new rules to take care of new conditions. Together these operate to guarantee the debate in Parliament which we consider necessary and to ensure that the Government will be subject at all times to effective scrutiny by the representatives of those in the country who do not agree with its policies. Our whole governmental system is based on the responsibility of the Cabinet to the House of Commons. It is the rules of the House that make this responsibility a reality.

Because the book is not intended to be a handbook it deliberately avoids minutiae, and tries rather to show procedure as an active force. I regret that some problems of exposition cannot be avoided, however. It is necessary for instance to use many technical terms which are not familiar to those outside of Parliament. Unfortunately, the rules of the House cannot be understood without some knowledge of parliamentary jargon. To assist the reader in understanding these unusual terms and procedures an attempt has been made, particularly in the early chapters, to cross-reference the more unusual of them so that a full description may easily be found.

It is more difficult to justify the arrangement of the chapters, and undoubtedly many will wonder why a discussion of Government bills must wait until nearly the end of the book. The only answer is that procedure is not a single thread; rather it is a network of threads, connecting only at intervals, but all depending on one another to a great extent. I have begun with a discussion of the general problems of procedure, a description of the constituent elements of procedure in Canada and an account of how they are changed. Following this are two chapters which do not seem on the surface to have any real connection with the general theme of the book. But the Speaker and privilege are central to all procedure, and without some knowledge of them the rest loses much of its meaning. With chapter 5 the discussion of procedure begins by setting out how the House arranges its time during the sitting day. The nine chapters that follow could, after this beginning, be arranged in numerous combinations. Some naturally go together, such as the chapters on motions and divisions. With others, there is no real, direct connection. The reason for arranging them as they are is simple—the general features of procedure have been considered first; the specific parts have been left to the end. Thus any discussion of the passage of bills must depend to a great extent on a knowledge of motions, divisions, committees, and the general rules of debate; any attempt to describe the passage of bills before dealing with these other elements would result either in confusion or in repetition. I can only hope that the arrangement used will prove to be reasonably satisfactory.

While this volume was in the hands of the printer a committee on revision of the rules reported to the House and had its recommendations adopted. These revisions have been noted in the text, but extended comment has, of course, not been possible. The changes, though small in themselves, clearly point up the divisions in the mind of the ordinary member of Parliament. On the one hand the members recognized the need for a drastic shortening of speeches on certain occasions and a narrowing of their opportunities for debate on the budget and the Address in Reply. On the other hand they took what can only be considered a retrograde step by reviving the pre-1955 question period which was both tedious and useless. This reversion may be the price that had to be paid for progress in another direction but the House should take care in the future that it does not lose more than it gains in such revisions.

The obligations which I have incurred in the writing and production of this book are numerous. The Social Science Research Council of Canada provided a pre-doctoral Fellowship, and Nuffield College a Studentship for study in Oxford. My appreciation for collective services must go to the staffs of the Parliamentary Library and Public Archives in Ottawa and Rhodes House Library in Oxford. Numerous friends and colleagues have also contributed time and effort on my behalf. Professor K. C. Wheare read the entire manuscript while it was being prepared in its first version for submission as a doctoral thesis, Professors J. A. Corry and J. E. Hodgetts provided invaluable assistance in transforming a thesis into a study of greater scope, and Miss Jean Jamieson of the University of Toronto Press steered the book through the final stages of production. Publication has been made possible by a grant from the Social Science Research Council of Canada out of funds provided by the Canada Council, and by a grant from the Publications Fund of the University of Toronto Press.

As much of the writing was done while I was Assistant Chief of the English Journals Branch of the House of Commons, my colleagues on the parliamentary staff spent considerable time discussing procedure with me. In particular I must mention Mr. E. Russell Hopkins, Law Clerk of the Senate, and Mr. J. G. Dubroy, Second Clerk Assistant of the House of Commons. Specific reference to these two does not absolve me from my debt to many others, particularly in the English and French Journals branches and the Committees Branch of the House who contributed so many little-known facets of procedure. Their help is gratefully acknowledged.

Finally, I owe an immense debt to my wife. She has lived with this book for years, has criticized it as a political scientist, and has typed its many drafts and revisions. Without her untiring help its production would not have been possible.

W.F.D.

University of Alberta
February 1962

CONTENTS

PROCEDURE IN THE
CANADIAN HOUSE OF COMMONS

PARLIAMENT
AND
PROCEDURE

1

MEMBERS OF PARLIAMENT NEVER WEARY of telling one another that the word "parliament" is derived from the French verb *parler* and that therefore it is their right and duty to talk. In fact, such unrestricted debate has never existed in Canada and has not existed for several centuries in the United Kingdom. Perhaps it is safe to establish the beginning of this attitude in the United Kingdom in the seventeenth century, when the House of Commons was in perpetual opposition to the Stuart government. During this period the British House developed its parliamentary procedure in such a way that no bill or resolution could be rushed through without proper scrutiny. Above all, parliamentary practice, which grew up without written rules, was designed to encourage opposition to the executive. As important as any feature of this period was the constant problem of sharing time. All members had equal rights, and ministers had to compete with private members for the time of the House.

By the nineteenth century in the United Kingdom the House had changed its position from one of constant opposition to the executive to the more familiar position of supporting a responsible Cabinet. Between 1832 and 1878 the House changed its rules so as to give the Government certain rights over the order of business and control of the time of the House. Thus the executive, after a long period, again controlled the activity of the House.

The Irish Nationalists, who brought parliamentary obstruction to such a high pitch of efficiency, made some further changes necessary. The House developed its rules to make it virtually impossible to bring the parliamentary machine to a halt. In this century the rush of business emanating from the Cabinet has led to other changes, and has, in effect, completed the development of the House. The Commons has thus gone from a talking chamber in opposition to the executive, through a period of moderate control, to the present situation where it has again become a talking chamber but one of a very different sort. The difference today, of course, is that the Government has a majority in the House to support it and rules which it can invoke to guarantee the passage of any legislation it likes.

As in so much else, the Canadian House has been spared several centuries of slow and difficult procedural development. In 1867 the Canadian House could and did adopt from the United Kingdom and from colonial legislatures many customs and rules which had already been tried and found satisfactory, not least of which was the rather weak relation between the Cabinet and the House. And as the United Kingdom had to develop its rules and practice to meet new conditions, so also the Canadian House. For the most part, the changes in Canada lagged many years behind those in the United Kingdom. The Liberals of 1913 corresponded to the Irish Nationalists of the 1880's and precipitated the introduction of the closure. The Second World War increased the volume of legislative business in Canada in the way that the early years of the century had done in the United Kingdom, and made necessary more stringent controls on the time of the House. The Canadian House has by now arrived at approximately the same stage as the British House, dominated by a Cabinet which insists on an ever-increasing portion of its time.

Out of this must come a revaluation of the position and importance of procedure in our parliamentary system. The old procedure, based almost entirely on custom with few written rules, was admirably adapted to the use of the private member. What was not forbidden was in order and ample opportunity was given for debate and obstruction. The second period, during which the Canadian House adopted its first set of rules, was little different, but with every rule that was written the Government tightened its hold over the House. The third period, which extends to the present day, is marked by the wide adoption of more and increasingly complicated rules, which limit the private member by outlining more efficient methods of Government control. Contrary to popular belief, it is not primarily the written rules of the House which protect the rights of the private member. The unwritten law of Parliament, which can be found in custom and precedent, ensures that the member of the House may speak. The written rules trim and prune these rights in the interests of efficiency and to the advantage almost exclusively of the Government.[1] Thus the perpetual conflict of parliamentary procedure is a clash between the extremes of unrestricted debate on the one hand, and unquestioned subservience to the Government on the other. It is a conflict in which there have been of necessity many compromises. No Government, regardless of its majority, is willing to expose itself to the charge that it is dictatorial in its relations with the House. But equally, no Government can hope to let debate in the House wander on unchecked.

Through the years, as we will see later, these threads run unbroken. In nearly forty years little was done to hinder debate in the Canadian House. Then gradually the Government asserted its claims to more time, and insisted that the time of the House should be put to better use. Restrictions were written into the rules which limited the motions which could be debated. The Government was given a greater portion of the time available; a rule was introduced which gave it the right to cut off debate on any subject. In fifteen years, further restrictions became necessary, and the length of speeches was limited. The most recent changes have limited the length of speeches still further and have also set time limits on several of the regular debates of the session. Most of these changes have been at the expense of free speech and in favour of Government domination.

But procedure in the House does not stop at the struggle for time. There is one other all-important theme which has become more crucial as the dominance of the Government has grown. This is the assumption that the opposition should have ample information at its disposal. The procedures in this respect have developed somewhat differently, and the opposition has been given increased powers of scrutiny to use as it sees fit. The question period is the most important feature here. Practice developed the question period and recent changes in the written rules have been designed to make questions more productive rather than to limit the rights of members. Less important are the rules related to the tabling of documents and ministerial statements of policy, both of which are designed to give the House information and which are relatively recent innovations.

The development of the committee system has been, at least partially, a result of pressure on parliamentary time, but has also given the opposition increased opportunities to gather information and to supervise Government operations. Canada has not yet developed a consistent policy of sending Government legislation to committee but in recent

[1]Lord Campion, "Parliamentary Procedure, Old and New" in Lord Campion, ed., *Parliament: A Survey* (London, 1952), p. 144.

years there has been a marked increase in the number of estimates which have been sent for examination.

There is a third, less conspicuous but not less important, part of parliamentary procedure, which finds its origin centuries ago and has maintained its major features intact. This is the method of conducting a debate and the protection which the House has provided for itself to enable it to carry out its functions with reasonable efficiency. Two features, brought to a high degree of development in the United Kingdom and adopted in a modified form in Canada, are prominent. The first of these is privilege—that peculiar addition to and exception from the common law, which protects the House from external pressures. The second is the institution of the Speaker who presides over the deliberations of the House and in whose hands the dignity and decorum of the House rests.

Other features of this branch of procedure are even less noticed but have contributed much to the respect in which Parliament is held. Perhaps the most fundamental rule which the British House of Commons devised and which the Canadian House has adopted is the one that requires all debate in the House to be based on a motion so that debate may always be concentrated on the point at issue. Other customs have also been adopted that contribute not only to orderly debate but also to moderation in debate. All speeches must be directed to the Chair, and should be extemporaneous. Members may not be referred to by name, nor may "unparliamentary" language be used. Above all, there is always the respect of the majority for the rights of the minority, a willingness to allow the opposition more time in debate than its size may warrant, and a desire on the part of the Government to answer argument by counter-argument and by persuasion rather than by votes.

The procedure of the House of Commons of Canada may be found in several places: in the constitution, the Canadian statutes, the less binding rules of the House, custom and tradition, and Speakers' rulings. Not all of these sources are of equal importance, but one has been built on the other until the whole of the present procedure has been developed.

Underlying all Canadian procedure is the British North America Act. Perhaps the most significant portion is the preamble which states that the government of Canada shall be similar in principle to that of the United Kingdom. This was, of course, no great change from colonial times. All previous Canadian experience in procedure had been within the British framework, even in Quebec. The importance of the preamble becomes evident when one notes the omissions from the actual text of the Act. There is no reference in the British North America Act to the most fundamental portions of the British and Canadian systems. The existence of responsible Cabinet government is completely outside the document and rests on tradition alone. Yet responsible Cabinet government lies at the centre of the governmental structure and it is from the assumptions inherent in it that much of Canadian parliamentary procedure springs. We accept the fact that there will be a Government in the House with a programme of legislation and an Opposition which will be given every opportunity to attack it in an attempt to have the legislation altered or rejected.

A grant of money or a tax bill must be looked on not only in the light of the written words which specify that they must be introduced in the Commons and only on the recommendation of the Governor General[2] but also with the understanding that members of the Cabinet are the only individuals capable of obtaining this recommendation, and that they are responsible to the House for the amounts involved and the uses to which the money is put. Similarly, the question period in all its aspects depends on the assumption that that portion of the "Queen's Privy Council for Canada" at present advising the Governor General is willing to submit its administration of public affairs to the scrutiny of private members and the Opposition. Behind the rules which limit debate—the closure and the "previous question"[3]—is the assumption that the Government, so long as it is able to command a majority in the House, will be able to pass such legislation as it wishes. The sparing use of these devices merely emphasizes the acceptance by the Opposition of the principles involved and the natural disinclination of the Government to appear to be neglecting the rights of private members.

Other sections of the British North America Act have a more specific application to procedure. Various sections apply to the Speaker, the quorum of the House, voting in the House, and procedure on money bills. One section in particular is important—section 18, which allows the Canadian House to adopt by statute as many of the privileges of the British House as it wishes.

Three Canadian statutes also have a direct bearing on procedure: the Senate and House of Commons Act, the Speaker of the House of Commons Act, and the House of Commons Act.[4] The Senate and House of Commons Act claims the privileges of Parliament allowed by the British North America Act, relates them to the "general and public law of

---

[2]B.N.A. Act, ss. 53, 54.

[3]For closure see chap. 7, pp. 120–33, and for the "previous question" see chap. 7, pp. 119–20, and chap. 9, p. 171.

[4]R.S.C. (1952), cc. 249, 254, 143, respectively.

Canada," and regulates the examination of witnesses by committees. The Speaker of the House of Commons Act approves the succession to the Chair of the Deputy Speaker and validates such acts as are performed by him in the Speaker's absence. The House of Commons Act is restricted in its application to procedure. It deals with the disqualification of members and their resignations and with the Committee on Internal Economy, and expands slightly on the rules which control the work of the officers of the House.

The most important of these three acts is the Senate and House of Commons Act, which establishes in Canada the same privileges which exist in the British House of Commons. Among these privileges, and the most important procedurally, is the right of the House to regulate its own proceedings. The House in Canada has taken advantage of this privilege and has from time to time set out and modified such rules as it has needed to have in written form. These written rules, which persist from session to session without renewal, are known as the standing orders of the House. They are passed in the House by a simple majority vote and may be altered at any time in the same way. The House publishes them periodically under the title *Standing Orders of the House of Commons*.[5]

In this volume the members will find 119 written rules which cover every aspect of the work of the House from the simple rule (S.O. 75) that "every bill shall receive three several readings on different days previously to being passed . . ." to the regulations (S.O. 83, 84, 85, 86, 88) governing the duties of the Clerk and Sergeant-at-Arms. Many of the rules are vital to the proper conduct of business. Methods of asking questions and making motions are detailed (S.O. 39, 43–51). They specify the order of the day's business and the hour at which the House will adjourn (S.O. 15, 6). Many questions of this sort may be answered by reference to the rule book itself.

Other sections are either outdated or are unnecessary under normal conditions. The rule (S.O. 5) which requires every member to "attend the service of the House" has survived every revision of the rules and yet has not been applied since 1877. Similarly, the rule (S.O. 89) which states that "It is the duty of the officers of the House to complete and finish the work remaining at the close of the session" dates back to the time when there was no well-organized Commons staff to do the clerical work of the House.

[5]Throughout, the term "Standing Order" has been used to denote the current rules of the House. When past rules are referred to they are noted as "Rules" and the date at which they appear in the rule book is used.

The House has occasionally found it desirable to adopt rules of procedure for only a limited period of time. These rules are called sessional orders and are passed under the same authority and in the same way as are the standing orders. As their name implies, they continue in force for only one session and are generally passed to enable the House to do its work more effectively over a limited period. Their content varies considerably, although the most common sessional orders have been those which alter the normal daily proceedings or extend the daily sittings hours of the House. Sessional orders have also been used to clear the agenda in extraordinary sessions. Sessional orders were thus passed to suspend some of the formalities of House procedure at the beginning of the First and Second World Wars and in the emergency sessions of 1930, 1950, and 1956–7.[6] Experiments in procedure may also be tried out through sessional orders before permanent changes are made. This has been done several times[7] although the House has never made full use of this device for such experiments.

Behind these written rules, and vastly more important, is the great legacy of custom and tradition which Canada has inherited from the British House and from the colonial legislatures. As Lord Campion has written: "It would be misleading to say that the standing orders are grafted onto the trunk of practice; they are like shears pruning the overgrowth of leaves and branches. . . . the standing orders everywhere presuppose practice. They are in no sense a code; they are amendments of the rules of practice."[8]

Some of the Canadian standing orders are quite unnecessary, as the practice of the House is so well established that no written reminder is required. A bill would be given its three readings in the House even if Standing Order 75 were removed from the rule book. The same is true of many parts of the normal proceedings. The strength of tradition is clear when one examines the elaborate ceremony which opens a new session. Black Rod proceeds to the Commons and informs the House that the Governor General desires its immediate attendance in the Senate Chamber. It matters little to any member that the traditional knock heard at the closed door of the Commons is no longer made by Black Rod himself but by a parliamentary doorkeeper. The tradition remains, and with it, many of the outward symbols inherited from England.

[6]*Debates*, Aug. 19, 1914, p. 3; Sept. 7, 1939, p. 5; Sept. 8, 1930, p. 5; Aug. 29, 1950, p. 4; Nov. 26, 1956, pp. 6–7; Nov. 27, 1956, pp. 43–4.

[7]E.g., *ibid.*, July 12, 1905, col. 9280; Feb. 21, 1944, pp. 676–91; Oct. 12, 1951, p. 5; Sept. 27, 1961, p. 8975.

[8]"Parliamentary Procedure, Old and New," p. 144.

On the other hand, traditions have grown up which are distinctly local. Divisions are not controlled by standing order and yet the British method of proceeding into two lobbies has been supplanted by a calling over of the names of those standing in their places in the House. A new method of asking questions has been developed in Canada although nothing like it exists in Great Britain. Above all, the position of the Speaker, although partly copied from the United Kingdom, acquired distinctive local traditions when transferred to Canada.

The development of both the written and unwritten rules of the House depends largely on the Speaker's ruling, which thus in itself becomes an integral part of procedure. These decisions, often delivered in the midst of debate, are the most uncertain part of procedure. The standing orders and even the practice of the House may be clear and consistent, but a Speaker's decision depends to a great extent on the individual incumbent. A Speaker with an interest in the rules and a knowledge of their intricacies will make a valuable contribution to a clarification of the procedure of the House. On the other hand, an inexperienced Deputy Speaker or Acting Chairman may give decisions which are both immediately unsatisfactory and a nuisance as precedents. Recent Speakers have tended more and more to defer decisions on complicated problems until they can present well-reasoned and well-documented statements on the relevant precedents and the proper procedure. These are of great value to any interested member of Parliament and to a student of the subject. If the practice is continued, the rulings of future Speakers will gain in certainty and consistency and the procedure of the House will gain immensely.

CHANGES IN
PROCEDURE

2

THE PROCEDURE IN ANY LEGISLATIVE BODY must be constantly changing. Just as the nature of the work of the legislature changes, so also its methods of work must change. Rules which were adequate in the leisurely days of the nineteenth century are no longer satisfactory. Parliament must find new ways of examining the growing amounts of money which are spent each year. It must develop new controls for the publicly owned industries. Above all, the demands of the Government on increasingly large amounts of the time of the House must be met. Canadian procedure has not been completely stationary over the years, but the House has been noticeably slow to reform its rules and practices. Indeed, one of the things that makes Canadian procedure such a worth-while field for study is the fact that Canada in ninety-five years has developed a procedure which is distinctive and which is more than a mere slavish adherence to British tradition. There is no question but that Westminster is still the most powerful single influence on Canadian procedure. The physical aspects of the House are copied: the Government faces the Opposition across the floor of the House; the Speaker's Chair and the Mace bear a close resemblance to those in Britain; the clerks may be found at the Table and the Sergeant-at-Arms at the Bar of the House. True to British tradition there is no formal recognition of the party system. There are only two sides, the "ins" and the "outs," those who support the Government and those who oppose it. The similarity is overwhelming at first sight.

First impressions are, however, deceiving. Even some of these basic British principles have changed in Canada. The Government may face the Opposition across the House, but the procedure of the House has been altered on several occasions to recognize the existence of minor parties.[1]

The bilingualism of the country has also produced profound effects on certain parts of procedure. A linguistic split has always been noticeable. When Lower Canada became independent in 1791 the French Canadians took advantage of their opportunities and both languages became the rule of the Assembly. This insistence was carried over into the Assembly of the Province of Canada in 1841. The Act of Union established English as the only official language of record, but did not forbid the use of French as a language of debate. This clause was repealed in 1845 and thereafter English and French were used for both the records and debates of the Assembly. This provision was perpetuated in the British North America Act. English and French may both be used in the House and all bills and records are printed in both languages. The use of both languages by members is, of course, not obligatory, but the occupants of the Chair in particular find it an advantage to be fluent in both.[2] In practice Speakers have often been bilingual, although in any event the rules provide that the Deputy Speaker shall have a full knowledge of the other language. Because of the bi-racial nature of the country, it has also been necessary, whether from a sense of equity or from political expediency, to alternate French and English Speakers with considerable regularity. The British practice of electing a Speaker for an indefinite period has given way to a tradition which forces the incumbent out of office at the end of each Parliament regardless of his ability.

The federal system of government in Canada naturally gives rise to the question of the relation of members of Parliament to their constituencies. The conditions of local politics and strong provincial interests make it almost inevitable that a member of Parliament should live in the area he represents. There is no legal requirement to govern this, but it is only in unusual cases that local feelings can be successfully ignored and an alien candidate be elected.[3] In practice there will therefore be

[1]Provision has been made for moving sub-amendments to certain motions (*infra*, chap. 12, pp. 213–14). Members may now abstain from voting in divisions (*infra*, chap. 10, pp. 184–6). The Speaker recognizes the leaders of minor parties on special occasions (*infra*, chap. 8, pp. 164–5), and minor parties are allowed representation on committees in proportion to their strength in the House (*infra*, chap. 11, pp. 197–8).

[2]This advantage has become less in recent years with the installation of a simultaneous translation system. Such a system does, of course, provide yet another contrast to the British House.

[3]This is most often accomplished by a Cabinet minister. Mackenzie King, for instance, sat for such widely diverse seats as North Waterloo, North York, and Glengarry in Ontario, Prince Albert in Saskatchewan, and Prince in Prince Edward Island.

a strong tendency for a member to express local views before national ones. Some members do indeed try to put the national interest first, but they are not common. One of these exceptions is Mr. C. G. Power who echoed Burke when he stated in the House in 1939: "A member of Parliament, when he is elected by his constituency . . . is elected, not to be the mouthpiece or delegate of any group or class in his constituency, but to represent in this House the whole people of Canada."[4] Experience has shown this to be an idealistic view. There is no question of a member's being a delegate from his constituency, for this is now forbidden by the Canada Elections Act, but many members accept a limited view of their representative function.

A typical statement of a member is that of Mr. J. M. Dechêne who spoke in 1951:

They [May, Bourinot, and Beauchesne] refer us to Westminster and tell us that once a member is elected for the far-flung constituency of Athabaska, for instance, he is supposed to cease to be a member for that constituency and to become a statesman and a legislator; he is supposed, as a statesman, to consider everything that comes before this House as it affects the whole of the people of this country. But these rules, sir, . . . apply to a country about the size of my own constituency, and in which 45 million or 50 million people live. . . . It takes only a few hours to travel from one end of the country to the other. How can I, with the best of good will, do that? How can you expect the member for Athabaska . . . representing a population of pioneer farmers, ranchers, trappers, fishermen and lumbermen, to come down here and call himself a statesman in order to offer solutions to the problems of Canada and of the whole world? No sir. I deem it my duty to represent, first, the people of my riding of every political faith.[5]

It is possible then to come to the conclusion that the Canadian member of Parliament plays several roles in the House. He can display a praiseworthy interest in national and international affairs. He may be acting as the agent for his party, his constituency, his geographic region, or his religious group. He may merely be following a particular interest of his own. All of these are possible, but a member on most occasions acts in one of two capacities: as a member of his party he follows the policy put forward by his leaders and accepted in caucus, and at the same time, as a representative of his constituency, he puts forward the wishes of his own particular locality. This dual attitude is not, on the surface, inconsistent with a fair degree of statesmanship. Local problems and needs should be heard in Ottawa and it is natural that private members should state them, and should describe the likely impact of various proposals on their sections of the country. This liberty, however,

[4]*Debates*, Feb. 24, 1939, p. 1307.
[5]*Ibid.*, Feb. 5, 1951, p. 79.

can soon turn into licence and the House must be willing and able to draw the difficult line between full debate and parochial politics.

Several unhappy developments in procedure come from this over-solicitude of members for their constituents. Debates on the Address in Reply to the Speech from the Throne and on estimates tend to become long tedious dissertations on the virtues and shortcomings of individual constituencies. Ordinarily members of Parliament are unwilling to send any large number of bills or estimates to committees for thorough study. Few members are willing to give up the opportunity of putting in Hansard, for distribution to their constituents, their views on legislation or their requests for new and larger public works. There is, of course, a fear in the mind of many members that some bills or estimates may be sent to committee, and they therefore insist on sitting on every committee which could affect their constituents. Thus not only are the parties in the House represented on the committees, but the geographical regions and even provinces must also be considered. As a result, those who wish to reduce the size of committees face constant strong opposition from back-benchers of all parties.

The other two possible influences on Canadian procedure—the continental French and the American—have been negligible. There are no signs in Canada of French influence. Quebec has followed British practices and forms ever since it achieved representative institutions and has thus never served as a source of alien traditions. The United States, which contributed much to the federal form of the country, has had only a slight influence which may be seen in the provision of desks for members, page boys to run errands, and roll-call votes. These are relatively insignificant borrowings.

These forces of inheritance, race, and federalism are always at work and are reflected in the outlook and the conduct of the members of the House whatever they do. They can (and have) affected the procedure of the House without formal action. The House has, however, not always been content to leave changes to chance, and has on many occasions seen fit to institute them to meet the needs of the times. Once again, it is perhaps as well to divide procedure into five parts: the constitutional portions, statutes, sessional orders, Speakers' decisions, and standing orders. Each of these is changed in a different way and in only one, the standing orders, is it possible to trace any consistent trend of change.

For many years the portions regarding procedure written into the British North America Act were the most difficult of all to alter. Fortunately a change was necessary on only one occasion and the British Parliament passed the necessary amendment. The British North America

(No. 2) Act of 1949 now enables the Canadian Parliament to amend the few sections of the British North America Act which relate to procedure; it has never done so, although bills have been introduced by private members to make such changes. The small amount of procedure that depends on statute may also be changed by the passage of an act through both houses of Parliament. Again, the need for this has been small and only rarely has it been necessary to pass new acts or amend the old.

Sessional orders by their very nature are rarely altered, as they expire at prorogation. If necessary, of course, they may be altered or removed by resolution of the House. Custom and Speakers' rulings can be altered even more easily. Speakers do not consider themselves firmly bound by previous rulings, although they will give them some weight in their decisions. Even if sustained on appeal to the House a ruling is not necessarily binding.[6] Custom may similarly be changed when the Speaker considers that it hampers the conduct of business in the House.

Amendment of standing orders is a much more serious and complicated affair. No uniform procedure for preparing amendments has been adopted. The final stage is clear enough: standing orders are amended by a motion approved by a majority of the House. Many routes however, may be followed to reach this point.

When the House contemplates extensive revisions in the rules, it has generally found it desirable to set up a special committee to study the rules and recommend changes.[7] The first permanent set of rules for the House was drawn up by such a committee in 1867 and revisions followed committee reports in 1876, 1906, 1910, 1927, and 1955. This method was also followed in the abortive attempts at reform in 1925, 1940, 1944, 1945, 1946, 1951 (twice), 1952, 1953 (twice), 1960, and 1961. But even here procedure has not been uniform. The terms of reference of the committees have varied widely: they have been asked to assist the Speaker in framing and revising rules; to examine the rules and report possible changes; and to consider with the Speaker the advisability of revising the rules. These variations in the terms of reference seem to have made little difference to the work of the committees. One cannot say so with any degree of certainty, however, as the committees invariably meet *in camera* and it is impossible to ascertain what differences there have been within the committees. However, there has

[6]Note the statement of Mr. Speaker Sproule in 1913: "It [the previous ruling] would be a precedent, but if I thought it was wrong of course I would not be bound by it." *Ibid.*, April 16, 1913, col. 7851.

[7]For a description of the various kinds of committee used by the House see chap. 11.

never been any significant difference in the form of the reports which have been presented, and it is likely that the terms of reference have had little effect on the work actually accomplished.

The size of the committees has also varied widely. The smallest of all was that of 1906 which had only seven members. From that remarkably small number, committees have ranged as high as twenty-one members. Again, however, there is no correlation between the size of the committees and the work accomplished. Both of the above committees produced lengthy reports and recommended numerous changes, almost all of which were accepted by the House.

Although revisions of the rules are supposed to be carried out in a non-partisan manner, the composition of the committees follows closely that of any special committee. The significant difference is that the Speaker usually acts as chairman and one of the clerks of the House as secretary. The Government maintains on the committee the majority to which it is entitled by its majority in the House. Revision committees do not, however, appear to have split on party lines and nowadays they customarily present unanimous reports.[8] If such unanimity cannot be reached the committee will not present any important recommendations —a tradition which has undoubtedly retarded considerably the reform of the rules in recent years.[9]

Unanimity is not a long-standing custom. The report of 1925, for instance, does not seem to have had the support of all parties, for as late as June 1926 the Prime Minister announced to the House that he was trying by means of inter-party conferences to eliminate the controversial parts.[10] Similarly, the committee of 1944 which suggested extensive reforms was not unanimous. R. B. Hanson, a leading member of the committee, said in the House that "the report represented a good cross-section of the opinion of the committee."[11] The same general feeling was expressed by Mr. Stanley Knowles when he supported the appointment of the revision committee of 1955: "I urge very strongly that it be recog-

[8]On one occasion the Speaker even refused in committee to present to the House a report approved by only a majority of the committee. *Debates,* June 7, 1956, p. 4817.

[9]The report of the committee of 1951 was a mixture. One section was passed unanimously by the committee but dealt only with the hours of sitting of the House. The second section, which would have limited the length of speeches in the House, was passed in committee on division, although the amendment suggested was to have effect for only one session on a trial basis. Neither section was accepted by the House. *Ibid.,* Dec. 13, 1951, p. 1858.

[10]*Ibid.,* June 14, 1926, pp. 4432–3.

[11]*Ibid.,* March 7, 1944, p. 1244. Five years earlier, however, one member had referred to the necessity for a unanimous committee before any changes were made in the rules. *Ibid.,* Feb. 14, 1939, p. 912.

nized right from the start, not that unanimity must be required for any change, but that there be pretty general agreement amongst the representatives . . . of all parties, before any very serious changes are made."[12] The warning may have been unnecessary; at any rate the committee was unanimous in its recommendations.[13]

The unanimous support of a committee does not ensure that its proposals will be carried out. According to R. B. Hanson the committee of 1944 was unanimous, at least in recommending that speeches in Committee of the Whole should be shortened.[14] This clause suffered the fate of the remainder and was never passed in the House.

The composition of the committees has varied almost as much as the numbers and the terms of reference. Even the Speaker, who would seem to be an indispensable member of a committee on the rules, has been excluded on occasion. The Speaker sat on the first rules committee in 1867. In 1876 the original motion for a committee merely called for a special committee, but in response to a request from a member to conform to what he termed the "usual custom," the motion was amended to include the Speaker.[15] In 1906 and 1910 the "custom" was ignored and the Speaker forgotten, but since that time he has been a member of every committee appointed. It has been suggested that the Speaker might, in future, be relieved of the duty of sitting on revision committees so that he would not be in any way responsible for making rules which he would later be called on to enforce.[16] It is questionable if the loss of his expert disinterested knowledge and his moderating influence on the committee would be sufficiently compensated for by any possible increase in his prestige in the House.[17] The British House has generally found it possible to divorce the Speaker from procedural reform but it seems unlikely that the Canadian Commons will do so.

The Prime Minister and the Leader of the Opposition have also served intermittently on these committees. The Prime Minister sat on all of the committees up to and including that of 1910, while in the same period the Leader of the Opposition was excluded from only the

[12]*Ibid.*, Jan. 14, 1955, p. 182.
[13]*Ibid.*, June 14, 1955, p. 4751. This does not mean that there was not a prolonged struggle in the committee itself, but the final report had the support of all parties.
[14]*Ibid.*, March 7, 1944, p. 1245.   [15]*Ibid.*, Feb. 14, 1876, p. 50.
[16]E. R. Hopkins, "Saving Parliament's Time," *Queen's Quarterly*, Winter 1955, p. 527.
[17]The moderating influence of the Speaker may be seen in the committee of 1955 where he forced the appointment of a subcommittee which broke a deadlock in the committee and enabled a unanimous report to be made to the House. *Debates*, June 7, 1956, p. 4817.

committee of 1867; since 1910 they have appeared on none of the major revision committees. Such leadership as Government and Opposition want is now provided by other prominent party leaders.[18]

The private members of these committees have also often had a thorough knowledge of procedure. As early as 1867 there were two former Speakers of provincial assemblies and a former chairman on the committee drawing up the rules. The committee of 1906 was perhaps the most unusual, as it numbered among its seven members not only the Prime Minister and Leader of the Opposition but also three former Speakers (two of whom had been in the Chair of the House itself) and one former Deputy Speaker. Since then the record has not been as good, but one or two experts with experience in the House or in the provinces have been on every committee. A number of the other members have also shown in the House their knowledge of the rules. Such an interest in procedure will generally ensure a place for them on the revision committees.

A special committee may also be used for more limited reforms.[19] In 1887 a special committee was established to assist the Speaker in a revision of the rules on private bills relating to the incorporation of railways. A similar motion in 1931 enabled a special committee to investigate the possibility of amending the rules and procedure followed in taking divisions. An attempt in 1952 to revise specific rules in this way was converted by a motion of the Prime Minister into a general investigation.

A joint committee of the House and Senate has been used on one occasion to revise minor portions of the standing orders. In 1903 the Senate requested the House of Commons to appoint members of a committee to consider similar Senate and Commons rules relating to private bills. The committee was appointed and its report was adopted by both houses.[20]

The reports of all revision committees are traditionally considered in Committee of the Whole when they are presented to the House, for it is generally felt that the absence of restrictions in debate in Committee of the Whole makes it a more satisfactory forum for discussion of such subjects than the House itself. Again, practice has not been uniform. Extensive reports, when proceeded with at all, have invariably been studied in Committee of the Whole. The report of the joint committee

[18]Recent committees have generally had two Cabinet ministers, a similar number of front-bench Opposition members, and leading members of the minor parties.

[19]See *Journals*, May 31, 1887, p. 195; May 6, 1931, p. 161; April 7, 1952, p. 190.

[20]*Ibid.*, Oct. 10, 1903, pp. 644–6.

of 1903 was also considered in committee. Reports on specific or relatively unimportant points are dealt with by the House itself: the specific and minor reforms recommended in 1887, 1931, and the second revision of 1951 were all passed without reference to Committee of the Whole.

The standing committees of the House have frequently advised the House to alter its rules. On at least six occasions the Standing Committee on Railways, Canals and Telegraph Lines has recommended amendments to the rules relating to private bills.[21] Five times the Standing Committee on Standing Orders has recommended similar changes. The Standing Committee on Miscellaneous Private Bills and the Standing Committee on Banking and Commerce have also suggested amendments.[22] These proposals have invariably related to the work of the committee involved and have affected a limited range of rules. No standing committee under its normal terms of reference could make any sweeping recommendations and so the committees restrict their attention to rules relating to private bills. Such suggestions rouse little interest and are generally passed with little or no debate. Occasionally they are either completely ignored or referred to a committee on general revision.[23]

Amendments have occasionally been suggested by the Government acting on its own initiative. The numbers and names of the standing committees of the House have been altered three times by a motion of the Government and the changes have passed with a minimum of interest.[24] On the other hand, debate may be long and bitter as it was in 1913 when Robert Borden, then Prime Minister, introduced the closure. This is the only occasion on which party divisions have been allowed to influence the revision of the rules. The closure and the two rules which accompanied it were never sent to a special committee or to Committee of the Whole. They were moved by the Prime Minister in the House with the consent of only the Cabinet and the party caucus.[25]

[21]Throughout, the distinction made between the various types of bills is that used by the House in its written rules. "Government bills" include all bills sponsored by the Government for any purpose. "Public bills" are bills introduced by private members to alter the general public law of the country. "Private bills" are bills introduced by private members to grant some special right to an individual or group, such as a divorce or the incorporation of a company.

[22]The Committee on Railways, Canals and Telegraph Lines in 1874, 1883, 1887, 1893, and 1909 (twice); the Committee on Standing Orders in 1874, 1886, 1906 (twice), and 1929; the Committee on Miscellaneous Private Bills in 1873 and 1883; the Banking and Commerce Committee in 1883 and 1887.

[23]Committee on Standing Orders, 11th and 13th reports, 1906.

[24]*Debates*, March 27, 1924, p. 729; Sept. 18, 1945, pp. 244–5; May 30, 1958, pp. 679–703.

[25]Henry Borden, ed., *Robert Laird Borden: His Memoirs* (2 vols., Toronto, 1938), I, pp. 413–15.

Oddly enough, the Government on its own initiative put a motion on the Order Paper[26] in the 1957–8 session for the repeal of the closure rule. The Leader of the House announced at that time that he had no intention of referring the motion to a special committee although it is possible that it might have been discussed in Committee of the Whole.[27]

Only moderate interest is shown in amendments proposed by back-bench members. Their recommendations have covered every aspect of the business of the House. Motions for shorter sittings and different hours have been common, as well as motions for altering the arrangements for private members' days and the disposal of estimates. A lively debate was begun in 1931 on a motion to amend the standing orders relating to divisions, and in recent years several long debates on procedure have taken place on private members' motions.

The fate of motions which have been proposed by individual members —whether front- or back-bench—varies. Those moved by a Minister with the blessing of the Government are almost certain to pass the House. The success of those moved by private members is by no means assured; most of them are withdrawn after debate. The Government is generally not willing to take such drastic steps as are proposed, and will be prepared to ensure the defeat of the motion should it come to a division. A proposer may be satisfied by a Government assurance that the matter will be looked into and perhaps an "arrangement" arrived at.[28] In 1925 three members had their motions referred to the special committee which had been set up for a general revision of the rules. A motion in 1931 was changed and a committee was set up to examine a larger question than the one originally proposed. On one occasion a motion for specific reforms was amended to become a motion for a general committee of revision.

The most notable individual to propose reforms of procedure was Mr. Speaker Fauteux. He drew up a comprehensive series of suggestions relating to the business of the House. These he placed before the House with the statement that it had the "undoubted right to alter, reject or adopt" the recommendations.[29] The report was considered by a special committee which made an interim report to the House and the question of reform lapsed.[30]

[26]The Order Paper (properly called the Routine Proceedings and Orders of the Day) is the daily printed agenda of the House. In it will be found entries for all the business that could properly be considered under the rules on any particular day. For the precedence of business on the Order Paper see chap. 5, pp. 95–8.

[27]*Debates*, Dec. 7, 1957, pp. 2027–8.

[28]For this and the following sentences see *ibid.*, Feb. 19, 1877, p. 101; and *Journals*, Feb. 25 and March 11, 1925, pp. 66 and 114; May 6, 1931, p. 161; April 7, 1952, p. 190.

[29]*Journals*, Dec. 5, 1947, p. 10.   [30]*Ibid.*, June 25, 1948, pp. 679–81.

When one considers the hazards in the path of any change in the standing orders, it is perhaps remarkable that any reforms of consequence are ever passed. The hazards do, however, provide a reason, if not an excuse, for the relative slowness of the Canadian House in making major changes in its rules. The progress of reform of the rules in Canada has been neither orderly nor (in most cases) timely. The House over the years has been remarkably unwilling to alter its procedure until impossible conditions have resulted from old rules. Nevertheless, the gradual economic and social development of the country has eventually been reflected in the changes in the rules of the House as the particular needs of the Canadian situation have dictated.

The first set of rules adopted in the House of Commons in 1867 was not marked by any great surprises or originality. The committee which drafted the rules was instructed to consider the rules of the assemblies of the three federating colonies as well as those of the United Kingdom. The committee merely recommended to the House the adoption of a set of rules which were copied almost verbatim from the Legislative Assembly of Canada. There was, of course, no thought of abandoning the British tradition, or even of altering it significantly. It had been found adequate in the colonies and was never seriously questioned. The principles of British procedure, rudimentary as they were in the light of modern practice, were taken over by the new Parliament along with its rules and have never been discarded. They have, of course, been altered in their details to adapt them to local needs, but there has remained a final appeal to British and not to American or other foreign experience.

Early procedure based itself on the British tradition of the seventeenth century which Lord Campion has described as being "leisurely, ceremonious, cumbersome; . . . individualistic, giving wide scope to the initiative of members and affording no special facilities to the Government; . . . designed to protect the rights of minorities in debate and to encourage opposition to the executive."[31] The natural consequence was not long delayed. For nearly forty years the House carried on unchecked. The period up to 1906 was marked by lengthy speeches, obstruction by the Opposition, and a total lack of efficiency in the conduct of business by the House. While the British Commons appointed six committees between 1867 and 1906 to study its procedure, the Canadian House appointed only one, and even that one did little to improve the situation. This neglect reflected the limited interest of the House and of the population. Canada was still a vast and empty country. Her first forty years were devoted to economic expansion and exploitation. One trans-

[31]Lord Campion, "Parliamentary Procedure, Old and New" in Lord Campion, ed., *Parliament: A Survey* (London, 1952), p. 142.

continental railway was built and others were started; and by the end of the period the great wave of immigration which settled the west had begun. The country was preoccupied with internal development, as shown by the mass of private bills which flooded the House. Along with this preoccupation went the fundamental differences between the two major parties on such basic policies as tariffs and settlement. These differences led to the cherishing of those rules which ensured the fullest possible expression of Opposition opinion on the small number of Government bills, and reforms were carried out to provide more efficient and expeditious handling of the large flow of private bills. In the revision of 1876 few rules relating to the conduct of debates were altered and none of them in any important respect. The House did, however, make substantial alterations in its rules on private bills.

Concern over private bill procedure began in 1873 and was to continue through numerous standing committee reports. Publication of notice, fees for bills of incorporation, the time for receiving petitions, and similar questions were constantly being reported on by standing committees and consideration of them absorbed the time, if not the interest, of the House. Little conflict was aroused, but the need for reform was recognized and the House responded to it.

Few rules dealing with the business of the House itself were altered in this period. The House changed the arrangement of the Order Paper, added a Deputy Speaker, and adopted several sessional orders as standing orders. Nothing further was done. Members presented resolutions from time to time which were designed to limit the length of sittings and speeches, but all were dropped after debate. Determined obstruction compelled substantial amendments in Government bills on at least two occasions,[32] but no move was made to increase the control of the Government over the House, or to speed up the work of the House. The House, therefore, moved towards the revision of 1906 with practically the same set of rules as it had adopted in 1867.

Between 1906 and 1913 two general revisions of the rules were carried out. In the report of 1906 the committee showed a growing realization of the changing needs of the House. Many of the rules dealing with private bills were amended but several methods of blocking or slowing progress on Government bills were also eliminated. Government business was given precedence. A more stringent rule was adopted which allowed certain questions to be treated as notices of motions and transferred to a different section of the Order Paper.[33] No member was to

[32]The franchise bill of 1885, and the Manitoba school bill of 1896.
[33]For the definition of a notice of motion see chap. 5, p. 96 n.

interrupt without permission while another was speaking; this may seem an insignificant change but the Prime Minister himself pointed out that there had been a tendency for members to obstruct business by this method.[34] Most important, the right of a member to move the adjournment of the House was severely curtailed. Up to 1906 this right was practically unrestricted and could be used at any stage of proceedings in order to debate matters of importance to individual members, but in that year it was eliminated and the present Standing Order 26 was adopted, limiting the moving of the adjournment to certain times and even then only in order to debate matters of urgent public importance. Minor amendments were also made to clarify procedure on public bills.

The revision of 1910 tended in the same direction. It became possible to present a petition by filing it with the Clerk of the House instead of presenting it in person on the floor of the House. The question period was considerably altered and more perfunctory answers to questions became possible. Two new provisions were added which enabled a Minister merely to hand an answer to a question to Hansard to be printed unless a member specifically asked for an oral answer, and also made it possible for the Minister at his discretion to turn a question into an order for a written answer to be tabled in the House at a later date. A member was enabled to get information more quickly by a new rule which allowed unopposed notices of motions for the production of papers a special place on the Order Paper ahead of those on which debate was expected.[35] On the other side, two rules were added to encourage speaking to the point in debate: one required relevancy in Committee of the Whole; the other gave a wide power to both the Speaker and the Chairman to enforce relevancy in the House or in Committee of the Whole.

The changes of 1906 and 1910 had reflected the increasing amount of Government work which the House was expected to do, but these amendments were not enough, and in 1913, which may be taken as the most important single year in the history of Canadian procedural reform, the House put into the hands of the Government the power needed to control the business of the House. In response to a Liberal filibuster on a Conservative naval bill, the Prime Minister introduced a motion which contained three new rules.[36] The most striking was the closure, which enabled the Government to end debate on any subject by a motion in

[34]*Debates*, July 9, 1906, col. 7469.
[35]For a description of notices of motions for the production of papers see chap. 8, pp. 160–4.
[36]*Debates*, April 9, 1913, cols. 7388–9.

the House after twenty-four hours' notice. The other new rules were less drastic, but have contributed more materially than the closure to the efficiency of the House in recent years. The new rule 17A limited the number of motions in the House which could be debated. It listed a small number of motions which were debatable and ended with the clause "all other motions shall be decided without debate or amendment." The other rule (17C) restricted debate still further, but only on a limited number of motions. Hitherto it had been necessary to make a formal debatable motion whenever the Government wished to discuss estimates or budget resolutions, with the result that at the end of the session nearly every day there was one motion which could be debated at length, and during the debate any subject could be raised. This was often done, and these debates could be used effectively to block the granting of supply indefinitely. Under the new rule, the motions for Committee of Supply or Ways and Means were eliminated on Thursday and Friday, so on those two days of any week the Government could be certain that its business would be reached. The rights of the Opposition were preserved but in a more limited form. Every department was still to be introduced for debate in committee only after a motion for supply had been moved and passed and grievances debated on one of the other three days of the parliamentary week. Thus the Opposition was certain to have an ample, although more limited, opportunity to attack the Government, and the Government could be certain that its proposals would at least come before the House for debate.[37]

These three new rules could have opened a new phase in the relations of the Government and the Opposition. They enabled a Government with a majority at its heels to limit debate at any time it saw fit, and to bring any question to a vote after two days' debate. It was more difficult to refuse supply at the end of the session than it had been in 1896 and 1908, and the endless number of opportunities for debate as a bill passed through the House were drastically cut. The hopes for a new era were not, however, realized. Governments have not used their powers to limit debate, and aside from four bills passed with its assistance in the first six years the closure has rarely been used or even threatened.

Between 1913 and 1925 the House rested content with its existing procedure. Virtually no changes were made and few serious suggestions were put forward. However, in these years the foundation was laid for the reforms of 1927. In 1919 one member made a motion for a limit on speeches. Two years later a member suggested a fixed adjournment hour. In 1923 a motion was made to permit a sub-amendment to be moved

[37]For a full discussion of Committee of Supply see chap. 12, pp. 211–16.

to motions for the House to go into Committee of Supply or Ways and Means.[38] This attempt to provide an opportunity for third parties to express their views was defeated at the time and accepted later. Some support could also be found in the House in these years for the idea that estimates should be sent to either standing committees or a special committee for more effective scrutiny.[39]

Increasing pressure from a few members led to the appointment of a revision committee in 1925. A private member precipitated the appointment by introducing a motion stating that a revision of the rules was desirable and that a special committee should be appointed to report on such a revision.[40] The motion was amended slightly on the suggestion of the Prime Minister and the committee was established. Three motions on the Order Paper were also referred to this committee. One member wished an increase in the number of private members' days, another wanted to send estimates to committees, while a third desired a reduction in the size of standing committees. Three months later the committee presented a comprehensive revision of the rules but no action was taken.

In 1927 the Prime Minister took the initiative and moved to set up another committee on revision; in the remarkably short time of one month it submitted its report, which was adopted by the House after several discussions in Committee of the Whole.[41] Few important rules remained unchanged. The general tendency was to advance peacefully along the lines of the reforms which had begun violently in 1913. In particular, the rights of the private members were curtailed by the introduction of the forty-minute rule[42] and an eleven o'clock adjournment. Another old problem was alleviated, although not solved, by imposing a limit on the number of members on the standing committees.

To parallel these new limitations on the freedom of members, certain concessions were made to the back-benchers. The rule which limited debatable motions was amended to permit debate on several motions

[38]*Debates*, Sept. 29, 1919, pp. 646–54; April 11, 1921, pp. 1828–45; March 19, 1923, p. 1299.

[39]*Ibid.*, March 3, 1921, p. 484; April 11, 1921, pp. 1828–45; April 18, 1921, p. 2193; May 25, 1925, pp. 521–39.

[40]*Ibid.*, Feb. 23, 1925, p. 412.

[41]*Journals*, Feb. 11, 1927, p. 103; March 22, 1927, p. 316. The short time necessary to produce a major reform of the rules may be partially explained by the fact that the report was virtually the same as that of 1925. But as there had obviously been difficulty in securing its adoption before, such an accomplishment may be remarkable. It is possible that the two elections that intervened between the reports had eliminated much of the opposition to the reforms.

[42]See chap. 7, pp. 133–7.

which, under a strict interpretation of the rule, had not been debatable since 1913; the House had, in fact, continued to debate them, but only by unanimous consent. The procedure on public bills was changed to make their passage easier. Private members' notices of motions were limited, but in the interests of the members themselves. The third parties were, at long last, given the right to move a sub-amendment to a motion for Committee of Supply or Ways and Means.

Numerous changes were also made in the rules relating to private bills. But these changes were for the most part clarifications of old rules and eliminations of obsolete sections. Private bills had lost the pre-eminence they had enjoyed in the nineteenth century and amendments to the rules regarding them were of negligible importance.

Between 1927 and 1955 the rule which governs standing committees was slightly altered, provision was made for a Deputy Chairman of Committees, and the hours of sitting of the House were changed. Aside from these amendments and in spite of intensive study in session after session nothing was done to bring the rules closer to modern needs. It was not that the House found itself able to cope with its work more easily than before or that it had less work to do. The war was looked on as an unusual period which put heavy strains on the existing machinery, but after the war there was no lessening in Government activity. The welfare state developed rapidly and defence took an unprecedented share of the peacetime budget. The Government was thus collecting and spending far more money and doing far more tinkering with economic and social conditions than ever before in peacetime. Parliament was faced with the problem of doing more work every year in roughly the same time as before and with much the same methods.

The House was not entirely insensible to the need for reform. In 1942 Mr. Ilsley referred to the House as being "more and more on trial at the bar of public opinion." The next year P. J. A. Cardin stated that the rules were obsolete and that there was an "urgent necessity" for a change in procedure; more strongly still, John Bracken, then Leader of the Opposition, described Canadian procedure as being "still in the oxcart stage of half a century ago."[43] Many members individually offered their solutions to the problem either in motions or speeches in the House.

Whatever the pressures, the Commons seemed almost incapable of effecting any widespread change. A motion for a committee in 1940 was withdrawn before the members were even named.[44] A committee in

---

[43]*Debates*, May 26, 1942, p. 2774; March 18, 1946, p. 35.
[44]*Journals*, May 21, 1940, p. 30.

1944 was more fortunate. It was not only appointed but survived to present a substantial report to the House.[45] It was moderate in its suggestions and included such innocuous amendments as a limit on the length of the debate on the Address in Reply to the Speech from the Throne and a restriction on the number and length of speeches which a member could make in Committee of the Whole. It rejected the radical suggestions that estimates be sent to committees and that there should be a thirty-minute limit on all speeches. The debate on the report was abandoned in favour of matters more important to the war effort. In 1945 a motion for a committee was passed but the committee never reported to the House.[46] The committee of the next year advocated fewer changes than the committee of 1944 but was more extreme in the ones that it did put forward. It recommended that the Speaker have the power to suggest and enforce a time limit on any debate. It also approved the idea of sending estimates to committees.

Mr. Speaker Fauteux's report on procedure was yet another extensive collection of suggestions for procedural reform. Among other matters he suggested a reference of estimates to committees, a division of the yearly session into three sections separated by lengthy adjournments, and a reduction in speaking time of private members.[47] The committee to which the report was submitted lagged far behind the Speaker in its recommendations.[48] It suggested limiting the speaking time of private members, but only in Committee of the Whole. It was also in favour of a cut in the length of the dinner recess and the elimination of debate on the resolution stage of money bills.[49]

All these suggestions were ignored and some recent committees have not even been able to submit reports. The changes suggested by a committee in 1951 were shelved although they were both sensible and moderate. Speeches were to be limited to thirty minutes and all members were to come under the new rule.[50] The Government was to be allowed to go into Committee of Supply or Ways and Means without a motion on Wednesday as well as the other two days provided for in 1913, and the whole committee system was to be "re-examined and reorganized."[51]

Four more profitless years followed. Only the hours of sitting and the general arrangement of the business of the House were changed.[52]

[45]*Ibid.*, March 3, 1944, pp. 146–52.   [46]*Ibid.*, Nov. 7, 1945, p. 232.
[47]*Ibid.*, Dec. 5, 1947, pp. 7–30.
[48]*Ibid.*, June 25, 1948, pp. 679–81.
[49]For a description of money bill procedure see chap. 13, pp. 231–3.
[50]The Prime Minister, Leader of the Opposition, and—under specified conditions—other members are given unlimited time (S.O. 31).
[51]*Journals*, Dec. 13, 1951, pp. 311–13.   [52]*Ibid.*, July 1, 1952, p. 624.

Three more committees were set up, none of which even suggested any reforms. The amendments of 1955 redeemed the situation briefly. The report of the special committee of that year was the result of a study which had extended over two sessions and was adopted by the House after a brief debate. Its provisions were markedly more restrictive of debate than any previous committee's had been, although a few earlier suggestions were adopted. The length of speeches in Committee of the Whole was cut and a maximum length was set for debate on the Address in Reply to the Speech from the Throne and the budget and on motions for the House to go into Committee of Supply. Private members' days were limited and minor alterations were made in many other rules to bring them up to date.

In the 1960 session the House attacked once again the problem of reform. The usual committee sat, but managed by the end of the session to suggest only relatively small reforms. These included a further shortening of speeches to thirty minutes during the Address and budget debates and of the over-all length of these two debates to eight and six days respectively. The committee recommended that these new rules be tried out for one session.[53] The House accepted this suggestion and set the committee up again to study further reforms in the session of 1960–1. This committee achieved as little as its predecessor. The temporary changes made in 1960 were to be continued for another session and it recommended further moderate experiments for the same period. Its only real achievement was the repeal of the nine standing orders which governed the lending of books by the Parliamentary Library.[54] The House accepted these suggestions without debate.

These revisions, however welcome, are only partial ones and leave many of the important defects of procedure untouched. The House still takes too long to do a relatively small amount of work. Debate during most of each session remains largely disorganized and repetitive. The committee system could be used to greater effect. The House does not give proper scrutiny to the public accounts and the estimates. These important problems are with the House today and seem likely to remain so indefinitely into the future.

[53]*Ibid.*, July 25, 1960, pp. 825–32.
[54]*Ibid.*, Sept. 26, 1961, pp. 949–55.

PRIVILEGE

3

THE BEST GENERAL DEFINITION of the privileges of Parliament can be found in Erskine May. There he states that "Parliamentary privilege is the sum of the peculiar rights enjoyed by each House collectively as a constituent part of the High Court of Parliament and by members of each House individually, without which they could not discharge their functions, and which exceed those possessed by other bodies or individuals. Thus privilege, though part of the law of the land, is to a certain extent an exemption from the ordinary law."[1] It is difficult to proceed far beyond this definition, for the privileges of Parliament are vague and have been kept so deliberately. Without any additions they have been adequate for centuries in the United Kingdom and for a shorter period in North America to protect the House against encroachment by the executive and the public.

Practically the only public acknowledgment in Canada of the vast powers of the House and the protection which is afforded the House and its members by the traditions of centuries is contained in the rather quaint formality which opens a Parliament. Each newly elected Speaker, when he leads the Commons to the Senate to hear the Speech from the Throne, claims on behalf of the House "all their undoubted rights and privileges, especially that they may have freedom of speech in their debates, access to your Excellency's person at all reasonable times, and that their proceedings may receive from your Excellency the most favourable consideration." This claim is, of course, immediately assented to by the Governor General. The privileges of Parliament, so

[1] Sir T. Erskine May, *Treatise on the Law, Privileges, Proceedings and Usage of Parliament* (16th ed., London, 1957), p. 42.

briefly summarized by the Speaker and so perfunctorily granted by the Governor General, are of two types. Some are personal to every member of the House and enable him to carry out his parliamentary duties without interference, and others are the additional privileges of the House as a whole, breach of which is considered to be analogous to contempt of court.

The former enable a member to speak on any subject free of any fear of legal responsibility for what he may say. He is free from arrest under civil process while the House is in session and for a reasonable time before and after the session. He is also exempt during the session from duty as a witness or as a juror. Threats against a member and attempts to bribe him are likewise considered as breaches of privilege. The privileges of the House as a whole have the same object as those of individual members. The House controls its own proceedings and its own members, including the right of a member to sit in the House. It may examine witnesses on oath and compel them to answer. As a last resort it can, and occasionally does, punish offenders by censure or imprisonment. Publications of the House are also privileged, and the House protects the publisher of its authorized records and also, to a more limited degree, the publishers of extracts from these records. The privileges of the House are also stretched to cover witnesses appearing before it or its committees and its own officers when carrying out their duties under the orders of the House.

The importance of privileges in the legislative system can hardly be over-emphasized. The statement of Pym that "Parliaments without Parliamentary liberties are but a fair and plausible way into bondage" remains as true today as it was 300 years ago. Historically, privilege in the United Kingdom has been used to protect the Commons, as the King's servant, from interference when engaged in the King's business; later to protect the Commons from interference by the Crown; and currently to protect the Commons from interference by individuals as it carries on the nation's business. The actual use today of privilege in its punitive forms is slight although the power remains with the House to use should the occasion warrant.

Canada, coming to nationhood relatively recently and with well-developed responsible political institutions, has never had to concern itself with the first two stages in the development of its privileges. Privilege in Canada has tended to protect members of Parliament against individuals and not against the Crown. And even here the public's acceptance of Parliament's rights and responsibilities has so increased, and political animosity has so diminished, that it is unlikely that the Canadian House will ever see a repetition of the stream of offenders who appeared at the Bar of the House in the last century. The more important and less spectacular aspects of privilege, such as freedom of speech, which protect an individual member of Parliament in his daily routine of business, are rarely mentioned in Canada and have achieved their purpose if he can carry out his duty without fear of anyone.

Privilege in the colonies, and later in the Dominion, never had the same foundation in common law as it had in the United Kingdom. The privileges of the imperial Parliament are derived from the ancient position of the House of Commons as an integral part of the High Court of Parliament and they are part of the *lex et consuetudo parliamenti* peculiar to England and not transferable to the colonies except by statute. The history of privilege in the American and other British colonies does not concern us here. It is interesting to note, however, that in all the colonies, the legislative assemblies asserted early, and often illegally, their right to the privileges of the British House of Commons and used them with success against the executive as the British House had earlier.[2]

The British North America Act laid the foundation of privilege in the Canadian House of Commons. Section 18 in its original form read: "The Privileges, Immunities and Powers to be held, enjoyed, and exercised by the Senate and by the House of Commons and by the Members thereof respectively shall be such as are from Time to Time defined by Act of the Parliament of Canada, but so that the same shall never exceed those at the passing of this Act held, enjoyed, and exercised by the Commons House of Parliament of the United Kingdom of Great Britain and Ireland and by the Members thereof." Within three weeks of the opening of the first session of the new Canadian Parliament in 1867, the House passed an act to "define the Privileges, immunities and powers of the Senate and House of Commons and to give summary protection to persons employed in the publication of Parliamentary papers."[3] By this act the House merely claimed the privileges held by the imperial House at the time of the passing of the British North America Act. At first sight this seems to be little advance on the terms of the British North America Act, but in fact it does contribute a definite

[2]See Mary P. Clarke, *Parliamentary Privilege in the American Colonies* (New Haven, 1943); F. MacKinnon, *The Government of Prince Edward Island* (Toronto, 1951); J. M. Beck, *The Government of Nova Scotia* (Toronto, 1957).

[3]31 Vict., c. 23. The provisions of this act, modified slightly by the Parliament of Canada Act, 1875, may be found today in the Senate and House of Commons Act.

claim to the broad privileges necessary to the proper functioning of a legislative assembly. The privileges claimed are not laid out in full, but in this Canada has followed the example of the United Kingdom and has avoided any statement which could be used to limit privilege in the future.

The result of this lack of precision is that the House of Commons has only three times had to define its privileges more broadly and has had no difficulty in maintaining and exercising its rights without question. Early in 1868 Parliament passed an act giving the select committees on private bills of both Houses the right to examine witnesses on oath and the Senate the right to examine witnesses at the Bar on oath, and in 1873 another act which extended this right to any committee of either House.[4] Both of these acts were *ultra vires* the Canadian Parliament by virtue of section 18 of the British North America Act, because the British House of Commons had acquired the right to examine witnesses on oath only in 1871.[5] Thus in 1873 the law officers of the Crown in the United Kingdom formally advised that the Oaths Act of 1873 was *ultra vires* and it was disallowed.[6]

The solution of the problem was provided in 1875 when the British Parliament, acting on the request of the Canadian Government, passed the Parliament of Canada Act. This amendment to the British North America Act changed section 18 so that at any time the Canadian Parliament could claim any privileges currently held by the imperial Parliament.[7] The British statute also set forth that the Oaths Act of 1868 "shall be deemed to be valid, and to have been valid as from the date at which the Royal Assent was given thereto. . . ." The next year Canada re-enacted the Oaths Act of 1873 in its original form.[8] The third clarification of privilege occurred in 1894 when the right to examine on oath was extended to the witnesses at the Bar of the House of Commons.[9]

Some of the formal privileges of the House claimed from the Governor General at the opening of every new Parliament are merely quaint anachronisms, and have been taken, along with many other

[4]31 Vict., c. 24, and 36 Vict., c. 1.

[5]As mentioned above, the privileges of the Canadian House under s. 18 of the British North America Act were limited to those possessed by the British Parliament in 1867.

[6]It is interesting that on April 30 Sir John A. Macdonald suggested in a memorandum to the Governor General that the Act was *ultra vires* and that "the attention of Her Majesty's Government should be called to its provisions and to the doubt that exists with respect to its validity." *Debates*, Oct. 23, 1873, p. 11.

[7]Parliament of Canada Act, 38–39 Vict., c. 38 (U.K.).

[8]39 Vict., c. 7.   [9]57–58, Vict., c. 16.

features of the system, from British and colonial practice. Neither "favourable consideration" of the proceedings of the House, nor "access" to the Governor General's person "at all reasonable times" has any meaning today. They may have been important in the United Kingdom and in the colonies, but their continuance is a matter of sentiment and tradition rather than necessity. However, the Speaker's claim for the "undoubted rights and privileges" is far from being an anachronism. This general statement, supported by the one significant illustration—freedom of speech—is the important portion of the request. Among other things, it covers the wide range of the personal privileges of the individual members which rest largely on British precedents.

Freedom from Arrest

The wide freedom from arrest and imprisonment which in England at one time included a member's servants, has never been enjoyed in Canada. The privilege extends only to civil actions and cannot be claimed for treason, felony, breach of the peace, or any indictable offence. The privilege is based on the right of the House to have the full attendance of its members at all times when it is sitting. The House has always recognized the distinction between arrest on a criminal charge for the protection of the community as a whole, and arrest in the course of civil proceedings which is a method of coercion to enforce private rights. Modern law has, however, provided a new form of arrest which provoked considerable interest in the United Kingdom in 1939, when a member of the British House of Commons was arrested and detained under the defence regulations without a formal charge. He appealed to the House as a matter of privilege and the House referred the question to the Committee of Privileges. The report of the committee illustrates the adaptability of privilege. It held that as the detention had been ordered under the provisions of an act of Parliament and was not ordered as a result of anything which the member involved had said from his place in Parliament there was no breach of the privileges of the House.[10] There has been no similar case in Canada, but it is likely that common sense would bring the House to a similar view of the situation.

Freedom from arrest, of course, is enjoyed only for a "reasonable" time before the opening and after the closing of the session. This time is

[10]H.C. 164 (1939–40).

generally held to be forty days, although in the case of *Pelletier* v. *Howard* a time limit of only twenty days after the end of the session was claimed.[11] Several cases and examples of this privilege and its limitations in action have been recorded.[12] In *Henderson* v. *Dickson* the Court of Queen's Bench of Upper Canada held that a court could commit a member for contempt although the imprisonment of the same person for debt would be impossible. In *Pelletier* v. *Howard* the privilege of a member was held not to extend to civil actions where there was no question of the arrest of the member involved. Bourinot also records the case of a member who was arrested and fined in 1885 for an assault committed in the lobby of the House. This action would apparently confirm the dictum of Mr. Justice Stephen in *Bradlaugh* v. *Gossett* which denies that an ordinary offence committed within the precincts of the House is thereby withdrawn from the ordinary courts. A better definition was provided by Mr. Justice O'Connor in *Regina* v. *Bunting* when he held that a member was not responsible in the ordinary courts for anything he might say or do "within the scope of his duties in the course of parliamentary business."

There is, however, no doubt that a member of Parliament can be arrested even during a session of the House for an indictable offence. In 1946 the question of the arrest of a member was considered and a report was made to the Minister of Justice on the subject.[13] The report concluded that "a member who had committed an indictable offence is liable to arrest at any time and any place except on the floor of the House when it is sitting." This advice was adopted and the member involved in the spy investigations of that year was arrested on the eve of a new parliamentary session. There is equally no doubt that had Louis Riel been caught in 1873 there could have been no question of the legality of his arrest.

One condition is imposed on the right of arrest—that the House should be informed through the Speaker of the cause of such action by the magistrate or judge concerned. Mr. Coldwell raised this point

11(1940) 43 Que. P.R. 258. The correct length of time was not settled by this case as the court refused to stay proceedings for any period in a civil action. A limit of forty days has been allowed at the provincial level (*R.* v. *Gamble and Boulton,* (1852) 9 U.C.Q.B. 546).

12(1860) 19 U.C.Q.B. 592 (C.A.); (1940) 43 Que. P.R. 258; [1884] 12 Q.B.D. 284; (1885) 7 O.R. 563.

13Letter, March 12, 1946, from F. P. Brais, K.C., to E. K. Williams, K.C., and G. H. Fauteux, K.C., printed in "Documents Relating to the Proceedings of the Royal Commission Established by Order-in-Council P.C. 411 of February 5, 1946, Including the First and Second Interim Reports of the Royal Commission." (This was the Royal Commission established to investigate the Gouzenko spy charges.)

briefly in 1946, commenting that the newspapers had reported that a member had been arrested and asking if the House should not have been informed. The Prime Minister answered by tabling several documents relevant to the prosecution and stated that he had intended to make a statement on the situation.[14] The traditional explanatory letter does not seem to have been written and it is likely that the House will accept any statement whether from the Government or Speaker as sufficient.

Attendance in Court

Tradition establishes two additional exemptions which add to the freedom of a member. He cannot be forced to attend court either as a witness or as a juror. These privileges, however, have not been widely used and as a rule the House does not insist on them. The same principle applies between the Houses themselves. The Senate, should it need the evidence of a member, informs the House that it desires his presence, and the House grants permission for him to attend.[15]

However often the House waives its privileges in the interests of justice, there is no doubt that the service of the House is paramount and the conscience of the member must be the deciding factor. In 1877, for example, a member moved to permit the Minister of Finance to be absent from the House to give evidence in Kingston, Ontario. The privileged nature of the motion was denied by the Speaker at the time and the matter was postponed. When the motion was made again the Minister made a statement in which he admitted that he had refused to attend the court owing to the condition of his work and the state of the session. He did volunteer to give evidence in Ottawa before a commission and contended that this practice had been followed previously. The motion was defeated in the House.[16]

On that occasion, the question of whether or not a subpoena may be served on a member arose only briefly. Sir Richard Cartwright noted in passing that an attempt had been made to serve a subpoena on him in the corridors of the House but did not pursue the matter. Such an attempt would undoubtedly be considered a breach of privilege in the United Kingdom as the service of process within the precincts of the House on a day when the House is sitting has been decided to be an offence against the House as a whole.[17]

[14]*Debates*, March 15, 1946, pp. 4–8.   [15]*Ibid.*, May 16, 1919, p. 2511.
[16]*Ibid.*, April 16, 1877, pp. 1540–1.
[17]Report from the Committee of Privileges, H.C. 31 (1945–6).

The officers of the House are covered by privilege in the same way as the members, and the House generally waives its privileges here also. There is little doubt that the House will allow its servants to give evidence in court, and on occasion it has even given permission for them to give evidence relating to proceedings in the House.[18] One privilege that has been maintained by the House is the immunity of its staff from jury duty. This has been exercised several times in recent years although the Attorney General of Ontario has not officially recognized the privilege of the House in this regard.[19]

Freedom of Speech

Freedom of speech is perhaps the most important and at the same time the least questioned of all privileges enjoyed by the House. In its most elementary form this privilege was stated in the Bill of Rights which declared "that the freedom of speech and debates or proceedings in Parliament ought not to be impeached or questioned in any court or place outside of Parliament." This right has never been seriously questioned in Canada.[20] Subject to the rules of debate a member may say what he likes within the House without fear of legal action. Should he care to publish his other speeches, he would then, of course, come

[18]Thus in 1892 the House passed a motion to enable clerks, stenographers, and other persons of the staff of the House to give evidence in the case of *Regina* v. *McGreevy*. The case was, however, an unusual one. The Committee on Public Accounts had investigated charges of corruption and had recommended prosecution. On a legal technicality the defendants in the case had retrieved from possession of the House certain damaging evidence and had presumably destroyed it. The motion was to enable the various members of the staff of the House to appear in court and give evidence about the missing documents.

[19]Several officers of the House have been summoned for jury duty in recent years. Application has then been made to the Sheriff to excuse them on the grounds of parliamentary privilege. The individuals have been excused, although on other grounds than those advanced by the House. The question was referred in 1954 to the Attorney General of Ontario without apparently eliciting an opinion. Under Ontario law, until 1941 the various parliamentary officials were exempt from jury duty (Jurors Act, *R.S.O.*, 1937, c. 108). In 1941 a new Jurors Act was passed which removed the exemption. This, in fact, does not affect the privilege concerned but makes any claim for exemption rest entirely on unwritten privilege rather than written law.

[20]A brief reference to this was made in the House in 1935 when Mr. Veniot rose on a question of privilege and noted that there had been news reports to the effect that a Crown prosecutor had asked that a writ be issued against Mr. Veniot for contempt of court for a speech made in the House. Nothing was done but Mr. Veniot noted that the prosecutor could be brought to the Bar for the offence against privilege. *Debates*, March 1, 1935, pp. 1348–9.

within the normal laws of libel. It has been felt at times that the privilege accorded members to refer to people outside the House is more unrestrained than the occasion warrants, and occasionally a member, on a question of privilege, has risen to the defence of the people referred to. Speakers have consistently ruled that such a defence is beyond the bounds of privilege, but have often stated that good taste should keep references to people outside the House within reasonable limits.[21] In Canada the House has never taken disciplinary action to punish a member for what he has said, beyond the normal retraction of unparliamentary expressions.

Constituency Control of Members

There seems little doubt that a strict application of privilege would successfully eliminate various delegate theories of representation favoured by some of the minor western parties in the past. The British House has taken a firm stand against any contractual agreements between members and their constituents and has held that it is improper for a member to enter into any relationship which would limit his complete independence as a member of Parliament.[22] The Canadian House did not see fit to assert its privileges to settle this problem, and instead amended the Dominion Elections Act to make recall agreements illegal.

The Exclusion of Strangers

A corollary of this freedom is the ability of the House to exclude the public from its meetings. This right is infrequently used. In early years, the House commonly began its sittings with a period during which the public was excluded.[23] This period of privacy appears to have been used to discuss the private internal affairs of the House. On one occasion the daily report included the statement that "according to the general report" a resolution was adopted abolishing the bar.[24] In 1929 R. B.

[21]*Ibid.*, Feb. 26, 1914, pp. 1119–25; June 24, 1922, p. 3493; Feb. 17, 1956, p. 1305; March 15, 1956, p. 2157, etc.

[22]Resolution of the House, July 15, 1947, quoted in May, *Parliamentary Practice* (16th ed., 1957), p. 52, and Report from the Committee of Privileges, H.C. 118 (1946–7).

[23]*Debates*, Nov. 8, 1867, p. 2; Dec. 6, 1867, p. 73; April 27, 1868, p. 194; June 1, 1872, col. 925; April 4, 1873, p. 63; April 13, 1874, p. 19; April 30, 1874, p. 62.

[24]*Ibid.*, Nov. 8, 1867, p. 2.

Bennett made a strong defence of this system. It was suggested that certain orders issued by the Speaker should be explained to the House, and Bennett added that "it is not well that matters of internal economy should engage the attention of the public; such matters should be discussed before the doors are opened."[25] He added that this method had been used recently to discuss the approaches to the Parliament buildings, and a few minutes later Hugh Guthrie noted that the House had also discussed the allocation of rooms to members behind closed doors. A few days later the House discussed the Speaker's action for an hour and a half *in camera*.[26]

Wartime conditions have also provided occasions for excluding the public. In 1918, 1942 (twice), and 1944 the House excluded strangers from its deliberations. In 1942 the exclusion was achieved by a Government motion. In the first instance the motion set aside a specific day for the session. The second merely allowed any day to be so designated without further notice. In 1944 the simple expedient of not opening the doors of the galleries after prayers achieved the same purpose. On all these occasions the House specifically excepted senators from the operation of the rule.[27] The British device of "spying strangers" is not recognized by Canadian practice, although, if used, it is accepted and translated by the Speaker into the form recognized by the rules.[28]

The process of clearing the galleries is not, however, as easy today as it was in the very early years of the House. From 1867 to 1876 the rule read that "any member may require the House to be cleared of strangers; and the Speaker shall immediately give directions to the Sergeant-at-Arms to execute the order, without debate."[29] The possibility, inherent in this rule, of arbitrary action on the part of any member is best shown by an incident in 1871. Mr. Macdougall complained in the House that a certain senator had referred to him in a "most scurrilous manner," and he gave warning that he would take the first opportunity to exclude the senator from the gallery. Three weeks later the senator appeared, Macdougall fulfilled his promise, and senator, press, and public were ordered from the gallery.[30] Five years later the House adopted the British practice and accepted its present rule (S.O.

[25]*Ibid.*, April 12, 1929, pp. 1508–11.
[26]*Journals*, April 16, 1929, p. 245.
[27]Senators are included, however, when a motion "that strangers be ordered to withdraw" is passed by the House under Standing Order 13.
[28]*Debates*, Sept. 7, 1950, p. 390.
[29]1867 Rule 6.
[30]*Debates*, March 6, 1871, col. 296–7; March 27, 1871, col. 655.

13) which took this unrestrained power from the hands of the individual member and gave it to the House as a whole.[31] It is now nearly impossible for a private member to secure the exclusion of strangers. Twice during recent years members have tried to clear the galleries during debates on divorce bills: in 1929 J. S. Woodsworth moved "that strangers in the Galleries do withdraw forthwith" and in 1951 G. M. Murray moved for their exclusion during committee stage. Both motions were soundly defeated.[32]

An offence against the House as a whole or any member thereof while the House is sitting is undoubtedly a breach of privilege and the House exercises its right to exclude individuals from its precincts. In recent years control over minor disturbances such as throwing pamphlets or shouting from the galleries has been left to the Sergeant-at-Arms and the protective staff. Offenders are normally merely escorted from the building by the constables on duty and the House takes no cognizance of the incident.

A more notable incident of this type, however, attracted considerable attention.[33] In the early years of the House, distinguished guests were permitted to sit on the floor of the Commons Chamber during debates. On May 10, 1879, one such visitor, John Macdonell, was heard to say to a member sitting near by: "You are a cheat and a swindler." Not unnaturally the member so addressed, L. S. Huntington, resented the remark and drew it to the attention of the Speaker. The Speaker promptly ordered "Strangers to leave the floor." Macdonell, ignoring this order, returned to the floor of the House and was removed by the Sergeant-at-Arms. After yet another appearance on the floor and another expulsion he wrote a note to Huntington in the following terms: "I desire to state out of the House what I stated in it, you are a cheat and a swindler." Two days later another member raised the matter as a question of privilege and called on the Prime Minister to take action. A formal charge was made and the Prime Minister moved that Macdonell be summoned to the Bar. A few days later the Sergeant-at-Arms reported that Macdonell could not be found to be summoned. The Speaker mentioned that Macdonell had made a personal apology to him,

[31]*Ibid.*, March 29, 1876, p. 906.
[32]*Ibid.*, June 4, 1929, p. 3228; May 22, 1951, p. 3288. It is interesting to note that at the time the 1951 motion was suggested the House was in committee and Murray suggested that the sense of the House should be taken as to whether or not the galleries should be cleared. Over the objection of Mr. Knowles the Speaker resumed the Chair and put the question. The manner of the proceeding seems unnecessary as the rule specifically permits the Chairman to put the question.
[33]*Ibid.*, May 10, 1879, p. 1940.

but had been warned of its insufficiency. Prorogation then intervened to prevent further action at that session.

Early the next year the Prime Minister moved that the relevant entries in the *Journals* of the preceding session be read and Macdonell was again summoned to the Bar. He appeared at the appointed time and was permitted to make a public apology to the House. He defended his actions on the grounds that the remarks were not directed to Huntington but to his neighbour on the floor. He also did not consider his note a breach of privilege as it was not written within the House and did not refer to Huntington in his official capacity as a member. The House decided otherwise, however, judged Macdonell to be guilty of a breach of privilege, and ordered the Speaker to communicate the decision to him. An amendment which would have added an apology to Huntington to the general apology was unaccountably defeated and Macdonell was discharged from further attendance.

Control over Publications

Control by the House over the publication of its proceedings is absolute. In the early years of the Commons, the House passed an annual resolution "that the Votes and Proceedings of this House be printed, being first perused by Mr. Speaker and that no person but such as he shall appoint do presume to print the same."[34] This motion has now disappeared, but as the *Votes and Proceedings* are published over the signature of the Speaker it is likely that the House would take speedy action should anyone outside the House publish a similar paper. Changes in the *Votes and Proceedings* are properly made by motion in the House, or if made by consent of the House are entered in the *Votes* the next day.[35] No member, even the Speaker, is permitted to alter the official record of the House. In 1875 both the Prime Minister and the Leader of the Opposition attacked a suggestion by the Speaker that he should himself order the amending of division lists in the *Votes and Proceedings* following the discovery that a member had voted before having properly taken the oath, but the alteration was subsequently ordered by the House following a report of the Committee on Privileges and Elections which recommended the change.[36]

The House achieved strict control over the publication of its debates

[34]*Journals*, Feb. 15, 1871, p. 10; March 27, 1874, p. 4; Feb. 10, 1876, p. 50; Feb. 8, 1877, p. 12.
[35]*Votes and Proceedings*, June 6, 1944, p. 434, and June 22, 1951, p. 604.
[36]*Debates*, Feb. 22, 1875, p. 260; *Journals*, March 8, 1875, p. 176.

only after an initial period of experimentation. From 1867 to 1875 there was no "official" report of debates. For three years newspaper reprints were produced in bound form and for the other sessions only collections of newspaper clippings have been kept.[37] After 1875 the reporting of debates was let out to a private contractor under the supervision of a committee of the House and continued in this unsatisfactory way until the establishment of the Government Printing Bureau in 1887 enabled the House to bring Hansard more closely under its control. At the present time the reporting staff are employees of the House and although Hansard is not accepted by the courts as the official record of the House it has attained this status in the popular mind.

In one aspect at any rate Hansard has a privileged position. The same act which defined the privileges of the House in 1868 also provided that should any person be prosecuted for the publication of any "report, paper, votes or proceedings," a certificate from the Speaker or the Clerk of the House stating that the document was published under the authority of the House would be sufficient to stay proceedings. Similarly, any extract from such documents, should it be printed "bona fide and without malice," is protected. These provisions have been kept in their original form and now appear in the Senate and House of Commons Act.[38] No Hansard report is, of course, made of any of the secret sessions of the House. Instead, the Speaker generally makes a brief report which is printed in place of the usual verbatim record.

The 1960 session provided an interesting breach of privilege relating to Hansard. A private member complained in the House that a company had reproduced a portion of Hansard including the cover. The question was referred to the Committee on Privileges and Elections which heard evidence from the Law Clerk of the House and decided that a breach of privilege had indeed occurred. In its report the committee summarized its findings thus:

Respecting the publication of a document by the Sperry and Hutchinson Company of Canada Limited, your committee finds that there has been a breach of the Privileges of this House committed by Byrne Hope Sanders in that she is responsible for the printing and circulation of a misrepresented report of the House of Commons Debates. Your committee is of the opinion that she has published as a Report something which is made to appear as an authorized official version, which it is not; and also that she has failed to obtain from the proper authorities permission to reproduce the cover of a document belonging to the House of Commons.[39]

[37]The so-called Scrapbook Hansard.   [38]R.S.C. (1952), c. 249, ss. 7–9.
[39]Minutes of Proceedings and Evidence, 1960, p. 4.

The evidence before the committee and its discussions of the offence are, unfortunately, not very revealing or convincing, but at least the finding constitutes a definite claim on the part of the House to exclusive control over its verbatim reports.

Members alter Hansard as a matter of privilege. The method is simple. A member rises in his place at the beginning of a sitting, states that he has said something (or had meant to say something) other than what has been printed, and asks that the record be changed. No question is raised, and the assent of the House to the change is assumed.[40] The authority of the Speaker to make changes is not clear. At times he has approved alterations in Hansard without reference to the House,[41] and at other times has ordered alterations subject to the approval of the House.[42] A recent incident, however, has strengthened the point of view that Hansard should not be amended by any member except with the permission of the House. On this occasion the Minister of Agriculture removed from the record, with the approval of the Speaker, a politically embarrassing statement. The remarks had, however, been heard and reported by the press and his action was thus easily brought to the attention of the House. The correction in itself was unimportant except in so far as it embarrassed the Minister, but it pointed up the danger of this form of correction.[43] At least once words have been removed from Hansard by formal motion. On this occasion a member had made an attack on the Speaker and had apologized for it in the House. The next day the Prime Minister moved that the words used "be expunged from the official report of the debates of this House."[44] The fact that the motion which eliminates the offending words from Hansard must repeat them in full and thus enter them in the *Journals* of the House has probably limited the use of this method of change.

Control by the House over documents in its possession includes even those desired by the Senate. In 1919 the Speaker notified the House that the Senate had passed a resolution requiring the tabling in the Senate

[40]The request for the change appears in the daily unrevised Hansard and the alteration is actually made in the final bound edition. When the change is made the original request is omitted, so that there is no record in the bound edition of these "points of privilege."

[41]See the statement of the Chairman, *Debates*, May 3, 1938, p. 2508, and the action of the Deputy Chairman, *ibid.*, July 11, 1956, p. 5861.

[42]*Ibid.*, May 12, 1921, pp. 3260–1; Feb. 28, 1933, p. 2536; April 5, 1933, pp. 3728–9; May 1, 1934, p. 2734; May 14, 1936, pp. 2811–12; April 28, 1938, pp. 2371–2.

[43]*Ibid.*, Feb. 12, 1956, pp. 1097–1113. See also statements, *ibid.*, July 13, 1942, p. 4135, and July 11, 1956, pp. 5861–2.

[44]*Journals*, March 21, 1912, p. 366.

of certain papers in his possession. The Speaker protested this action to the House as a breach of privilege and the Acting Prime Minister immediately moved that a message be sent drawing this breach to the attention of the Senate. All agreed that the papers should be made available to the other House, but also agreed that the proper method of obtaining them would be to convey a message to the Commons with the request.[45]

The general provisions of secrecy of debate apply also to the committees of the House. In 1875 a member claimed that there had been a breach of privilege when a Toronto newspaper published the report of a committee before the committee had presented it to the House. The point was not accepted. The Speaker ruled that reporters should not have been present while the committee considered its report. If the committee permitted their presence, it could not complain when the results were reported.[46]

For the most part meetings of committees are open to the public and many of them publish verbatim reports of their proceedings. Their rights are, however, unquestioned, and many exclude the public. The most notable of these are the committees on procedure which traditionally meet *in camera*. Closed sessions are universal when committees are preparing their reports, and even members of the House who are not members of the committee are generally not present. A striking example was the Joint Special Committee on Capital and Corporal Punishment and Lotteries which met *in camera* throughout 1956 although in the previous two sessions its meetings had been public and fully reported. The committee spent the whole of the session preparing its four reports for presentation to both houses.

There has never been a clear statement in Canada on the question of whether or not it is a breach of privilege to publish the proceedings of a committee that is meeting *in camera*.[47] Newspapers regularly speculate on these meetings and publish reports whose accuracy is often open to doubt. On May 10, 1956, D. F. Brown, the House Chairman of the Joint Special Committee on Capital and Corporal Punishment and Lotteries complained, as a matter of privilege, of a leakage of confidential information which had been reported in the newspapers. He stated that

[45]*Debates*, March 20, 1919, pp. 642–3.   [46]*Ibid.*, March 23, 1875, pp. 861–7.

[47]It has been ruled, however, that a reference by a member to what takes place at a committee meeting *in camera* is not a breach of privilege, as members of the House cannot be excluded from the meeting (although those who are not members of the committee are expected to withdraw by courtesy) and when the committee has reported, its proceedings are the property of the House. *Ibid.*, June 14, 1955, p. 4790.

the report was false, and the matter was dropped.[48] A later report which related to a vote in the same committee gave the result of the vote and claimed that proxies had been counted.[49] No official notice was taken of this although the report was completely inaccurate. It is probably fair to say that the House is unlikely to take any action in cases of this sort, as the responsibility for the leakage rests square on the shoulders of the members of the committee. Should a committee clerk or other similar person be responsible, the House might take a different view.[50]

The House has always taken a stand against any other form of publication of its debates or of the proceedings of its committees. No debate has ever been broadcast, and recent attempts by the Canadian Broadcasting Corporation to obtain permission to broadcast the ceremonial of the opening day of the session as a regular feature have been resisted. The Senate has allowed television broadcasts of this ceremony, and the opening day of the 1957–8 session was televised in both houses. However, there is no reason to believe that this will be a permanent feature. No strong feeling has been expressed. In 1956 the Speaker asked for advice on this subject in Committee of Supply while his estimates were before the committee but no member even commented.[51]

A much stronger stand has been taken on two other forms of publication. In 1954, the chairman of a standing committee, with the consent of the Speaker, had the proceedings of his committee recorded. The Leader of the Opposition raised an objection in the House that the practice was undesirable and that the committee had overstepped its powers. The chairman of the committee defended the experiment as an attempt to help the reporters get more accurate accounts of committee proceedings.[52] The question was not pursued further. There is no doubt, however, that there is little or no support in Ottawa for any such method of recording the proceedings of the House. The danger inherent in a tape-record which may easily be erased or altered would seem to weigh

[48]*Ibid.*, May 10, 1956, pp. 3751–2.

[49]Toronto *Globe and Mail*, June 29, 1956, and Montreal *Gazette*, June 29, 1956.

[50]The Canadian attitude is decidedly more lax than that in the United Kingdom. A report of the British Committee of Privileges in 1947 was quite definite on the subject: "if a Committee had resolved to transact its proceedings behind closed doors this decision, although it does not exclude the right of other members of the House to attend, would no doubt result in any publication of what had taken place constituting a contempt." H.C. 138 (1946–7), p. x.

[51]*Debates*, Aug. 13, 1956, p. 7486.

[52]It is interesting to note that at its 1957 session the legislature of Ontario used a tape-recorder to enable the Hansard reporters to check the accuracy of their notes. After a further attempt to use such recorders to replace reporters the legislature found that tape-records were markedly inferior and returned to the more conventional reporters.

against any adoption of this method of reporting debates in future. The House also expressed its disapproval of the actions of the Prime Minister when he had an extension from the amplifying system of the House installed in his office. The connections were made without the knowledge of the Speaker or the House. The House generally agreed that the principle was unsound and that the secrecy surrounding the operation was reprehensible. No formal protest was made, but by the next session the extension had been removed.[53]

Protection of Witnesses

The House claims the right to protect its witnesses against prosecution for evidence given in the House or before one of its committees. This principle, of course, stems from the same general principle that enables the House to conduct its business in secret—the principle that no proceedings of the House shall be reported outside except by leave of the House. A witness before a committee or at the Bar of the House has no right to refuse to answer a question even if he may consider that it will incriminate him.[54] Thus in 1892 there was a long debate on a motion to order the employees of the House to attend court and produce records referring to an investigation that had been carried on by the Public Accounts Committee. In the same motion the House maintained its right to protect witnesses and to reserve such evidence as it saw fit in the public interest. In 1913 the House insisted on its right to have an answer from a witness even over his objection that it would incriminate him. He persisted in his refusal to answer and was committed to jail for contempt.

Reflections on Members

The House exercises only a minimum of control over external reports of affairs in the House. In Britain control is strict in theory, but in fact the House will ignore any reports until an individual has made a complaint.[55] Occasionally even the Committee of Privileges decides that

[53]*Debates*, July 19, 1958, pp. 2447–9; Aug. 9, 1958, pp. 3294–8; Jan. 27, 1959, p. 362.
[54]*Ibid.*, May 30, 1887, pp. 616–36; April 12, 1892, cols. 1289, 1283–1311; Feb. 20, 1913, col. 3740.
[55]The British House retains as its final authority a resolution of March 3, 1762, which holds that any publication of reports of speeches by members is a breach of privilege.

action is not necessary or desirable.[56] In Canada the practice is more lax. The House has never claimed that all reports of debates are a breach of privilege. Several times, however, the House has taken action with regard to newspaper reports which it has felt were a reflection on members of the House. On three of these occasions members of the staff of the House were implicated as having been the source of the reports.[57] On the first occasion the staff member was summoned to the Bar to admit his authorship; punishment was left in the hands of the Speaker as a matter of internal administration and the man was removed from the staff. The culprit on the second occasion was not even examined at the Bar, but the House was informed that he had been dismissed from the service. In the third instance, a member of the Law Branch was apparently given an opportunity to retract his "serious reflections" on members of the House and was dismissed only after he refused to do so.

On the occasions not involving members of the staff of the House, one author was found to be a leading Liberal member of Parliament who was to become Speaker a year later; the House heard the article read, and decided by vote that it was a "scandalous, false, and malicious libel upon . . . this House" and a "high contempt of the privileges and constitutional authority of this House." A later article was similarly judged on motion to be "a scandalous, false, and malicious libel upon the honour, character and integrity of the Speaker of the House." In neither case did the House take further action or examine the authors at the Bar. Early in this century the House took a more serious view of an attack on a front-bench member of the Opposition. The House called the author, E. E. Cinq-Mars, to the Bar and examined him not only on the authorship of the article but also on his reasons for believing it to be true. After hearing him, the House decided that the article exceeded "the bounds of reasonable criticism," and that it constituted "a breach of the privileges of this House." The most recent attempt to censure those writing in the press took place during the session of 1956. Mr. Cameron asked that two letters to the editor be read at the Table and moved that the statements therein were "derogatory of the dignity of Parliament and deserving of the censure of this House." This motion

[56]For example, the report from the Committee of Privileges on a complaint made regarding an article in the *Daily Worker*, H.C. 31 (1953–4). More recently, however, a newspaper editor was summoned to the Bar and allowed to apologize for an article he had written which had been judged by the Committee of Privileges to be a breach of the privileges of the House. H.C. 38 (1956–7).

[57]*Debates*, April 7, 1873, p. 67; May 2, 1878, pp. 2368–9; Sir John G. Bourinot, *Parliamentary Procedure and Practice in the Dominion of Canada* (3rd ed., Toronto, 1903), p. 153 n.

was never debated at length by the House: the next day the Speaker ruled the matter out of order as a matter of privilege since the content of the letters did not go beyond the bounds of fairness.[58]

Whatever the reason may be, there is no doubt that the old method of dealing with offences arising from newspaper articles is falling into disuse. The current practice is a very superficial one. The member involved rises "on a question of privilege," reads the article referred to, comments on its unfairness or inaccuracy, and resumes his seat. Usually he does not make a motion condemning the article or its author. Twice in the 1956 session the Speaker explained the exact procedure which should be followed to make a formal complaint about a newspaper article; on one occasion the member reluctantly made the necessary motion, and on the other the member asked "whether some action cannot be taken to maintain, or to restore, if it has been lost, public confidence in this institution." The Speaker explained the remedy and the member quietly resumed his seat.[59] It seems obvious, on all this evidence, that the House has never taken the serious view of reflections on its members or on the Speaker that the British House has. In the nineteenth century, articles which alleged insobriety on the part of Canadian members of Parliament were common and went largely unchallenged, perhaps because so patently true.[60] A jocular suggestion was even made that a cheap edition of Hansard could be expected "for the special benefit of cabmen and omnibus drivers . . . whose vocabulary of abuse and retort would be greatly enlarged by a careful study of that interesting publication."[61] Such remarks could hardly be overlooked in the United Kingdom. The most recent attacks in Canada took place in the session of 1956, as has already been mentioned. The charges made were more

[58]Journals, April 17, 1873, pp. 167–9; Debates, April 25, 1894, cols. 1958–65; June 14, 1906, cols. 5266–320; May 31, 1956, pp. 4529–34. This last motion should not be taken very seriously as it formed part of the procedural wrangling which accompanied the most bitter debate the House had seen in thirty years. It is likely that the motion was made to block progress on the bill under consideration at the time rather than as a serious attempt to save the reputation of the House.

[59]Debates, June 26, 1956, pp. 5378–9. The motives of the member may be open to question, as he read several of the choicest epithets from a particularly vulgar attack on the Speaker and quite evidently had no intention of proceeding, or even of denying the allegations. It is interesting to note that this article bears a striking resemblance to that condemned by the House in 1894.

[60]On one occasion at least, one of these articles was questioned as being improper, and on a point of privilege a member denied the allegation. Ibid., April 17, 1878, pp. 2057–67.

[61]Quoted in N. Ward, "The Formative Years of the House of Commons, 1867–91," Canadian Journal of Economics and Political Science, XVIII, Nov. 1952, p. 434.

serious than most, as the Speaker, Deputy Speaker, and Deputy Chairman of Committees were all abused editorially and in letters to the editor for partiality and subservience to the Government. Such journalistic comment would be unlikely in the United Kingdom and, if attempted, would be dealt with severely.

Two recent cases show clearly the position of the House in that country.[62] A reference in a letter to the editor in 1941 to "seeming irregularities in the procedure by which [a Draft Order] has been advanced to its present Parliamentary stage" was raised by the Chairman of Committees as a reflection on himself as Chairman. The writer of the letter was cleared of the charge but not without a lengthy investigation. Ten years later, an obscure newspaper reported that in a political speech in the Midlands a woman had mentioned that she thought a recent decision of the Deputy Speaker "very deplorable." The Committee of Privileges held this remark to be a breach of the privileges of the House as was a further statement in the speech which contained an "imputation of partiality upon the Chair." Although the Committee recommended that no further action be taken, the principle was firmly stated that "a comment upon the conduct of the Chairman with regard to the business of the House which would be construed reasonably by those who hear or read such comment as charging him with partiality, is a breach of the Privileges of the House." The application of this dictum to the Canadian newspapers of May and June 1956 would have kept the Committee on Privileges and Elections busy until the end of the session processing the contempts committed. In 1941, on the other hand, Mackenzie King, when moving for the appointment of a special committee, noted that the imputation made by various newspapers that a member of a committee could not act impartially was a breach of privilege and would be treated as such.[63] It may be that the newspapers involved did not pursue their criticism but nothing further was heard of the threat.

Attempts at Influence

The House has taken a more serious view of attempts to influence its members. Since 1867 there has been a rule of the House which forbids as a "high crime and misdemeanour" any attempt to bribe a member. It has been invoked only once. In 1873 Robert Cunningham read a

[62]Second report from the Committee of Privileges, H.C. 103 (1941); report from the Committee of Privileges, H.C. 235 (1950–1).
[63]*Debates*, March 4, 1941, p. 1234.

statement to the House in which he charged that an Ottawa alderman, John Heney, had attempted to buy his vote for the Government. The House ordered the arrest of Heney and his appearance at the Bar, but prorogation (and later dissolution) intervened a few days later and prevented any further action against him.[64] Similarly, in 1939 a member of the House stated from his place that he had been threatened with exposure of some alleged irregularities that had occurred fifteen years previously. The Prime Minister asked for the name of the person who had made the threat and assured the member that the Government would take action should he not wish to himself.[65] The matter appears to have been dropped at this point as no further reference to it can be found. More recently, one member who received a threatening letter from an unknown person merely turned the whole matter over to the police. No question of privilege was raised or even suggested.[66] It would seem likely that this more effective course would normally be followed for any real threat to a member.

Control of Members by the House

The House also reserves the right to control its good name within itself. There is no doubt about its power to judge its own members and decide their fitness to serve in the House. Between 1867 and 1874 it retained the right to try controverted elections, and even after it turned that duty over to the provincial courts it maintained a watchful eye over the members elected. The House has held many investigations to determine the propriety of members serving. An old conviction for forgery was considered by one committee, and on another occasion the House refused to examine a charge that a member had misappropriated municipal funds.[67] In 1891 and 1892 some of the members were investigated and one was convicted of corruption connected with the Department of Public Works. One of these men, Thomas McGreevy, shares with Louis Riel the doubtful distinction of being the only member of the Canadian House actually expelled for his actions. Riel was expelled twice: the first time, the House decided that he was a fugitive from justice and that he had refused to obey an order of the House to attend in his place

[64]*Ibid.*, Nov. 5, 1873, pp. 55–6. The rule was passed as a sessional order every year until 1876, when the House accepted it as a permanent rule. It now appears as Standing Order 79.

[65]*Ibid.*, Feb. 1, 1939, p. 519.

[66]*Edmonton Journal*, Feb. 18, 1960.

[67]*Journals*, March 16, 1876, pp. 145–60; March 3, 1880, pp. 87–8.

and answer charges; he was re-elected, and when he was judicially declared an outlaw the next year, the House took cognizance of the verdict and again expelled him.[68]

Procedure Regarding a Breach of Privilege

The procedure to be followed in raising and examining a breach of privilege has never been very clearly established in Canada. The House itself has generally considered that it should sit in judgment on the cases submitted to it—the Committee on Privileges and Elections, in spite of its name, has been given little work to do in this regard.[69] A major question of privilege, then, that requires action by the House is normally raised by an individual who makes a suitable motion. The House takes the motion under consideration, debates it, hears witnesses if it wishes, and divides on it. Most of the actions of the House in connection with cases of privilege are governed by custom. The only relevant standing order (S.O. 17) is clear as far as it goes: "Whenever any matter of privilege arises it shall be taken into consideration immediately." It is clear that no notice of motion is necessary should the member who raises the point include a motion in his statement. It is also accepted that in cases of urgency the proceedings of the House may be interrupted to deal with a matter of privilege, and that if the matter is not urgent, it should be raised during routine business at the next sitting.[70]

Should the House wish to examine a witness at the Bar, the practice is reasonably certain. After a complaint has been made or the general point to be raised has been set out, the member responsible moves "that Mr. Speaker do issue his warrant summoning . . . to the Bar of this House." A specific date may be attached,[71] or the vague term "without delay" may be used instead.[72] On occasion, if the individual is available, he may be ordered to appear "forthwith."[73] The cause of the summons may or may not be added to the motion or included in

[68]*Ibid.*, April 15, 1874, pp. 64–70; Feb. 24, 1875, pp. 122–4.

[69]The only significant exceptions have been investigations of charges made against members either by other members directly, or by way of petition by individuals outside. The committee was also used in 1960 to investigate a breach of privilege relating to a reproduction of Hansard by a private company, as mentioned previously in this chapter.

[70]For the proper time to raise a question of privilege see chap. 5, p. 000 n.

[71]The orders issued to John Macdonell on February 16, 1880, M. Connolly on June 5, 1891, A. Sénécal on August 27, 1891, and E. E. Cinq-Mars on June 6, 1906, all specified the day.

[72]*Journals*, May 12, 1887, p. 121.

[73]The order for E. Tassé, a member of the staff of the House, required him to appear "forthwith." *Ibid.*, April 7, 1873, p. 133.

the summons. At the appropriate time the Sergeant-at-Arms reports on the attendance of the individual. Should he not be present, his absence is reported to the House, and a motion is made for the Sergeant-at-Arms to take him into custody, and "that Mr. Speaker do issue his warrant accordingly."[74]

When the culprit or witness arrives at the Bar the Clerk reads the original complaint, and the examination begins. When a charge has been laid against the individual he may request, and is generally granted, counsel both to advise him and to speak for him. The examination proceeds by question and answer. Each question is a separate motion properly proposed and seconded, put to the House by the Speaker, and if passed, put by the Speaker to the witness at the Bar.[75] These questions when in motion form are amendable and may be voted on should the House desire. Any objection to a question by counsel or by a member must be made before the question is put to the House, and the Speaker decides on the admissibility of the objection; the early custom, before the days of proper Hansard reports, was for a clerk to take down the witness's answer and read it to the House. Should the witness be unwilling to answer any question he is ordered to do so by the Speaker, and if he should persist in his refusal he may be committed for contempt. If the House desires to discuss any procedural point, or if it is satisfied that its examination is completed, the witness is ordered to withdraw. He is also excluded while the House considers its verdict. If necessary, he is then recalled while the Speaker delivers the message of the House.

The whole system is admittedly cumbersome and unsatisfactory. Not the least factor in this is the constant doubt about the exact function of the individual at the Bar. On occasion he has been simply a witness and nothing more: in 1874 the Attorney General of Manitoba and two Ottawa policemen appeared solely as witnesses to answer questions relating to Louis Riel. On the other hand, the individual at the Bar has occasionally been accused of a specific offence: Connolly in 1891 and Miller in 1913 had both been formally accused before their summonses to the Bar. These cases were clear, but those of a returning officer in 1887 and two journalists in 1873 and 1906 were not. The returning officer was summoned to "answer for his conduct" but was not accused specifically of any offence. Similarly, the two journalists were called "to give evidence" relating to articles they themselves had written It is these doubtful cases which demonstrate most clearly the problem facing the House when it sits in judgment.

[74]It will be recalled that in the case of the Ottawa alderman, John Heney, the charge was such that his immediate arrest was ordered without the preliminary call to the Bar. *Ibid.*, Nov. 3, 1873, pp. 134–5.
[75]For the procedure used by the House when voting see chap. 10, pp. 181–2.

The worst feature of the procedure in these cases is the partiality of at least a portion of the court. The situation is largely inevitable in Canada. The charge involved is generally of a political nature—an attack made in a newspaper or an awkward question unanswered in a committee. It is hardly surprising that one side should enter the court with a crusading zeal and the other with a determination that little should be done. There is no doubt that the verdicts of the House on these occasions have generally been justified, but little of the impartiality of the British House has been used in arriving at them. Exceptions may be found at the highest level and Sir Robert Borden paid tribute to Sir Wilfrid Laurier on one such occasion as one who was "always mindful of the dignity of the House and determined to uphold its powers."[76] This attitude has been rare, however.

It is undoubtedly within the power of the House to punish for breach of privilege or contempt. In its most mild form punishment takes the guise of a declaration on the part of the House that an action or article is a breach of privilege. In most of the aggravated cases the reprimand is delivered to the offender personally at the Bar. In extreme cases the offender is committed to the Carleton County jail for such term as the House may direct. On the one occasion on which the House decided to imprison an individual no term was specified when he was committed on February 20; the prisoner was, therefore, released only by prorogation on June 6. It is accepted, although not stated, that prorogation ends any committal, and there is equal agreement that recommittal in the next session for the same offence is possible on another order of the House, though the House has not, in fact, ever given such an order. The right to punish by fine has never been exercised in Canada either. It was a common punishment in colonial times, but has never been suggested as suitable in any of the cases brought before the House. It is interesting that the Speaker suggested this form of punishment as a possible form of redress in 1956.[77]

The Modern Concept of Privilege

Privilege, then, has little real significance in Canada today. Three hundred years ago the Earl of Clarendon wrote in his *History of the Rebellion*: "It is not to be believed how many sober and well-minded

[76]Henry Borden, ed., *Robert Laird Borden: His Memoirs* (2 vols., Toronto, 1938), I, p. 394.
[77]*Debates*, June 26, 1956, p. 5379.

men . . . had their understanding perverted by the mere mention of privilege of Parliament." In a somewhat different sense these words might easily be applied to the Canadian House of Commons. At best, privilege in the Canadian House is little understood and little used. At worst, it is looked on as being a convenient excuse to make any remark in the House which cannot be made in the normal course of business.

There have always been matters raised on points of privilege which have, on examination, proved not to be privileged, and Speakers have tried unsuccessfully to prevent abuses of the rules. Very early, the practice began of allowing a member to rise and correct a newspaper article referring to himself. Although occasionally a Speaker would cast doubt on the propriety of such a point, the custom grew quickly and by 1908 the Speaker admitted a member's right to make the correction from his place in the House.[78] Today this right is used by members virtually unchecked. The same right is used to correct mis-statements in Hansard and in members' speeches.

The House sanctions another practice by which the Speaker may draw the attention of the House to the presence of distinguished strangers in the galleries. This was stretched by private members to include reference by themselves to groups of school children, clubs, or sports teams from their own constituencies. In 1951 Mr. Coldwell raised an objection to this abuse of "privilege." He contended that those members who observed the rules and made no reference to constituents in the gallery would be misunderstood. Mr. Speaker Macdonald made a statement on the subject a week later and "suggested" that the practice be discontinued.[79] Since then, members have abandoned this custom.

A more prevalent habit is still maintained by which the members draw frivolous items to the attention of the House under the guise of a question of privilege.[80] In 1951, for instance, a member referred to a discussion he had had with the Minister of Finance over a definition contained in the Excise Tax Act. He concluded with the statement:

the manager of the W. T. Hawkins Company of Tweed, Ontario, Mr. Armand Turpin, has sent a package of caramel corn snacks for the Minister so that he may have the opportunity to decide whether the

[78]*Ibid.*, Feb. 20, 1877, pp. 122–3; April 11, 1878, p. 1869; March 10, 1908, col. 4668–9.
[79]*Ibid.*, May 23, 1951, p. 3309; May 29, 1951, p. 3494.
[80]*Ibid.*, May 10, 1951, p. 2873; March 7, 1951, p. 995; March 17, 1955, p. 2101; Nov. 30, 1953, p. 443 ("When the Secretary of State for External Affairs kicked off the ball on Saturday afternoon [at a championship football game], did he have his eye on the ball or on Miss Saskatchewan?"); June 5, 1956, p. 4751; May 8, 1956, p. 3702; May 4, 1956, p. 3563.

product is comparable to popcorn. He also has sent a standard package of Cheezies, another product made by this company. . . . He has also sent a standard package for every member of the House and I will have them distributed. In addition there will be an aerial view of the village of Tweed sent with the compliments of the Tweed Chamber of Commerce.

Earlier in the year, again on a question of privilege, a member had corrected a Minister's statement that a firm in his constituency did not make brooms and presented him with one of their products on the floor of the House. Similarly, questions of privilege have been used to protest the suspension of a popular hockey player, to ask questions both humorous and serious, to "take great exception" to the remarks of another member, to ask for a ruling by the Speaker, and even to question a statement made by the Speaker.

These examples illustrate clearly the concept of privilege in the mind of most members. The word "privilege" is well known, and is recognized as a magic word which may be used to excuse the most flagrant irrelevancies. The occupants of the Chair have tried on occasion to limit these interruptions but have had little success; they have often tried to draw distinctions between privilege and fraudulent points raised under the same name, but even these attempts have met with strong resistance from the House.[81] As usual, a convenient instrument is not to be surrendered easily.

At the root of the problem is the ignorance of the Canadian House of the true meaning of privilege, which is essentially the defensive weapon of a legislature which has been used to protect itself against interference. The Canadian House has never had to fear such trouble and has never bothered to develop a defence. Such sporadic attempts as have been made to assert the authority of the House have been made from partisan motives and have been treated as such by the House. There is little hope that the Commons will alter this part of its procedure. Interest in the problem is too slight, and the convenience of the present practice is too obvious to every member. But perhaps in future the House should remember the words of Lord Chancellor Lyndhurst in 1831, who stated: "The Privileges of the House are part of the Law of the land; they were given to the Houses of Parliament for the sake of the subject, and not for the convenience of the Member."[82]

[81]Even the term "fraudulent" relating to these "questions of privilege" has been resented by members of the House. *Ibid.*, May 17, 1956, p. 4030.
[82]Quoted in *Spectator*, Feb. 1, 1957.

THE SPEAKER

4

FOR NEARLY SIX HUNDRED YEARS the office of Speaker of the House of Commons has been recognized in England. It has not, of course, always filled the same place in the procedure of the Commons as it does now. The first half of this period saw only a slow development. The Speaker maintained his position as an officer of the Crown and a link between the Crown and the Commons until the time of the Stuarts, when the struggle between Charles I and the Commons began the development which has produced the modern Speaker. Two well-known incidents marked the change and foretold the future: Mr. Speaker Finch was prevented by physical force from adjourning the House at the King's command in 1629, and Mr. Speaker Lenthall, thirteen years later, delivered his famous speech when King Charles entered the House to arrest the five members. The first real victory of the House, however, was won in 1689 when the Commons, having had their choice of Speaker rejected by the King, in turn rejected a royal nominee and elected a compromise candidate. The royal influence in the election of a Speaker was not thereby eliminated, but the open interference of the King was at an end.

The eighteenth and early part of the nineteenth centuries saw the influence of the Crown over the Speaker replaced by party influence. The outstanding exception was Mr. Speaker Onslow (1727–61) who resigned a government post immediately on being elected to office. Onslow's successors were by no means so independent. In 1801 Addington moved from the Chair to the prime ministership and other Speakers maintained their right to take an active part in House debates. Mr. Speaker Manners-Sutton was the last to take an active political part in debates in the House and paid the price for it in 1835 when he was defeated by the same party that had elected him to the Chair two years previously.

The modern tradition of the Speakership began in 1839 when Mr. Speaker Shaw-Lefevre took office. He established without doubt the principle that the Speaker should refrain from all connection with politics both inside and outside the House. The Speaker is now generally elected to his constituency without opposition from an official candidate of any party.[1] He is re-elected to the Chair for as long as he wishes to offer himself, and when retired generally goes to the House of Lords with a pension.

Statutory Provisions in Canada

The Canadian House fortunately has not had to undergo this long and often difficult development to achieve a reasonably satisfactory Speakership. The Speaker has not always been free from political influence, and has occasionally even been a strong partisan while in the Chair, but the House has never had to contend with royal influence in either the appointment or the conduct of its Speaker. The existence of the Speaker is not only recognized in the Canadian constitution but his election is made mandatory. Section 44 of the British North America Act contains the bald command that "The House of Commons on its first assembling after a general election shall proceed with all practicable Speed to elect One of its Members to be Speaker." The three succeeding sections continue to provide for the Speakership. If a vacancy occurs in the office the House shall proceed to elect another of its members to be Speaker (s. 45), and should the Speaker be absent for more than forty-eight hours the House may elect a temporary Speaker to continue in office during such absence (s. 47). Section 46 provides, almost as an afterthought, that "The Speaker shall preside at all meetings of the House of Commons." This clause provides for only part of the Speaker's functions. A further elaboration of his duties may be found in the House of Commons Act.[2] Here the Speaker appears as an administrative officer, presiding over a department. The Act sets up a Committee

---

[1]This is by no means as universal a practice as common belief would have it. The Speaker has been opposed in 1885, 1895, 1935, 1945, 1950, 1951, and 1955. Most of this opposition has been provided by unofficial candidates. The opposition poll, however, may be heavy. In 1955, for instance, the Speaker polled 25,372 votes and his opponent 12,394.

[2]R.S.C. (1952), c. 143.

on Internal Economy to help supervise the affairs of the House, and gives the Speaker disciplinary authority over his staff.[3]

Various other references are made to the Speaker in these and other acts, but they do not affect the position of the Speaker. The House itself, of course, has enacted many standing orders which affect the Speaker in his capacity as a presiding officer and these provide a much more comprehensive code of conduct than do the statutory provisions. The rules cover the actions of the Speaker from the time he takes the Chair at the opening of the sitting through all the various routine and other business to the time he adjourns the House without question put each evening. It is in these rules that one can see the traditional picture of the Speaker presiding over the House, putting all questions as they arise, settling points of order, and maintaining the dignity and decorum of the House.

The Election of a Speaker

At the beginning of each new Parliament when the members meet in the Commons Chamber for the first time, the Clerk occupies his usual place at the head of the Table. The Gentleman Usher of the Black Rod appears at the door and, as is customary for royal assent, summons the House to the Senate. Led by the Clerk, the House attends the Deputy Governor General in the Senate, only to be sent back to elect a Speaker.[4] On its return to the Commons Chamber, the House proceeds with the election in the same fashion as the House at Westminster. The Clerk rises in his place and points to a member who desires to speak. This member makes a short speech and moves that his nominee "take the Chair of this House as Speaker." The question is seconded by another member and is put by the Clerk. Should the opposition have no objection, the leaders of the opposition parties make short laudatory speeches and the Clerk declares the member elected. His proposer and

[3]Substantially the same provisions may be found in two acts passed in the first session of the House in 1867–8: "An Act further securing the independence of Parliament" and "An Act respecting the internal economy of the House of Commons and for other purposes."

[4]The House is not sent away with the command to elect a Speaker as it is in Great Britain. The Deputy Governor General merely announces that "the Governor General does not see fit to declare the causes of his summoning the present Parliament of Canada until a Speaker of the House of Commons shall have been chosen according to law. . . ." It is assumed that the British North America Act is sufficient authority to enable the House to proceed with the election.

seconder conduct him to the Chair, where his first official act is to thank the House and "disable" himself by expressing his unfitness for the high office to which he has been summoned.[5] The Mace is placed on the Table[6] and the House adjourns to await the attendance of the Governor General for the formal opening of Parliament. For this the House is again summoned to the Senate, the new Speaker presents himself to the Governor General, claims the privileges of the Commons, and prays that any "errors" should be imputed to him rather than to the House.[7] After the gracious granting of these requests, and the reading of the Speech from the Throne, the Commons return to their Chamber to proceed with the work of the session.

On the surface, the procedure at the opening of a Parliament is copied direct from the British House and, indeed, much of the spirit of the ceremony. In detail, however, the Canadian House has developed its own traditions and customs which make the Speakership vary widely from its British counterpart. The form of election of the Speaker is symbolic of the position of the office in Canada. There is no attempt to separate the Government front-bench from the nomination of the Speaker. On every occasion since Confederation, the Prime Minister or Leader of the House has made the nomination.[8] On all but three occasions a leading member of the Government has been the seconder: the exceptions to this rule were the elections of Mr. Speaker Beaudoin in 1953 and Mr. Speaker Michener in 1957 and 1958 when the Leader of the Opposition seconded the nomination.

This front-bench domination has perhaps led to the tradition that the Opposition never offers a candidate of its own. The Opposition does

[5]The form of acceptance varies widely. Several Speakers have used the same formula, and others have accepted in rather more flowery terms. The Speaker usually delivers his speech in his own language, although bilingual Speakers generally repeat their acceptance in both official languages.

[6]The Mace is always on the Table while the House is sitting. When any Committee of the Whole is sitting the Mace is placed on supports slightly below the level of the Table and is usually referred to as being "under the Table." In fact, the only time that the Mace is literally under the Table is before the Speaker is elected. Then it rests between the legs of the Table virtually at floor level.

[7]It is an interesting variation from British practice that the Canadian Speaker has never submitted himself to the Governor General for confirmation of his election. The colonial practice varied, but in the Province of Canada approval was never asked, presumably as a result of the refusal of the Governor of Lower Canada to approve the election of Louis Papineau in 1827. Nova Scotia, New Brunswick, and Prince Edward Island, however, all submitted their Speakers for approval.

[8]On the occasions when the Prime Minister has not made the nomination it has been only because of his unavoidable absence. In 1916 Sir Robert Borden was ill and in 1925 Mackenzie King had not yet found a seat in the House.

not, however, always agree that the best man has been chosen. In 1874 Sir John A. Macdonald expressed surprise at the Liberal nominee and suggested another prominent Liberal who might have been chosen. He openly opposed the re-election of T. W. Anglin in 1878 on a procedural point,[9] and forced a recorded vote on his election. This is the only occasion on which a Speaker has been elected on a recorded division.[10] In 1935, R. B. Bennett strongly opposed the election of P. F. Casgrain, not on personal grounds, but rather on his actions in dismissing House staff before his election to office. This motion, however, passed "on division" and without further nominations or a recorded vote.

As a result of this remarkable unanimity of opinion in the House, the case law relating to the election of Speakers is rather sparse. No procedure exists which could be followed should the Opposition as well as the Government nominate a candidate. Still more doubtful is the question of the proper method of breaking a tie vote. When the Government which nominates the Speaker has a majority in the House, this is of little importance, But on two occasions, in 1925 and 1957, the Government has met the House without a majority. The danger was apparent enough in 1925 for the Clerk of the House to address an inquiry to the Clerk of the British House. The answer was clear and for lack of a precedent will probably stand as the proper procedure: Sir T. Lonsdale Webster was certain that should there be a tie vote on the first name the question should be treated as void, and the question put on the second name;[11] the Clerk of the House does not have a casting vote.[12] The

[9] Anglin, who had occupied the Chair for four years, automatically vacated his seat when it was discovered that some years before he had accepted a government contract. He was returned in a by-election after prorogation, signed the roll, and took his seat as soon as the House met. The Government nominated him again for the Speakership. Macdonald opposed the motion on the grounds that Anglin could not properly take his seat before a Speaker was elected. Perhaps the most interesting feature of this incident is the fact that the House had for four years a Speaker who was legally a "stranger."

[10] The propriety of dividing the House when only one name had been suggested was questioned at the time, but no decision was given on the point of order. Anglin himself abstained from voting in this division in accordance with general practice. Under British practice (re-established in 1959) there could not be a vote on this motion. In that year the Clerk of the House let it be known that no vote could take place if only one candidate was nominated.

[11] A further point which is not settled by this answer is what would happen should there be a tie vote on a division like that of 1878 where only one candidate was nominated. Presumably the vote would be void and the Government would nominate a second person, although it might, on the grounds that the election of a Speaker is the right of the House as a whole, leave further nominations to the other members of the House.

[12] This situation arose in Australia in 1909 when the Clerk of the House attempted to settle the election of a Speaker by his own vote. His right to do this was vigorously challenged by the members present.

conclusion that this is the proper procedure is borne out by the objections raised by Sir John A. Macdonald in 1878 when the Clerk assumed the duties of a presiding officer and announced vacancies in the membership of the House and the election of new members before the Speaker was elected. The same announcements have been made by the Clerk in more recent years without complaint, although it is doubtful whether they should be made at such time. There is no doubt, however, that the Clerk does not preside over the House. He is merely chairman of a meeting called to elect a Speaker.

The Unwritten Conditions of Office

Certain unwritten conditions come into play with regard to appointments to the Chair. It has, for instance, been the practice to change Speakers after each Parliament, although this tradition has been broken. It has also been a general practice to alternate Speakers between the major linguistic groups in the country, but this is not invariable, and often an uncompleted term is not considered in the rotation scheme.

CHANGE OR PERMANENCE

These conditions have not always been looked on as ideal. In 1873, when Macdonald nominated James Cockburn for a second term, he noted that he was trying to copy the British system that a Speaker who served well should not be changed "capriciously" at the beginning of each Parliament. Hansard noted that the motion passed "amid loud applause from the Ministerial benches and a solemn silence on the part of the Opposition."[13] This silence was prophetic, for in 1874 when the Liberals assumed power, they passed over Cockburn in favour of T. W. Anglin, a leading supporter of the new Government. Oddly enough, Sir John A. Macdonald did not reproach the Government for its action; rather, as has been mentioned, he suggested that a different member of the Liberal party might have been a better choice.

The practice of changing Speakers was more firmly established in 1879 when Macdonald, in power again, passed over both Cockburn and Anglin, who were still in the House, and nominated a French Canadian. The gibes of Mackenzie, then Leader of the Opposition, reminding him of his statements in 1873 in favour of the British practice did not move the Prime Minister. The same quotations were used by Blake in 1883 when Macdonald nominated yet another Speaker; Blake was even more direct in his attack than Mackenzie had been and noted

[13]*Debates*, March 5, 1873, p. 1.

that while the Prime Minister deplored the scarcity of good men for the Chair, he did not suggest re-electing the previous Speaker who was still in the House. The same question was raised by Laurier as Leader of the Opposition in 1891 and 1911, and by other members in 1922.[14]

The problem is not always a simple one. Sir Wilfrid Laurier appears to have supported the principle of a permanent Speaker, although he did not himself nominate a candidate for two terms. When nominating Charles Marcil in 1909 he stated in the House that he had approached the former Speaker with the suggestion that he should remain, but that Sutherland had refused to serve another term.[15] The arduous nature of the job and the possibility of promotion from the Chair do not encourage an able Speaker to remain in the post.

A distinct pattern can, however, be found in all this. Whichever party is in power generally considers its duty to be the guarding of the valuable Canadian tradition of rapid replacement of Speakers, and the party out of power supports the great British practice of a permanent Speaker. Occasionally the positions are reversed and the Government, with a great demonstration of loyalty to the British tradition, renominates a Speaker for a second term; at these elections the Opposition may be found suggesting that the old Canadian practice of rotation is perhaps better than the British.[16] It is significant, however, that it is always a member of the Government party who is re-elected. One can hardly accuse Arthur Meighen of being overly cynical when in 1926 he remarked that he would believe the trend to the British tradition the first time it was used with a member who had been elected to the Chair by the Opposition.[17]

ROTATION OF FRENCH AND ENGLISH SPEAKERS

The rotation of French and English Speakers has also been uncertain in its application. T. W. Anglin succeeded James Cockburn in 1874 without any question being raised. The first French Speaker followed in 1879, although the Government did not formally state the principle of alternating according to language. The rotation scheme in fact was

[14]*Ibid.*, Feb. 13, 1879, p. 2; Feb. 8, 1883, pp. 1–2; April 29, 1891, col. 2; Nov. 15, 1911, cols. 3–5; March 8, 1922, p. 3.

[15]*Ibid.*, Jan. 20, 1909, cols. 2–4.

[16]*Ibid.*, Dec. 9, 1926, p. 2; May 12, 1958, p. 3.

[17]His statement was made on the occasion of the renomination of Rodolphe Lemieux (*ibid.*, Jan. 7, 1926, p. 2). Only once has an opposition member been considered for the Chair. In 1957 Mr. Diefenbaker offered the nomination to Mr. Knowles, a leading member of one of the minor parties in the House. The exact reasons for this offer are doubtful and it is difficult to assess its significance. The offer does not seem to have been repeated, either to Mr. Knowles or to any other member.

followed through the next three Speakers until with the change of Government in 1896 Sir James Edgar succeeded Peter White. The tradition was mentioned at that election, as might be expected under the circumstances, by the Opposition: Sir Charles Tupper regretted that the "time-honoured precedent" of alternating Speakers had been forgotten. An English Speaker, Thomas Bain, completed Edgar's unfinished term. The next Parliament elected a French Speaker and the rotation has continued in principle to this day. A few minor exceptions can be found: four Speakers—James Cockburn, E. N. Rhodes, Rodolphe Lemieux, and Mr. Roland Michener—have all spent more than one Parliament in the Chair; on two occasions Speakers of the same language have been elected to fill out uncompleted terms, although on another occasion even this opportunity was used to change to a Speaker of the other language.[18]

Alternation of Speakers has never been a guarantee of bilingualism in office: all the French Speakers have been completely bilingual but the English have rarely been as accomplished. The question first arose with Cockburn in 1867. The French members attacked his nomination on the ground that he was not sufficiently acquainted with their language. The Government defended its choice, and Cartier stated that although Cockburn was not fluent, he understood French well enough. He does not seem to have been particularly competent, however, for within two weeks another French member protested, and suggested that all routine business should be done in both languages. Anglin, who succeeded in 1874, spoke no French. Kirkpatrick, the next English Speaker, was "not as conversant with the French as with the English language" but his seconder held that he knew enough to follow the debates. Ten years later White was forced to admit to a French member whom he called to order that he was not fluent enough to understand what was being said, but asked him to remain within the rules.[19]

More recent English Speakers have at least made an effort to become familiar with French. Sir Robert Borden related a story which illustrates the industry, if not the ability, of one of these Speakers. When Thomas Sproule assumed the post in 1911 he knew no French, but thought it necessary to learn at least enough to read the daily prayers, and after three weeks' study, he felt fluent enough to take over the duty from the Clerk Assistant. The prayer was written out phonetically for him and he read it to the House. The irreverent comment of one member that "I

[18]N. A. Belcourt succeeded L. P. Brodeur in 1904, and J. L. Bowman succeeded George Black in 1935. Albert Sévigny succeeded Thomas Sproule in 1916 and was in turn followed by E. N. Rhodes in 1917.

[19]*Debates*, Nov. 6, 1867, p. 1; Nov. 22, 1867, p. 38; Feb. 8, 1883, p. 1; March 30, 1893, col. 3475.

have no doubt that Almighty God would understand it" is an indication of his proficiency. Borden concluded the story by writing: "After a time the Speaker became confused between the French diphthongs 'au', 'eau', and 'eu' and he read the Lord's Prayer with a pronunciation which greatly astonished the French-speaking members, as his pronunciation of the French word for 'heaven', sounded to them like the French word for 'bucket'."[20] Other Speakers have adopted the same co-operative attitude to the French language. Sutherland, when accepting the post of Speaker, attempted a few words of French in his speech of thanks.[21] Mr. Speaker Macdonald is reputed to have acquired a working knowledge of the language while in the Chair.

GEOGRAPHICAL REPRESENTATION

There has been no other tradition in the selection of Speakers. Various sections of the country have been represented, apparently at random: Quebec and Ontario naturally have provided the bulk of the incumbents, Quebec nine, Ontario ten; Manitoba has provided two; and New Brunswick, Nova Scotia, and the Yukon have each had one. The alternation of French and English Speakers has, of course, provided a large proportion of Speakers from Quebec, but with the spread of French-Canadian influence, it is by no means impossible that there will be French Speakers from Ontario, New Brunswick, or Manitoba.[22]

PROFESSIONAL BACKGROUNDS

The professional backgrounds of the Speakers have not been as varied; no less than seventeen out of twenty-four have been lawyers; the remainder have been scattered among the occupations of newspaper publishing, journalism, business, farming, medicine (two), and dentistry. Certainly a legal training is an advantage and the judicial nature of the job and the necessity of having a thorough knowledge of the law have been stressed many times.

EXPERIENCE AND TRAINING

Length of service in the House also seems to be no indication of eligibility. Mr. Speaker Rhodes, one of the outstanding Speakers of the Canadian House, had been a member for only nine years when called to the Chair, and Mr. Speaker Michener for the remarkably short period

---

[20]Henry Borden, ed., *Robert Laird Borden: His Memoirs* (2 vols., Toronto, 1938), I, pp. 335–6 n.

[21]*Debates*, Jan. 11, 1905, col. 4.

[22]During the speculation which followed Mr. Beaudoin's offer to resign in 1956, one of the names most prominently mentioned was that of Mr. René Jutras, a French-speaking member from Manitoba.

of four years. Early Speakers, on the other hand, often contested five elections before attaining the Speakership. Mr. Speaker Sproule's service in the House covered thirty-three years before he was elected, and Mr. Speaker Lemieux's twenty-six.

On a few occasions these years of training included terms in the lesser offices of Deputy Speaker and Deputy Chairman, the qualifications for which will be discussed later in this chapter. Six Speakers have served an apprenticeship in these minor posts. There has been little feeling in the House, however, that this is necessary, or that the Deputy Speaker should succeed to the Chair. In 1909 Laurier mentioned that "it is a tradition of our Houses and it is the fitness of things that the member of the Houses who ranks next to the Speaker in the previous Parliament should be called to the chair."[23] It is hard to accept this statement as the step had been taken only once previously, when in 1901 L. P. Brodeur, who had been Deputy Speaker for five years, was made Speaker. Laurier had, however, attempted to establish this practice in 1891 when Sir John A. Macdonald nominated Peter White for the Speakership. Laurier, after noting that the custom of re-electing Speakers was not to be followed, suggested that John Wood, who had been Deputy Speaker, might properly be promoted.[24] Arthur Meighen made the same suggestion in 1922 when he referred to the "custom" of promoting Deputy Speakers.[25] There was by this time a custom that had been followed on four occasions, but G. H. Boivin's membership in the Conservative party was against him, and the Liberals passed him over in favour of Rodolphe Lemieux. The custom has been revived in recent years; both Mr. Macdonald and Mr. Beaudoin had had previous experience. Whenever these promotions have been made, the training which the member has acquired and his proved quality have always been noted as valuable assets. It is even possible that, as in the case of Mr. Beaudoin, the post of Deputy Chairman can be used as a source of trained Speakers for the House.

Party Activity

Lord Ullswater notes in his autobiography that when he was appointed Deputy Speaker at Westminster he "had never been a strong party man." Lord Hemingford says of Mr. Speaker FitzRoy that he "never sought popularity, publicity or prominence." These two observations on the

23*Debates*, Jan. 20, 1909, col. 3.
24*Ibid.*, April 29, 1891, col. 2.   25*Ibid.*, March 8, 1922, p. 3.

character of the men who are elected to the British Speakership are indicative of the tradition of the British Chair over the past century.[26] There has never been such an approach to the Speakership in Canada. Indeed the Canadian House has shown a remarkable tolerance of the nominations of the Government and has accepted numerous men whose reputation for partiality was notorious. Mr. Speaker Anglin, for instance, was well known by the time he was elected to the Chair: he had been a member of the House for seven years, and was even better known for his work outside the House. In 1873 he had written an article in his newspaper in which he referred to the behaviour of certain Conservatives in the House as "loathsome" and "disgusting," and spoke of them as men who would "wade through filth so vile to Governorships, Judgeships, places in the Cabinet, places out of the Cabinet, profits and so-called honours." This article, as will be remembered from chapter 3, was judged by the House to be a "scandalous, false, and malicious libel upon the Honour, integrity and character of this House, and of certain members thereof, and a high contempt of the privileges and constitutional authority of this House." Nevertheless, within a year Anglin had been elected to the highest position in the gift of the House without any question being raised about his fitness for the post.

In 1883 the nomination of Kirkpatrick was questioned by the Opposition on the ground that he had taken a prominent part in defending a stranger who had insulted a member on the floor of the House. There was a strong suggestion that actions of this sort did not lend weight to a member's qualifications.[27] The nomination of Mr. Speaker Marcil in 1909 was accompanied by similar moralizing: Borden reflected at length on the practice of bribing constituencies with promises and emphasized that the Speaker could not go running to the Government looking for favours. Members took notice also of "strong partisanship" on the part of Black, Casgrain, and Sproule. In the case of the

---

[26]Lord Ullswater, *A Speaker's Commentaries* (2 vols., London, 1925), I, p. 257; Lord Hemingford, *Back-Bencher and Chairman* (London, 1946), p. 51. There have been notable exceptions. Both Brand and Peel were Government chief whips before their election to the Chair. W. S. Morrison was a Cabinet Minister from 1936 to 1945 and the present Speaker moved from his post of Solicitor General to the Chair. Sir Henry Campbell-Bannerman was an even more striking exception. He made every effort to attain the Chair in 1895 while he was a member of the Cabinet. His election to the Speakership was opposed only by his constituents and his Cabinet colleagues. These finally prevailed. In 1899 he was made leader of his party in the House, and in 1905 became Prime Minister. See J. A. Spender, *The Life of the Right Honourable Sir Henry Campbell-Bannerman* (2 vols., London, 1923), I, pp. 173–7.

[27]*Debates*, Feb. 8, 1883, p. 2. For discussion of this incident, see *supra*, chap. 3, pp. 39–40.

last of these, Sir Wilfrid Laurier referred to him in terms which would certainly have disqualified a British Speaker: "he is a Tory, a Tory of Tories, the very quintessence of Toryism. . . ."[28] It is interesting that Rodolphe Lemieux, one of the most distinguished Speakers of the House, not only was a strong party supporter, but actually had held three Cabinet posts before he was elected to the Chair. A speech made by Mr. Beaudoin illustrates a modern Speaker's attempt to minimize his party ties: he stated that from his election as Deputy Chairman in 1949 until 1956 he had not attended any political meetings except during the general election of 1953.[29] Such a restraint shows a commendable isolation from party politics and might well be emulated by future occupants of the Chair.

Occasionally the Canadian Speaker has been a popular and relatively non-partisan member. In 1887 Blake greeted happily the nomination of Ouimet and welcomed him as a Tory rebel who had bolted his party to vote with the Opposition in the debate on Louis Riel two years previously.[30] On other occasions the nomination has merely been met with a casual acceptance by the Opposition, who have admitted the member's impartiality and concurred in his election. A new practice may have started in 1953 when the Prime Minister moved and the Leader of the Opposition seconded the nomination of Mr. Beaudoin.[31] This symbolic unity of opinion had never been known before, and has since been followed on two other occasions.[32] If continued in the future it could do much to offset the stigma of Government front-bench nominations.

Participation in Debate

There does not seem to have been any tradition which prevented the occupant of the Chair from participating actively in debate when not actually presiding. In 1878 Anglin spoke at length in Committee of the Whole against a temperance bill. The practice was followed many times later, both at the committee stage on bills and in supply.[33] However,

[28]For these examples, see *Debates*, Jan. 20, 1909, col. 5; Sept. 8, 1930, p. 3; Feb. 6, 1936, pp. 3–10; Nov. 15, 1911, col. 4.

[29]Speech to the Empire Club of Canada, Toronto, Oct. 25, 1956.

[30]*Debates*, April 13, 1887, pp. 1–2.

[31]*Ibid.*, Nov. 12, 1953, pp. 1–2.

[32]*Ibid.*, Oct. 14, 1957, pp. 1–3; May 12, 1958, pp. 1–3.

[33]*Ibid.*, July 29, 1891, col. 3083; July 31, 1891, col. 3245; Aug. 24, 1891, col. 4300; March 31, 1892, col. 817; June 20, 1892, col. 3908; June 27, 1894, col. 5049; July 5, 1895, col. 3924; March 25, 1909, col. 3278, etc.

Mr. Speaker Lemieux precipitated a brief debate on the subject in 1927 when he rose in committee to offer some observations as a former Postmaster General on some non-controversial amendments to the Post Office Act. The propriety of his action was questioned at once and he defended his position with British precedents. In concluding he made his position clear: "I repeat that I quite agree with the principle laid down by the honourable gentleman and by all authorities that the Speaker from the Chair must not take part in the debate; that he must not vote unless there is a tie, but in committee he has a right to speak and to vote. I never speak unless on an exceptional occasion like this morning, on a non-party matter on a purely moral issue, and I would not even vote."[34] Recent Speakers have taken a more restricted view of their rights and have managed to confine their desire to participate in the House to brief and rather dull explanations of their departmental estimates in Committee of Supply.

Removal from Office

The removal of a Speaker from office is less complicated than his appointment. Most Speakers in Canada, of course, are removed automatically by the dissolution of the House over which they have presided. However, one Speaker died in office and four Speakers vacated the Chair before the expiry of their terms, and when a Speaker either dies or resigns many of the formalities of the opening of Parliament must be carried out anew. The fact that a vacancy exists is communicated to the House, the Governor General gives his assent to an election, and the new Speaker presents himself to the Governor General to ask that any faults be imputed to himself and not to the House. The privileges of the House are not requested again, because they are granted to the House for the duration of a Parliament. They cannot be abrogated by the death or resignation of a Speaker.

Of the four Speakers who have voluntarily left office before the dissolution of Parliament, only one resigned his office in a regular manner. On that occasion George Black placed a letter of resignation in the hands of the Prime Minister who communicated it to the House as it met for business at the beginning of a new session. The other resignations from the Chair were accomplished with a minimum of formality. Three Speakers accepted other appointments during the parliamentary recess and vacated their seats and the office auto-

[34]*Ibid.*, April 7, 1927, p. 2038.

matically.[35] The House met without a Speaker, and on its return from the Senate with the Governor General's consent to elect a successor, discovered that the incumbent had vacated his seat by his appointment. No formal notification was ever given by these three that they had left the Chair.

There is no doubt that some definite action on the part of the Speaker is necessary to effect his removal before the dissolution of Parliament. His death or loss of his seat are the most obvious. Beyond this the method is doubtful. A resignation announced from the Chair while the House is sitting is possible, but would leave the House in the awkward position of having to disperse without doing any further business. A letter of resignation to the Clerk or the Prime Minister which states a definite date of resignation is the only easily effective method. Certainly the House itself cannot be called on to act in the matter: it may express its regret at the loss of a valued presiding officer, but no action on its part is necessary to put the Speaker's wish into effect. It is hard, therefore, to explain the unusual "resignation" of Mr. Speaker Beaudoin on July 2, 1956, and to understand the attitude of the House to its withdrawal a week later—questions which will be discussed in detail later in this chapter. The resignation followed the disclosure in the press of a letter the Speaker had written which indicated a partiality in the Chair. He made a "farewell speech" from the Chair and placed his resignation before the House, asking only that action be deferred until the return of the Prime Minister from London a week later. The resignation was faulty in two respects. First, and most obvious, it contained no effective date: it was placed before the House with the expressed hope that it would be "accepted as soon as possible." Second, the resignation was to take effect "at the pleasure of the House": no indication was given of how the will of the House was to be made known, and thus the door was left open for a later reversal. The next week, at the request of the Prime Minister, Mr. Beaudoin withdrew his resignation. The reaction of the Opposition to the sudden reversal was as unusual as the action complained of. The Prime Minister was assailed for persuading the Speaker to remain in office and accused of arrogating to himself the right of appointing the Speaker of the House. The Prime Minister went to the nub of the problem when, in his own defence, he said: "A Speaker who chooses to resign, does resign, and it is the act of his own will that creates the vacancy required under the British North America

[35]L. P. Brodeur and Albert Sévigny both accepted portfolios and T. S. Sproule was summoned to the Senate.

Act to make way for the election of a new Speaker."[36] The debate ended the incident and Mr. Beaudoin remained in office until the dissolution of Parliament nearly a year later.

Prospects after Retirement

The future of a Speaker when he leaves the Chair of the Canadian House is uncertain. On the last day of the session of 1883 Alonzo Wright followed a common practice and delivered a eulogy of Mr. Speaker Kirkpatrick. He concluded by expressing the hope of all members that when the Speaker was "exalted into the political arcana," all members would be able to join in saying "well done good and faithful Speaker, enter thou into the new governorship, collectorship or judgeship prepared for you from the beginning of this Parliament."[37] There has been a general belief that the Canadian Speakership has been widely used by members as a step towards a Cabinet post.[38] This belief may easily be exaggerated. The Government does not appear to have looked on the post in this way, although several occupants of the Chair undoubtedly have: both Kirkpatrick and White, for example, pressed this claim to promotion on the Prime Minister, who met them coldly. Six Speakers have made the change, however: four of the six completed their terms of office and moved to the Cabinet after an election and the other two left the Chair in the middle of a Parliament. Almost as many Speakers have remained in active politics in the House. Charles Marcil sat as a private member for no less than twenty-six years after leaving the Chair. Surprisingly enough, the Senate has not been widely used to remove Speakers from the House and from active participation in politics. Two of the three Speakers who have been summoned to the Senate have desired a quiet haven and have earned their appointment by long service in the House: Thomas Sproule resigned for reasons of ill health before the end of his term as Speaker but he had previously served as a member of the House for thirty-seven years; Rodolphe Lemieux retired at the end of three terms in the Chair and thirty-four

[36]*Debates*, July 10, 1956, p. 5857.
[37]*Ibid.*, May 25, 1883, p. 1396.
[38]Only one member has gone from the Cabinet to the Chair—Rodolphe Lemieux who was in Laurier's Cabinet from 1904 to 1911 was made Speaker of the House in 1922 instead of being reappointed to the Cabinet. See R. MacG. Dawson, *William Lyon Mackenzie King: A Political Biography*, I, *1874–1923* (Toronto, 1958), pp. 362–73.

years in the House. Mr. Ross Macdonald, on the other hand, went to the Senate to become Government Leader and Solicitor General. The occasional judgeship, lieutenant-governorship, and even the post of collector of customs have all been used as suitable rewards for Speakers. Recently, Speakers have been appointed to the Privy Council after their term of office has expired—Speakers Fauteux, Macdonald, and Beaudoin—but it is difficult to tell whether these three appointments represent a definite trend, for the two preceding Speakers—Casgrain and Glen—went direct from the Chair to the Cabinet.

The Deputy Speaker

In the early years of the Canadian House of Commons the lengthy sittings made the Speaker's job a very arduous one, but no provision had been made in the rules of 1867 for a Deputy Speaker. They did provide that "in forming a Committee of the Whole House, the Speaker before leaving the Chair shall appoint a Chairman to preside,"[39] but the trouble was that the member thus called to the Chair quite often knew little of the rules and as a result was incapable of settling points of order satisfactorily. The problem was not faced until 1885, when Sir John A. Macdonald proposed an amendment to permit the appointment of another officer who would be called the Chairman of Committees. The questions that were raised on the need for this new post were merely an attempt to embarrass the Government;[40] the questions that were raised on its legality were more important. The Opposition pointed out that the office of Speaker was governed by the British North America Act, and that although Parliament could alter certain of its provisions, it could not do so by a mere resolution of the House. The Prime Minister accepted this objection and moved first reading of a bill "to provide for the appointment of a Deputy Speaker of the House of Commons." The rule subsequently accepted for inclusion in the standing orders was based on the provisions of this Act.[41]

[39]1867 Rule 76. The legality of the actions of temporary occupants of the Chair was also guaranteed by an Act Respecting the Office of Speaker of the House of Commons of the Dominion of Canada, 31 Vict., c. 2.

[40]The comment of Edward Blake, the spokesman of the Opposition, that "it is a case not of an office for which a man is wanted, but of a man who wants an office" indicates the doubts raised about the reason for the appointment. *Debates,* Feb. 10, 1885, p. 70.

[41]48-49 Vict., c. 2. At first the rule was included in the rule book merely as a resolution of the House (1904 Rules, pp. 60-1); it was not formally written into the rules until 1906 (1906 Rule 13).

POWERS, ELECTION, AND QUALIFICATIONS

The Act vests in the Deputy Speaker all the legal powers of the Speaker should that officer be absent from the House. Two possibilities are covered. First, should the Speaker wish to leave the Chair briefly during a sitting, he is empowered to call on the Chairman of Committees (who is also the Deputy Speaker) or any other member to assume his duties as presiding officer. This is often, of course, done. Second, should the Speaker be absent from the beginning of a sitting, the Clerk informs the House of his "unavoidable absence"; the Chairman of Committees at once takes the Chair and reads prayers. These formalities are repeated at each subsequent sitting until the Speaker returns. In the event of an adjournment of more than one day, the Deputy Speaker retains his extraordinary powers for only twenty-four hours. The provision is rarely invoked: Mr. Speaker Beaudoin, for instance, was never "unavoidably absent" in his four years in office; Sir James Edgar, however, was absent for some days prior to his death in 1899, and other Speakers have been absent occasionally.

The standing orders are more exacting:

A Chairman of Committees who shall also be Deputy Speaker of the House shall be elected at the commencement of every Parliament;[42] and the member so elected shall, if in his place in the House, take the Chair of all committees of the whole including the committees of Supply, and Ways and Means, in accordance with the usages which regulate the duties of a similar officer, generally designated the Chairman of the Committee of Ways and Means, in the House of Commons of the United Kingdom of Great Britain and Northern Ireland. (S.O. 52(1))

He must, in addition, possess "the full and practical knowledge" of the language which is not that of the current Speaker (S.O. 52(2)). This provision has not always been followed. Admittedly the first incumbent, Malachy Daly, who served under an English Speaker, was not fluent in French. In nominating him, Sir John A. Macdonald contended that he would be "quite competent" in the language, but there is no evidence to support this claim. Generally, however, the letter as well as the spirit of the law has been observed. As a natural consequence, even though there seem to be no geographical conditions attached to the office,[43]

[42]There was an attempt in 1887 to rescind the rule relating to the election of the Deputy Speaker. It was argued that the Deputy Speaker's main duty was as Chairman of Committees of the Whole and that the old practice of calling any member to the Chair could be continued. The motion was defeated. *Debates*, May 5, 1887, pp. 296–9.

[43]There is on record a letter to Sir Wilfrid Laurier in which W. S. Fielding questions the advisability of having a Deputy Speaker from the same province as the Speaker of the Senate. P.A.C., Laurier Papers, pp. 51205–6.

there has been some emphasis on representatives from Quebec, which has supplied over half the Deputy Speakers. Most of the rest have come from Ontario; Nova Scotia has supplied three and Saskatchewan one.

The nomination of the Deputy Speaker, who holds office until the end of the life of each Parliament (S.O. 52 (3)), is moved and seconded by the Government, and there is some indication that the opinion of the Speaker is taken into consideration.[44] The election generally proceeds without debate and almost always without a division. Occasionally, however, the election has met with opposition. Normally the point at issue has been the nominee's ability to be impartial, but in 1962 a division was forced on the election of a Deputy Speaker on the ground that the Government was using the office as a training ground for the Cabinet. On this occasion the protest was not aimed at the individual concerned, but at the Government for promoting three Deputy Speakers into the Cabinet in three years.

PARTY ACTIVITY

Actually the Deputy Speakers have never made any real effort to remain aloof from party conflict. Like the Speakers, they did until recently retain their right to speak in the House when not in the Chair, and exercised the privilege often. In 1931 A. R. Lavergne defended this right with the strong words: "A Deputy Speaker is not supposed to be impartial when he is not in the Chair. Truth holds a greater place in the House than the opinion of my honourable friend."[45] Even today the Deputy Speaker votes in all divisions except on appeals from his rulings in a committee, although he generally does not speak in the House.

Nevertheless, in 1911 the election of P. E. Blondin was opposed on the ground that he was an extreme nationalist and therefore unsuitable for the post.[46] It is not very surprising that two years later a motion of censure was moved against him, and that the third year after, Sir Wilfrid Laurier moved "That in the opinion of this House in the discharge of the duties and responsibilities of Deputy Speaker towards this House, he is bound by and subject to the same rules as apply to Mr. Speaker, and that therefore, he is disbarred from taking part in electoral contests."[47] This motion represents the only real attempt that has been made to achieve impartiality in the Deputy Speaker. Oddly enough, Borden, the Prime Minister, opposed the idea. He admitted that there

[44]See letter from Sutherland to Laurier, Jan. 4, 1905, *ibid.*, p. 93374.
[45]*Debates*, June 19, 1931, p. 2840.
[46]*Ibid.*, Nov. 29, 1911, cols. 519–25.
[47]*Ibid.*, March 5, 1914, p. 1362.

had been several very partisan appointees and that the question of the Deputy Speaker's participating in by-elections had been raised previously.[48] The status of both the Speaker and Deputy Speaker was based on custom and should the House feel it necessary to establish rules for the Deputy Speaker it would undoubtedly be necessary to do the same for the Speaker. No decision was taken and Sir Wilfrid withdrew his motion.

The same general position was taken in 1931 by Mackenzie King when he questioned the propriety of a Deputy Speaker's speaking in the House. He referred to the Laurier motion and pointed out that the Deputy Speaker had a salary to ensure his independence. The Deputy Speaker involved maintained his right to speak for his constituents and for the country, and offered, if necessary, to resign to regain his freedom. It was generally agreed that no action could be taken, and that the good taste of the Deputy Speaker must govern his actions.[49]

PROSPECTS AFTER RETIREMENT

The rewards for Deputy Speakers, aside from the six who have been promoted to the Speakership, seem as varied as those for Speakers. Surprisingly enough, the most common event is for a Deputy Speaker to retire into private life for at least a brief period after a defeat at the polls. No less than nine have done so, although three have later returned to the House. Five have also entered the Cabinet direct.[50] Continued membership in the House, retirement, the Senate, and the judiciary have accounted for the remainder.

The Deputy Chairman

In 1938 the standing orders were further amended to permit the House each session "or from time to time as necessity may arise" to elect a Deputy Chairman authorized to exercise all the powers of the Chairman (S.O. 52 (5)). The Deputy Speaker was to be absent from the country

[48]He mentioned the debate which had taken place in 1897 on the question of whether L. P. Brodeur should absent himself from the House to campaign while in receipt of a salary as Deputy Speaker. He could also have mentioned that a similar question had been raised in 1888 over the absence of C. C. Colby on similar business. The Speaker at that time was quick to suggest that the Deputy Speaker was absent from the House on "private affairs" with permission. *Ibid.*, April 26, 1888, pp. 1005–6.

[49]*Ibid.*, March 20, 1931, pp. 173–80.

[50]This does not include the three who entered the Cabinet after a term as Speaker.

for a considerable time and it was thought advisable to appoint another full-time officer. Mackenzie King suggested that the post would not be permanent but would be filled only when circumstances dictated.[51] The first appointment of J. F. Johnston in 1938 was as temporary as King suggested it would be, and after the session the office was left vacant for nearly ten years. It was revived in 1947 and, is now, in practice, a permanent one: when nominating Mr. Applewhaite in 1953, the Prime Minister referred to the appointment as "completing the organization of the personnel of the House."[52] It is also the custom to reappoint the same person to this position each session.

Impartiality of the Chair

There is a certainty in the minds of all members that the Speaker and his deputies are partisan appointees who in any difficult situation will be sympathetic to, if not actually partisans of, the Government. In a normal session this makes little or no difference. Should the Speaker not allow an amendment to a bill, or should he prevent debate on some subject, however important it may be to the opposition, the decision will be taken with equanimity. Even if it results in a heated debate at the time the matter will soon be forgotten as new issues arise. However, in a session in which feelings are running high and the opposition is determined to follow a particular course of action, an adverse decision by a Speaker will inevitably be looked on as partisan and influenced by Government policy. The fact that the Speaker was practically appointed by the Government and the possibility that he may be looking for advancement when his short term of office is over then become important to the opposition. The outcome of this line of thought is the motion of censure which the Opposition moved against Mr. Speaker Beaudoin in 1956.

CENSURE OF THE SPEAKER

The debate on a bill to establish a Crown corporation (the debate popularly termed the pipeline debate because of the purpose of the particular corporation) had proceeded with great bitterness for three weeks. Closure had been used at each stage and notice had been given of a new closure motion. By adroit tactics the Opposition had postponed the application of closure for one day and had hoped to postpone it still

[51]*Debates*, Feb. 11, 1938, pp. 370–1.
[52]*Ibid.*, Dec. 16, 1953, p. 963.

further. On June 1, the Speaker, in a series of actions, re-established the Government's dominant position and precipitated the rioting and disorder which characterized "Black Friday." That evening, Mr. Drew, the Leader of the Opposition, gave notice in the *Votes and Proceedings* that on Monday he would move: "That in view of the unprecedented actions of Mr. Speaker in (a) improperly reversing his own decision without notice and without giving any opportunity for discussion; (b) repeatedly refusing to allow members to address the House on occasions when the Rules provide that they have the right to be heard; (c) subordinating the rights of the House to the will of the Government, this House resolves that it no longer has any confidence in its Presiding Officer."[53]

The motion appeared on routine proceedings on Monday, June 4, and was debated on four days that week.[54] The debate was carried on with restraint. The House listened in what a local paper described as a "hushed, uneasy, expectant" atmosphere as the Leader of the Opposition outlined his case against the Speaker and demanded a dissolution. Members spoke on both sides of the question while the Speaker himself presided.[55] All the members paid tribute to the outstanding qualities of the Speaker up to the beginning of the pipeline debate; what his accusers contended was that it was only his actions in that debate, and particularly his actions on June 1, that had precipitated the motion of censure, and they pointed out that only twice before in his three years in office had his rulings been appealed. The motion was defeated on a party vote, 35 to 109, the Progressive Conservative and C.C.F. parties voting for it and the Liberal and Social Credit parties against.

It is difficult to assess fairly the objectives behind this action of the two opposition parties. Two points, however, stand out which indicate their motives were not exclusively the obvious ones. First, the tenor of the debate denied that the Speaker was the real object of censure. The Government was under constant attack and a dissolution of the House

[53]*Journals*, June 4, 1956, p. 692.

[54]The debate was adjourned on Monday after one speaker from each party had spoken. It was superseded on Tuesday by a motion to pass to the orders of the day; the House adjourned early on Wednesday in tribute to a member who had just died, and the division took place on Friday. Thursday was the only full day's debate.

[55]The propriety of the Speaker's presiding over his own trial was questioned but the Prime Minister defended the Speaker's decision to preside and the matter was dropped. *Debates*, June 4, 1956, p. 4661. The authorities support this course of action. Sir John G. Bourinot, *Parliamentary Procedure and Practice in the Dominion of Canada* (4th ed., Toronto, 1916), p. 179; A. Beauchesne, *Rules and Forms of the House of Commons of Canada* (4th ed., Toronto, 1958), p. 52.

while the pipeline issue was still fresh was the objective.[56] A statement made by Mr. Knowles is most illuminating: on the final day of the censure debate, he answered a remark of the Minister of National Health and Welfare with the interjection "we are after the Government for what you did to our Speaker." Clearly, a dissolution at this time would have been most advantageous to the opposition: for the first time in years they had an issue which they were sure would carry the country. But they had found that they could not get an election by opposing the bill: the Government was adamant that it would not fight an election on that issue. The issue of the Speaker was then accepted as a desirable means of forcing the Government's hand. There was no question of the resignation of the Speaker and the succession to office of either of the subordinate occupants of the Chair or of some other member. The issue, in spite of the wording of the motion, was the institution of the Speakership and its relation to the Government. The only means of resolving it was an election.

Second, notice of motion was made when the opposition was still suffering intense annoyance over a disastrous tactical defeat. When the House rose on Thursday night, the opposition had complete control of the business of the House with the expectation that it would be able to maintain its dominant position for at least another day. In ten minutes on Friday morning one ruling by the Speaker had handed control of the House back to the Government. It is understandable, then, that all the bitterness and frustration of three weeks of debate would be turned loose at such a time. Earlier there had been a feeling that the Speaker had been ruling suspiciously often in favour of the Government, a feeling which was expressed almost involuntarily on May 23 when Mr. Coldwell remarked, after appealing a ruling, "I think we must be right occasionally."[57] The Speaker realized this and took the opportunity on May 28 to suggest that his record be submitted to a committee of opposition members for judgment so that his impartiality should be beyond question.[58] Three more days of largely unsuccessful procedural wrangling brought the situation to a climax in the motion of censure.

Unfortunately, the motion moved by the opposition is inconsistent with its attitude in debate. The Speaker is an officer of the House

[56]It was suggested by a Government member that the motion of censure was yet another form of obstruction to the bill under consideration (*Debates*, June 4, 1956, p. 4659). This is unlikely as the bill was only one stage away from final approval and the censure motion could be, and was, easily postponed for the necessary time.

[57]*Ibid.*, May 23, 1956, p. 4262.

[58]*Ibid.*, May 28, 1956, pp. 4370–1.

itself, not a servant of the people of Canada. Unlike the Government he is responsible neither in theory nor in practice to any person outside the House of Commons. Similarly, his relations with the Government or the opposition are matters of internal interest to the House alone and cannot be resolved by an appeal to the country. Had the opposition succeeded in its attempt to force a dissolution, the situation would not have improved no matter which party was returned. The Government would have had a public pronouncement on its general policies, and another party might have succeeded to power, but the Speakership would have remained substantially unaltered. Had the Government been returned, the situation would have been even more unsettled, as the opposition would have been unlikely to accept this verdict as the final one on the question.

Under the conditions of the time the problem was really insoluble. It is improbable that, had the opposition parties succeeded in forcing the Speaker from the Chair, they would have accepted as an impartial Speaker either the Deputy Speaker or the Deputy Chairman, both of whom had rendered unpopular decisions while in the Chair during the pipeline debate,[59] or any other Liberal member who might have been proposed as a substitute. The only alternative was a dissolution and a new Parliament. But this, in turn, would put in the hands of the opposition the power to force a dissolution on the Government merely by moving a vote of censure on the Speaker. The motion would not need to be passed, or the charges even properly substantiated, as indeed on this occasion they were not. This would be an intolerable power placed in the hands of the opposition and one totally at variance with the normal practices of parliamentary government.

Under certain conditions, the Speaker could be removed without this dilemma. Three weeks after the above motion of censure was defeated, a Montreal newspaper, *La Patrie*, printed in an editorial excerpts from a letter written by the Speaker to a free-lance journalist, in which the Speaker stated that in the censure debate his "accusers had distorted the facts for their own political ends." Oddly enough, this disclosure of bias on the part of the Speaker did not lead to a motion of censure—a motion which would have been justified. The Speaker tendered his resignation and the Prime Minister refused to accept it. Comment in the House was limited to a few remarks on a supply motion. In circumstances of this sort the resignation of a Speaker could be demanded and accepted by the opposition, another member elected to his place, and

[59]The Opposition had already made a half-hearted effort to censure the Deputy Speaker as well in this debate. See *infra*, pp. 78–9.

the work of the House continue. The matter was a personal one, affecting on the one side the Speaker alone, and arose at a time when the other possible occupants of the Chair were not under attack. The opposition again made the Government's actions the target of its attack and again demanded a dissolution. Here dissolution was even more unjustified than it had been before. Whether a Prime Minister is right in refusing to accept the resignation of a Speaker under these conditions may be disputed, but certainly he is not obliged to go to the country. A motion of censure moved at this time might easily have removed the Speaker and probably should have done so, and a refusal to accept a resignation, even were such a motion defeated, could not be defended.

CENSURE OF THE DEPUTY SPEAKER

The Deputy Speaker has also come under attack on two occasions. On May 13, 1913, a private member, E. M. MacDonald, moved:

That the action of Mr. Blondin, the Deputy Speaker, as Chairman of the Committee of the Whole House, while the committee was considering Bill No. 21, entitled: "An Act to authorize measures for increasing the effective Naval Forces of the Empire", in refusing to permit Mr. Carroll, the member for South Cape Breton, to move to add an additional section to said Bill, and also in declining to put the motion that the Chairman do now leave the Chair, as moved by Mr. Pugsley, the member for the City of St. John, was a violation of the rules and constituted an infringement of the privileges of this House.[60]

This motion was also made in the midst of a turbulent debate. It was, however, based on two isolated incidents in Committee of the Whole and merely expressed the belief that the occupant of the Chair was biased in his actions during a limited part of the debate. The charge was made with vigour and with many appeals for justice. It was a personal attack, and the Government was criticized only for its support of the Deputy Speaker. At no time was there an appeal for a dissolution to clear the charge. The whole day's debate was a highly technical one revolving around the new rules of procedure introduced a month earlier, and whether the members named had any right under the new rules to make the motions they had. The motion was defeated on a party vote, and the Deputy Speaker continued in office until he entered the Cabinet in 1914.

The other attack took place in the pipeline debate of 1956. The Deputy Speaker, who had been in the Chair continuously for several days during the committee stage of the bill, made several most unpopular

[60]*Debates*, May 13, 1913, cols. 9710–11.

rulings. The sitting of the House on Friday, May 25, reached its climax when a leading member of the Opposition was suspended from the service of the House for defying the Chair. Immediately before the suspension, the Leader of the Opposition stated that "the Chairman who was sitting in the Chair does not command the confidence of members on this side of the House, and such appropriate steps as should be taken, will be followed."[61] On the Monday following, the Leader of the Opposition moved the adjournment of the House to discuss a definite matter of urgent public importance,[62] "namely the subordination by the Government of the Office of Chairman of Committee of the Whole to serve the partisan interests of the Government."[63] The Speaker rejected the motion because a censure of the officers of the House may be debated only on a substantive motion after notice. Mr. Drew made a brief defence of his motion, contending that it was a motion of censure of the Government. In spite of the careful explanation of the Speaker of the proper procedure to be followed in such motions of censure the Opposition did not renew its complaint. The Deputy Speaker, however, did not take the Chair for the remainder of the passage of the bill.

APPEAL OF RULINGS

Censure of the Speaker and his deputies is not restricted in Canada to formal substantive motions. It has always been possible under the rules to show dissatisfaction with the Chair through an appeal of rulings.[64] If the Speaker is in the Chair the appeal is direct: any member may call for a decision by the House, and should he be supported by four others, a recorded division takes place on the appeal.[65] If the House is in Committee of the Whole an appeal also lies to the House:[66] when the Chairman's ruling is appealed he reports the matter at once, the Speaker takes the Chair without a motion, and submits the Chairman's report on the point of order to the House for its decision. The Committee does not rise and report progress, and when the appeal is settled, the Committee resumes its work at once.

[61]*Ibid.*, May 25, 1956, p. 4350.
[62]For a description of this procedure see chap. 9, pp. 173–6.
[63]*Debates*, May 28, 1956, p. 4365.
[64]Such an appeal is not recognized in Great Britain. The undesirable features of the procedure are discussed below.
[65]S.O. 12. The rule does not specifically require the support of five members for a division on an appeal, but the ordinary provisions of Standing Order 9 have been held to apply.
[66]There is no appeal from the committee to the Speaker. Beauchesne, *Rules and Forms* (4th ed.), cit. 232, p. 197. See also *Debates*, May 31, 1956, pp. 4518–27.

The Future Considered

Lord Ullswater concludes his autobiography with a quotation from the *Daily News* which refers to himself, but could equally describe the qualities desirable in a good Speaker.

A plain man without a touch of genius, almost without a touch of brilliancy, but with all the qualities of the average man in perfect equilibrium . . . , he is essentially an ordinary man in an extra-ordinary degree. His instinct for justice sound, his spirit firm and masculine. . . . He is the type of practical man, who does his task honestly, firmly, and good humouredly. The office of Speaker does not demand rare qualities. It demands common qualities in a rare degree.[67]

It is not impossible to find men of this sort in the Canadian House of Commons. An attempt must be made, however, to ease the strain on the occupants of the Chair and to make their tenure of office more fruitful and enjoyable. There is no doubt that some members of the House, however well qualified, would refuse to accept the office under any circumstances. In 1877, for instance, T. W. Anglin related to the Committee on Privileges and Elections that he had at one time refused the Speakership. "I had always regarded the Speakership as most irksome and unpleasant, and with my habits . . . accustomed as I was to take an active part in the business of the House and a large share in the debates of the House—I felt that the occupancy of the Chair would be for me a particularly unpleasant position."[68] Such members, however, are few in number.

The effect of the Canadian system of appointing Speakers for short terms and retiring them quickly has, of course, done much harm to the institution. The Canadian House can point to few, if any, great Speakers in the tradition of Lowther, Denison, Brand, or FitzRoy. Lack of experience in the office is largely responsible for this unfavourable comparison: aside from the four who have been in the Chair for more than one term, no Canadian Speaker can have hoped to be more than five years in the post. Mr. Speaker Denison has written that "I spent the first few years of my Speakership like the captain of a steamer on the Thames, standing on the paddle-box, ever on the look-out for shocks and collisions."[69] After a Canadian Speaker has spent his first few years in this precarious position he finds that a new election has

[67]Ullswater, *A Speaker's Commentaries*, II, p. 298.
[68]*Journals*, 1877, App. 8, p. 3.
[69]Lord Ossington, *Notes from my Journal when Speaker of the House of Commons* (London, 1900), pp. 2–3.

been held and that he is quietly dropped, just as he is reaching maturity in office.

The most important single step which could be taken to make the post of Speaker more attractive to able men and to improve its occupants would, therefore, be to make it permanent. The four Speakers who have continued beyond their normal terms have all been recognized as outstanding men. In particular, Rhodes and Lemieux rank among the foremost Canadian Speakers. There is no hope of achieving a lasting tradition of impartial Speakers until permanence is secured. The Chair ought not to be regarded merely as a step on the way to higher office. Its occupants should be selected at a relatively early age and should be allowed to prove their ability as Deputy Speaker or as Deputy Chairman. It must be accepted by all parties that a man elected to the Chair will be re-elected, as is traditional in the United Kingdom, no matter which party is returned at the polls, and that he will remain in office until he chooses to leave. At the end of his period of service he must retire from active politics. His reward at the end of his tenure of office would be somewhat more difficult to determine than it is in the United Kingdom where a peerage is convenient and effective: a senatorship is not particularly satisfactory as it tends to bring the Speaker back into active politics again;[70] other offices in the gift of the Government are even less satisfactory as the Speaker then reverts to the present situation of depending on the Government of the day for a desirable post. A substantial pension in addition to his pension as a former member of the House is the most satisfactory alternative at the present time, and if made a statutory draft on the Consolidated Revenue Fund would not even be open to annual review in Parliament.

The member who accepts nomination under such a scheme must, as has already been pointed out, put behind him all his outward political loyalties. He should, as he does in the United Kingdom, sever all party connections. In recent years the Speaker has refused to participate in debates in the Canadian House or in committee except to answer questions on his own estimates. There are also signs that the Speaker is willing to limit his constituency work to the bare minimum necessary to be re-elected. These are all trends in the right direction, and the Government and the House should give them impetus. Hansard still lists the Speaker among the other members and continues to attach to him

[70]Should a reform of the Senate along lines which have often been proposed bring large numbers of politically unaffiliated persons into that House, then a former Speaker of the Commons could take his place in their ranks without prejudicing his political anonymity.

a party label. A seat is also kept for him in the House on the front bench on the Government side. These small but significant symbols of party allegiance should be eliminated. No one, of course, expects the Speaker to be without opinions on any matter before the House. As an ordinary individual he has opinions and even strong prejudices. They must, however, be kept under strict control, and no suspicion of them must be seen at any time. In the United Kingdom Sir Percy Harris has paid tribute in this respect to Mr. Speaker FitzRoy: "He was a high Tory in his outlook and found it very difficult to swallow some of the opinions ventilated in the House. But so great is the tradition of this office that never once did I see him allow his own opinions to influence his judgment in the Chair."[71] No Speaker could ask for a more fitting epitaph.

All doubt of the Speaker's impartiality must be removed. In Canada this does not necessarily entail slavish adherence to the British practice. The tradition, for instance, of having two back-bench members nominate the Speaker is not worth transplanting to Canada. All members know that even in Great Britain this form of nomination has only a symbolic value, and the permanent adoption of the present Canadian practice of having the Leader of the Opposition second the Prime Minister's nomination would accomplish much the same end. Similarly, there is no justification for considering the British suggestion that the Speaker should have a sinecure seat. However, if permanency of office were accepted, it would be possible and desirable for the major parties to adopt the British practice of refusing to nominate official candidates in the Speaker's riding. As in the United Kingdom this would not preclude any individual who felt so inclined from opposing the Speaker, but it would make it unnecessary for the Speaker to take part in active campaigning, and would allow the other parties to show their confidence in his neutrality.[72]

There is no doubt that the abolition of appeals from the Chair would

[71]Sir Percy Harris, *Forty Years in and out of Parliament* (London, 1946), p. 168.

[72]This suggestion was put forward unsuccessfully by Sir Robert Borden in 1917 when he suggested to Sir Wilfrid Laurier that Mr. Speaker Rhodes should be re-elected. He wrote Laurier that "the question [whether Rhodes should be re-elected to the Chair] is of some urgency at the moment, for the reason that the Speaker ought not to be opposed if the proposal is to be carried out. Naturally his influence over the House and his status as its presiding officer would inevitably suffer if he should come before the new Parliament fresh from a party conflict." P.A.C., Borden Papers, OCA, 93, p. 73282. Although Borden's suggestion was not accepted, Rhodes was re-elected to the Chair for another Parliament.

be a useful step towards improving the Canadian Speakership. The futility of this rule can hardly be over-emphasized, and the reputation of the Speaker must inevitably suffer whenever it is used. First, and most important, why is a ruling appealed? There are a few who would contend that rulings are submitted to the House because they are patently wrong and should be reversed. But few, if any, rulings are so completely wrong as to justify a vote of this sort. More commonly, those who appeal merely do not like the decision which has been made and take the easiest way to protest it. Appeals may also be made to delay progress on a bill. A series of points of order may be raised, often without a shadow of a basis in fact, and are followed by a series of rulings and appeals. These take up a vast quantity of time: the sitting day is limited under the rules and each point of order may well cover an hour. The wastage, when cleverly used, may thus be substantial. It is also possible that some members believe that a vote against a Speaker's ruling is a vote against the Government. A more striking display of ignorance of the true position of the Speaker would be hard to imagine.

Second, what does an appeal mean? It is, in its bare skeleton, an opportunity for two hundred and sixty-four members to vote on a matter of which they know little or nothing. A handful of members of the House know enough about the rules to look up citations in the authorities and to use them properly. The rest are bored by the whole proceeding, but after a discussion of the point in the House and a ruling by the Speaker, these very members are called on to decide the issue by their votes. The decision is made simple for them as the whips are put on and the parties line up to vote as if it was a major item of Government policy. No thought has been given to the question of whether a proper ruling has been made. The division could as easily and as intelligently have been made without hearing the arguments presented.

The result is unfortunate. Usually the Government is on the defensive and uses its majority to protect the Speaker. Inevitably many energetic opposition members make motions and amendments which are out of order, and when the rulings on them are appealed, the Government appears to be siding with the Speaker. On the other hand, the House knows the Speaker is always dependent on a Government majority to defend his rulings. He, therefore, always seems to be a partisan when he rules in favour of the Government. The alternative is worse. If the Government decides to use its majority to reject rulings it dislikes, the rules of the House become a farce, and the authority of the Speaker to enforce them disappears. Should this use of the majority become common,[73] irreparable damage would be done to the whole principle of parliamentary procedure.

Two solutions are possible. Appeals could be abolished by a simple amendment to the rules. With a Speaker in whom the House had faith, and who might hold office for a long period, such a limitation could have only a salutary effect. The Speaker would then be free from any suspicion of subservience to the Government and would be released from the embarrassing necessity of submitting his conduct to the House at the whim of a disgruntled minority or majority.

If any large body of opinion can be found to support appeals, a compromise might be devised. The new rule should, however, be designed to achieve a constructive end, and should be made difficult enough of application that only serious appeals will be considered. Mr. Speaker Fauteux, for instance, suggested a measure of reform which could be used as the basis of a new rule. An appeal from a ruling would be submitted to the Standing Committee on Privileges and Elections. The member who lodged the appeal would be forced to commit it to writing along with his authorities and precedents. The Committee would then examine all sides of the question and would make a fully documented report to the House.[74] Many points of order which may be raised in Parliament are of a particularly abstract nature, and it is possible that the Speaker in the haste necessary in many situations may not make a perfect ruling. A careful review of the matter by a small body of experts would give a more satisfactory review than the present partisan vote in the House.

The solutions to the problem of the Canadian Speaker do not seem to be insuperable. One change—to a permanent Speaker—would necessitate a major change in tradition, but even in this field tradition seems to be weakening. In the past few years the idea has been receiving considerable attention. It is ironic that Mr. Speaker Beaudoin, the one Canadian Speaker against whom a motion of censure has been moved, should have been the first to be seriously considered for this post by all parties. In 1955, Mr. Fulton spoke on a motion for adopting major

[73]It has, in fact, happened only rarely. On two occasions the Government has reversed the ruling of a Chairman of Committee of the Whole (*Journals*, March 22, 1948, pp. 275–6; Dec. 13, 1957, pp. 270–1). The second of these shows the possible danger of this form of action. The Chairman made a ruling which was accepted by the House. The next day the ruling was repeated, and the Government, apparently desiring to eliminate an awkward precedent regardless of its propriety, appealed and reversed the ruling.

[74]*Ibid.*, Dec. 5, 1947, p. 24.

changes in the standing orders. In the debate he noted that as the rules developed in pace with the adoption of new "codes of self-discipline" in the House, certain sanctions would have to be applied by the Speaker. To fulfil this duty to the satisfaction of all, the Speaker should be known to be above party conflict.[75] Mr. Coldwell supported the idea a year later when he spoke on the censure motion, and mentioned that he had discussed the appointment of a permanent Speaker with some of his friends; they had come to the conclusion that Mr. Beaudoin should be offered the post on that basis.[76]

The debate on the pipeline and the events which followed put an end to speculation on this personal basis but raised the question in a more general way. The press in particular took up the debate in 1956 and generally agreed that a permanent Speaker would be desirable.[77] This spate of editorials does not mean that the House will take action, but it does indicate a growing public interest in the problems involved. Should the House take steps to introduce a new concept of the Speakership, the pipeline debate, with all its bitterness and animosity, will have served an entirely unexpected purpose and the Chair will have moved closer than it has yet in Canada to being the ideal "guardian of the powers, the dignities, the liberties, the privileges of this House of Commons."[78]

[75]*Debates*, July 1, 1955, pp. 5565–6. The position, of course, has been recognized in the United Kingdom where the authority of the Speaker over closure motions is dependent entirely on the confidence of the House in his impartiality.

[76]*Ibid.*, June 4, 1956, p. 4650.

[77]See editorials in *Ottawa Citizen*, May 29, June 5, June 20, July 4; *Ottawa Journal*, July 5; *Globe and Mail* (Toronto), June 8; *Winnipeg Free Press*, July 2; *Montreal Gazette*, July 3, July 9; *Maclean's*, July 21.

[78]*Debates*, Feb. 6, 1936, p. 4.

EACH SITTING DAY, a few minutes before the hour set for the meeting of the House, the Speaker walks in procession through the corridors of the Parliament buildings. Three members of the protective staff of the House and the Sergeant-at-Arms, who bears the Mace, precede him; a page and the three clerks at the Table follow. The Speaker enters the House by the door farthest from the Chair and, the members standing, proceeds up the centre aisle of the House. The Speaker then takes the Chair, the Mace is placed on the Table, and prayers are read.

Prayers

It was in 1877 that the House decided to add prayers to its daily routine. A private member moved that the prayers read daily in the Senate be read also in the House.[1] Other members raised the obvious objections which centred chiefly around the practical problem of selecting prayers for an assembly of varied faiths. Some expressed a preference for silent prayer and one went so far as to suggest that there was no more need for prayer in the House than there was in a dry goods store in Toronto. Nevertheless, the House appointed a committee, representative of all faiths, to consider and report on the desirability of using a form of prayer. Surprisingly, the committee reported within a week and not only accepted the desirability of prayer but also submitted a draft which was non-sectarian in character. The report and the prayers

[1] *Debates*, Feb. 12, 1877, p. 26.

were both adopted. These prayers, which bear a close resemblance to those of the Anglican Church of Canada, are still used. They have been changed slightly over the years through the necessity of altering references to the royal family; such changes are made informally and not by motion in the House.[2] The House also faced and settled the immediate problems of the time at which prayers should be said and the language of delivery. It was agreed that they would be said before the doors of the House were opened,[3] and the fact that the Speaker of the day spoke no French led to the suggestion that they be read in the language most familiar to the Speaker. A suggestion by Sir Wilfrid Laurier that the Almighty could safely be addressed in either English or French had little effect on his purely French-speaking colleagues, and a translation was arranged for the French-speaking members.

This system prevails to the present time. Every sitting day prayers are read by the Speaker from the Chair; the clerks stand at the Table and the members stand in their places. The Speaker may use either French or English as he chooses, but bilingual incumbents generally alternate the two. At the end of prayers the Speaker announces "Let the doors be opened," press and public enter the galleries, and the remainder of the daily routine is begun.[4]

Attendance

The House must have the attendance of at least twenty of its members before it can transact any business, though in practice the Speaker waits until the leading members on both sides have arrived. The quorum was set at twenty by the British North America Act (s. 48) and has never been changed. The same provision may also be found in Standing Order 3. There has been little concern over this rule. The committee of revision of 1925 suggested that the British North America Act be amended to raise the quorum to thirty, noting that the old number had been set for a House of only 181 members and was too small for the 1925 House

[2]*Ibid.*, March 22, 1957, p. 2589.

[3]This custom has always been observed. Even on the opening day of the 1957–8 session when the proceedings of the House were televised, the doors of the House were not opened to strangers present in the Parliament buildings until after prayers, although millions were able to see and hear the ceremony on television.

[4]As has already been noted (*supra*, chap. 3), the House can hold a secret session by requesting the Speaker not to order the doors to be opened. Other private business of the House is also transacted behind closed doors at this time.

of 245 members. The committee in 1927 quietly dropped the proposal and serious discussion lapsed for twenty-five years. The British North America (No. 2) Act, 1949, gave the Canadian Parliament the right to amend the British North America Act in matters relating exclusively to the federal government. Undoubtedly the quorum of the House of Commons is one of these matters, and in 1952 and in 1953, Mr. Knowles, a private member, introduced bills to amend the British North America Act to increase the number stipulated. The House referred the subject-matter of the 1952 bill to the committee on the revision of the rules which was then sitting, and defeated the 1953–4 bill on second reading.[5]

With such a small quorum, attempts to count out the House have been unusual. The House has been counted out a few times in its history, but rarely so as to interfere with important business. The system used to request a count has not changed over the years: a member rises in his place, refers directly to the absence of a quorum and requests a count. The Speaker, when requested, instructs the Clerk at once to count the House,[6] though a case is recorded where a member, having noted the absence of a quorum, withdrew his request for a count after an exchange with the Speaker.[7] Should less than twenty members (including the Speaker) be present, the names of those present are recorded in the *Journals* and the House adjourns automatically until the next sitting day.[8] The same procedure is followed to count a Committee of the Whole. Should there not be a quorum, the committee immediately rises and the Chairman reports to the Speaker.[9] The Speaker then proceeds to count the House, and if he does not find a quorum, the House rises for the day;[10] if he does find a sufficient number, the committee resumes its work.[11]

When the House is counted out, the business before it lapses and must be reinstated on the Order Paper by formal motion. It has been established that the motion to restore the dropped order to the agenda

[5]*Debates*, Jan. 23, 1953, pp. 1281–2; May 25, 1954, p. 5075.

[6]The division bells are not rung before the count is taken as they are in the British House.

[7]*Debates*, March 9, 1898, col. 1508.

[8]S.O. 3(2). There is one example of the Speaker's counting the House twice. On the first count, only eighteen members were present; on the second, a quorum was found. *Debates*, April 17, 1925, p. 2143.

[9]Should there be more than twenty members present in the committee, it will, of course, not rise to be counted again. *Debates*, May 2, 1885, p. 1535; June 19, 1934, p. 4113; July 15, 1943, p. 4893.

[10]*Ibid.*, June 9, 1938, p. 3704.

[11]*Ibid.*, June 6, 1899, col. 4461; March 30, 1915, pp. 1780–1.

is one that is made without notice and without debate.[12] When the Committee of Supply or of Ways and Means is counted out, it rises without reporting progress and without leave to sit again. It must, therefore, be reconstituted by formal motion, and the committee may properly consider whether or not any resolution passed at the preceding sitting and not yet reported to the House should be so reported.[13]

The revision committee of 1906 attempted to go beyond the establishment of a minimum attendance in the House and suggested that moral pressure should be exerted to compel attendance at the sittings of the House, recommending an amendment to the rules which would have provided a record of attendance for each sitting day. The suggestion met with little favour. The Prime Minister and the Leader of the Opposition both defended it, but for once the back-benchers exerted effective pressure and the reform was defeated on the motion of a private member. The suggestion has rarely been revived and absenteeism in the House remains high. Attempts have been made to accomplish the same end by public bill to amend the Senate and House of Commons Act, but nothing has come of them. A financial penalty is provided against members who spend their time outside Ottawa during the session; the exceptions allowed in the act, however, make its effect negligible.[14]

Standing Order 5, which has remained unchanged since Confederation, contains the bald statement that "every member is bound to attend the service of the House, unless leave of absence has been given him by the House." For the first ten years of its life the House of Commons enforced this rule. A member who wished to leave Ottawa requested leave from the House through a colleague. Reasons for the absence were generally given and examples may be found of the plea of "urgent private business," "family affliction," and "severe illness," to excuse a member from his duty.[15] No member was exempt from the rule and failure to obey it was dealt with severely.[16] If this rule, which has been

[12]*Ibid.*, July 3, 1917, pp. 2877–80; March 12, 1919, p. 398. The analogy was drawn between this and the procedure following the passage of an amendment to a motion for Committee of Supply. See chap. 7, p. 141.

[13]*Debates*, June 10, 1938, pp. 3705–6.

[14]For a full discussion of the act and its application see N. Ward, *The Canadian House of Commons* (Toronto, 1950), pp. 98–114.

[15]*Journals*, May 8, 1868, p. 301; Feb. 15, 1871, p. 10; April 13, 1877, p. 257.

[16]In 1873, Sir John A. Macdonald, the Prime Minister, was absent without leave from a meeting of an election committee. The Opposition took advantage of his lapse and moved to have him appear at the Bar of the House to offer his explanation. He appeared in the custody of the Sergeant-at-Arms and presented his defence in the form of a doctor's certificate, thoughtfully provided by one of his fellow Cabinet ministers. *Ibid.*, May 12, 1873, pp. 327–8.

ignored since 1877, were applied today, the problem of attendance in the House could easily be solved.

Time of Sittings

Once a quorum is ensured, the House may proceed to the business of the day. The House of Commons in Canada shares with the House in Westminster the tradition of regular afternoon and evening sittings, but the custom has not been meekly accepted in Ottawa, and every major revision of the rules has provided some change in the hours of sitting, as will be seen in the discussion that follows. Back-bench opinion seems to make itself felt in this regard more effectively than in any other aspect of the rules. There has certainly not been a tradition in Canada of electing members who carry on a business or law practice during the early part of the day and attend the House in the evening, because too few members live within daily commuting distance of Ottawa. There is, however, still a tradition of amateur members, but most of these come from outside the Ottawa area and carry on their business during the parliamentary recess. There is also a custom by which large numbers of members from Quebec and Ontario attend sittings of the House for only three days in every week. These "Tuesday to Thursday" members carry on their private businesses on the other four days. The Government, however, feels strongly that ministers ought to be free for a portion of the day to attend to departmental affairs, and the private member accepts his morning freedom as a valuable opportunity to attend to constituency affairs and committee business. Some few members still maintain that a House which sat in regular "business" hours would complete its work in less time and with less effort than at present, but these members are in a small minority.

In 1867 the rules of the House provided that the Commons would meet at 3 P.M. every sitting day. With a dinner break of an hour and a half the House then sat until an adjournment motion could be passed. This arrangement did not last long: by 1876 members were asking that the House sit earlier and rise at a reasonable time. It was pointed out for the first, but not the last, time that a member could hardly be expected to sit in the House until 2 or 3 A.M. and still be in proper condition to act on a committee later the same morning.

The first definite move to correct the situation was made by a private member the next year. D. Blain moved an amendment to the rules to provide that the Speaker should leave the Chair at 10 P.M. without putting any question, unless a majority of the House was against his doing so. He added that the time mentioned was merely a suggestion and that any other time would be satisfactory. The motion was attacked by leaders on both sides who saw in it a destruction of the rights of Parliament, and the Prime Minister suggested that the motion be dropped in exchange for an arrangement by which the House would agree informally to adjourn earlier.[17]

This was far from satisfactory. Within a month a member complained that a sitting the previous night was a "gross breach" of the arrangement.[18] A year later Blain repeated his motion. He noted that the arrangement had worked well for part of the session but that at the end "the old habit of turning night into day became the rule and not the exception."[19] Again, in the face of strong opposition, the motion was withdrawn on the understanding that the House would adjourn at 11 P.M. whenever possible.

Blain's feelings can best be appreciated by looking at a few examples of the abuses of which he complained. In the last thirty-one days of the session of 1882, for instance, the House sat until after midnight twenty-four times; on the other seven days the earliest time it rose was 11:10 P.M. In 1896 a similar situation arose in the last thirty days: seventeen times the House rose at midnight or later and only five times earlier; on eight occasions there was no adjournment at all. Overnight sittings were not common but were by no means unknown: in 1885 the House had one sitting of thirty-one hours and one sitting of fifty-seven hours;[20] in 1896 it once sat for six days without adjournment and was released only by the religious feelings of the members which led them to adjourn over Sunday.[21]

The general question of hours of sitting was not ignored. A leading member of the Opposition complained vigorously in 1885 that the House should sit regular hours, and two years later a plea was made for sittings from 1 P.M. to 6 P.M. only, thus leaving the evenings free for the private study of legislation.[22] Agitation by back-bench and Opposition members continued over the years. A long motion was introduced in 1889, when the health of members was used as the

[17]Debates, Feb. 19, 1877, pp. 99–102.   [18]Ibid., March 15, 1877, p. 777.
[19]Ibid., Feb. 20, 1878, p. 393.
[20]Journals, April 27–28, 1885, pp. 343–53; April 30–May 2, 1885, pp. 354–7.
[21]April 6–11. The record sitting was that held in 1913 when the House sat from Monday, March 3, at 3 P.M., to Saturday, March 8, at midnight, and from Monday, March 10, at 3 P.M., to Saturday, March 15, at 11:32 P.M.
[22]Debates, July 2, 1885, pp. 2996–7; June 23, 1887, p. 1270. Considerable doubt was expressed whether members would be likely to settle down by themselves after dinner for a study of legislation.

excuse for cutting the evening sittings short at midnight.[23] The motion concluded with a draft rule by which the Speaker would leave the Chair without question put at midnight. As before, the Government opposed the motion. The Prime Minister foresaw the Opposition's seizing on this opportunity to talk out every contentious measure. He also stated that most important work was carried after one o'clock in the morning. Once more, the House was content with the promise that an agreement would be reached for an early adjournment. These agreements seem to have been of short duration, and in the following years the subject arose again, but the Conservative Opposition was now attacking a Liberal Government on the same grounds.[24]

The committee of revision of 1906 began the gradual change. On June 7 of that year W. S. Fielding wrote Sir Wilfrid Laurier and recommended a night off in mid-week, stating that he had approached the Leader of the Opposition on the matter and had received a favourable reply. He pleaded in particular for those whose sense of duty did not permit them to take time off whenever they pleased.[25] The committee accepted the suggestion and recommended a new rule to the House: the old 3 P.M. meeting time was to be retained for every sitting day except Wednesday, when the House was to meet at 1 P.M. and adjourn automatically at 6 P.M. The House received the committee's report with differing reactions. Many accepted the change merely as a recognition of what was being done by many members in any event. Those who opposed the new rule saw the change as interfering with committee meetings, "revolutionizing" the lunch hours of hotels, and deranging the digestion of members by upsetting their routine.[26] The House finally agreed to meet at 2 P.M. on Wednesdays and adjourn at 6 P.M.; it also lengthened its dinner recess to two hours.

This revision did not entirely satisfy the House. In 1907 a member introduced a motion similar to those moved earlier. Once again the health of members and the plight of both Hansard and newspaper reporters were used to sway the House in favour of a fixed adjournment. Even the working hours of the "little pages" were brought into question.[27] The Prime Minister produced the panacea of an "agreement" and the motion was withdrawn.

[23]*Ibid.*, March 11, 1889, p. 526. A description of the heating and ventilating systems in the Chamber lends some weight to the arguments of those who complained of the effect of long sittings on their health. *Journals*, 1873, App. 4.

[24]*Debates*, March 28, 1890, col. 2667; June 22, 1900, col. 8073.

[25]P.A.C., Laurier Papers, pp. 110967–9.

[26]*Debates*, July 9, 1906, col. 7464; July 10, 1906, cols. 7613, 7614.

[27]*Ibid.*, Dec. 12, 1907, col. 586.

The question of Wednesday evening as well as the hours of sitting continued to interest the House over the years. In 1909 a motion to reserve Wednesday evenings for estimates was withdrawn after debate and in 1913 a universal sitting hour of 2 P.M. was suggested and briefly discussed.[28] After the First War, Opposition interest in these matters revived. In 1920 Mackenzie King made a plea for more sensible hours, and stated that discussion after 11 P.M. was "wearisome" and "protracted." Sir George Foster, for the Government, held that experience had always shown that a firm adjournment time was unsuitable, and that the House guided itself by what was fitting and reasonable. The next year another front-bench Opposition member moved to amend the rules to alter the Wednesday meeting hour to conform to the rest of the week and to guarantee an early and fixed adjournment.[29] The motion was met by the usual Government arguments and was withdrawn.

Four years later, the Liberal Opposition had become the Government and the House established a committee to revise the rules. This 1925 committee was the first to bring in a definite recommendation to provide for a compulsory adjournment. The draft rule resembles closely the suggestion put forward in 1921. The committee reported that the Speaker should adjourn the House without question put each evening at 11:30. Should the House be in committee the Chairman at that time should leave the Chair and report. In the event of an emergency, the House, or Committee of the Whole, could decide by majority vote to sit later.[30] This part of the report was shelved with the rest.

The committee of 1927 was even more definite in its report. It drafted a simple rule which called for compulsory adjournment at 11 P.M. The rule made no provision for special occasions or for its suspension, except that, when the closure rule was in use, adjournment was to be at 2 A.M. The move produced an outcry in the House. On the one hand the rule was supported by members such as G. G. Coote who suggested a general shortening of the sittings in the interest of the health of members and of the staff of the House. On the other hand members such as Mr. C. G. Power raised the old cry that more work was done after eleven o'clock at night than at any other period of the sitting. From these points the debate degenerated into an exchange of experiences of various members relating to the amount of sleep needed during a parliamentary session. The House passed the rule

[28]*Ibid.*, Dec. 15, 1909, cols. 1536–7; Jan. 28, 1913, col. 2282.
[29]*Ibid.*, May 3, 1920, pp. 1893–5; April 11, 1921, pp. 1828–45.
[30]*Journals*, May 29, 1925, pp. 358–9.

without a division. In the same report the committee recommended that the Wednesday sitting hours be revised to conform with those of other days of the week. Whether this was the result of overwhelming pressure from near-by hotels or the more insistent demands of the deranged digestive systems of the members affected by the reforms of 1906 is unknown, but the committee noted that for the last two sessions the House had passed sessional orders to permit a meeting at 3 P.M. on Wednesday. The committee therefore recommended, and the House accepted, a permanent change.

The House has been generally satisfied with the results of the 1927 revision. There have been suggestions for further changes but the protests have been moderate in tone compared with the earlier ones. Members put forward vague suggestions for changing the sitting hours in 1936 and 1938 but had no specific plans to suggest. During the war, Wednesday sittings were abandoned entirely for most of one session as a temporary measure.[31] The experiment was designed to allow more time for Cabinet and committee meetings, but did not prove successful and was abandoned.

After the war the House considered its hours of sitting along with the rest of the rules.[32] One member suggested afternoon sittings from 1 P.M. to 7 P.M. and the Speaker recommended the elimination of the dinner recess. In 1948 the Clerk of the House concurred in this latter suggestion and added that the House should not sit on Friday evenings. The committee which considered the memoranda of both Speaker and Clerk reported to the House in June 1948. It recommended a permanent adjournment at 10 P.M. on all sitting days except Wednesday. It also suggested shortening the dinner break to one hour. The report was never accepted. The House again considered the question of sitting hours in 1951.[33] A committee drew up five plans and the House tried four of them for short periods. None was entirely satisfactory, and at the end of three months of experiments the committee made a firm recommendation for an amendment to the standing orders. The House did not accept the report of the committee at that session, but in July 1952 passed a virtually identical report. The hour of meeting was advanced to 2:30 P.M. and the adjournment hour was changed to 10 P.M.

[31]*Debates*, June 18, 1936, p. 3846; Feb. 23, 1938, pp. 738–55; Feb. 21, 1944, pp. 676–91.
[32]*Ibid.*, June 25, 1947, pp. 4617–9; *Journals*, Dec. 5, 1947, p. 26; *The Table*, XVII, 1948, p. 235; *Journals*, June 25, 1948, p. 680.
[33]*Journals*, Oct. 12, 1951, pp. 7–8; Oct. 26, 1951, pp. 49–50; Nov. 2, 1951, p. 65; Dec. 13, 1951, pp. 311–12; July 1, 1952, p. 624. The 1951 report had also recommended a further alteration in the Friday sitting.

The committee of 1955 completed the amendment of these rules. The meeting hour of 2:30 P.M. has been confirmed for the first four days of the week. On Friday the House meets at 11 A.M., has a lunch recess from 1:00 to 2:30, and rises at 6 P.M. for dinner. Three days each week—on Monday, Tuesday, and Thursday—it resumes at 8 P.M. and sits until the automatic adjournment at 10 P.M. Each Wednesday and Friday it adjourns at 6 P.M. until the next sitting day (S.O. 2 and 6).[34] Few exceptions are made. The House sits at 11 A.M. when it is debating the Address in Reply to the Speech from the Throne (S.O. 2). As the session advances it gradually extends its hours of sitting by sessional order. Morning sittings become universal, as well as sittings on Friday evenings. Saturdays are added, and finally Wednesday evenings. In the last few days the House often extends its adjournment beyond 10 P.M. but only by unanimous consent. This extension, however, is unusual and depends entirely on the goodwill of the House. One disgruntled member, dissatisfied with the answer of a Minister in supply, is sufficient to force the House to rise for the evening. In the normal course of the session the sitting hours are not altered or suspended except in unusual circumstances and then only with unanimous consent.

Arrangement of Daily Business

The rule (S.O. 15) which lays down the daily business of the House reflects more than any other the growing dominance of the Government over the time of the House and the decreasing importance of private members' business. The arrangement of daily business has varied immensely over the years, and has been changed in every major revision of the rules since 1867.

The Order Paper of the House is divided into two main sections: "Routine Proceedings" and the "Orders of the Day." "Routine Proceedings" do not vary from day to day and under this heading reports from committees may be presented, bills and Government notices of motions are introduced, and other motions are made. It is rare for this portion of the day's work to consume more than a few minutes at any sitting, although a long debate may ensue. A motion relating to a question of privilege appears in this section as does a substantive motion dealing with censure of the Speaker. Both of these, of course, may be debated at length.[35] The remainder of the Order Paper (under

[34]For other forms of adjournment see chap. 9, pp. 172–6.
[35]*Routine Proceedings and Orders of the Day*, June 1, 1956, p. 2; and June 4, 1956, p. 2.

the heading of "Orders of the Day") is the business for a specific day and varies in a set pattern under the standing orders. Since 1962 every day of the week has been officially allocated to the Government, and the entry "Government Orders" may be found. This covers virtually all Government business, whether bills, motions, or the orders for the House in Committee of Supply and of Ways and Means. In the time allocated to private members (which was a limited number of whole days up to 1962, but is now a similarly fixed number of one-hour periods) a variety of entries is possible, indicating the type of business to be discussed. Private bills, public bills and orders, or notices of motions may have precedence.[36] The amount of time spent on any of these depends on the state of the Order Paper and often on the wishes of the House at the moment.

In 1867 the standing orders set out a daily routine of business which consisted of the presentation and reception of petitions, reports by committees, and routine motions. Then followed the various daily agenda. On Monday private bills had precedence, on Wednesday and Thursday notices of motions and public bills were taken first, and on Tuesday and Friday Government business had precedence. In addition, one hour immediately after dinner each Wednesday and Friday was reserved for private bills.

As early as 1876 some dissatisfaction was felt with the arrangement and several amendments were made. For several years it had been the practice of the House to give consent to consider Government business after private members' business on Monday, but consent had to be unanimous, so of course a single member could foil the wishes of the rest. In that year the practice was confirmed by standing order. Government business was also permitted on Thursday after private members' business had been exhausted.

The revision of 1906 marked the beginning of the period of Government control of the time of the House. The most significant change was in the Thursday sitting.[37] For the first time the rules recognized the familiar practice by which the Government acquired extra days for Government business after a few weeks of the session. Under the new rule, after four weeks Thursday ceased to be a private members' day

[36]A private member's notice of motion is a resolution, generally of a broad and vague nature, which he has not yet moved in the House. After he has moved it, and the debate on it has been adjourned or interrupted, it is listed under "Public Bills and Orders" on the Order Paper.

[37]Minor changes were also made in the order of business on Wednesdays as a result of the elimination of Wednesday evening sittings. The after-dinner hour for private bills was also changed from Wednesday to Tuesday in this revision.

and the Government took precedence. Even the Leader of the Opposition was willing to defend the change, in terms which have become increasingly familiar to Parliament: "The Government work is taking so large a proportion of the time of the House as compared with what it did formerly that some change seemed to be necessary. . . ."[38] It had been suggested in the revision committee that Thursday be a Government day from the beginning of the session, but the compromise of retaining the first four Thursdays as private members' days was finally reached. As Thursday had been appropriated to the use of the Government by motion in the House for some years past, the revision in fact only consolidated and simplified existing practice. Some private members raised objections, but the principle was finally accepted and the new rule adopted.

Few changes were made in the next fifty years. Verbal amendments were made in 1910 and slightly more important changes in 1927, when private members were allowed more time for their public bills. Members had asked for an extra day each week for this purpose, and although the committee rejected this request, it agreed that an effort should be made to advance public bills further than second reading. The result was a recommendation that they be considered in the private bill hour on Tuesday and Friday after private bills were exhausted, but this change has, in fact, made no difference in the number of public bills adopted by the House.

The situation in those years was not particularly satisfactory to the private members. A strict adherence to the written rules would have given them more than enough time for all their business. However, at intervals as the session advanced, the Government regularly passed a series of sessional orders which gave it precedence even on those days reserved by the rules for the private members. These left only short periods during the week for private and public bills. One or more of the Thursdays reserved for private members was also generally used to debate the Address in Reply to the Speech from the Throne. Complaints from the members were never wanting, but protests were rarely successful and at best could wrest the concession of a few days only.

The worst feature of the system was the uncertainty. The private members' time was entirely at the mercy of the Government's legislative programme and was arbitrarily cut short. The revision of 1955 changed this situation: for the first time private members were guaranteed a set number of days for their business. Under the new rule the first six Mondays and the first two Thursdays after the Address in Reply

[38]*Debates*, July 9, 1906, col. 7476.

had been passed were given to the private members. Should the Government wish to take one or more of these Mondays for a supply motion another Monday had to be substituted for the one taken.[39] In the revision of 1962, private members' days were eliminated. In their place, private members now have forty one-hour periods scattered through the early days of the session.

Importance of Private Members' Business

With the dominance of the Government over the private members growing steadily, the usefulness and importance of their business becomes of interest. The existence of private members' business is, of course, based on the parliamentary fiction that all members are alike in the House and that it is the duty of every member to bring his suggestions for legislation before Parliament. Today few members even bother to assert the equality of all in the House. The facts are too obvious. The Government has its rights and responsibilities and the official Opposition has its rights. Any independents, and even the members from minor opposition parties, who attempt to move amendments in the Address debate and on similar occasions, rapidly discover the elusive nature of their equality.

Private bills are of little significance. Today the overwhelming majority of them deal with divorce. They are all sponsored by one member[40] and are passed with a minimum of interest. Public bills are of little more use. Only the C.C.F. has consistently used this vehicle to develop a platform in Parliament. Each session it puts forward a dozen or more bills affecting labour and agriculture. Year after year the same bills appear before the House.[41] They rarely come to a vote but they remain on the Order Paper as visible proof of the devotion of the party to its ideals.

[39]In the 1958 session, which was a normal session in most respects and ran for ninety-two sitting days, the Government reverted to the pre-1955 practice and eliminated three private members' Mondays to speed the passage of its own legislation. *Debates*, Aug. 4, 1958, pp. 3043–63.

[40]The present custom is that divorce bills are sponsored by the chairman of the Standing Committee on Miscellaneous Private Bills to which the bills are referred after second reading.

[41]Note for instance the statement of Mr. Stanley Knowles in 1957 when he moved second reading of a public bill to amend the Industrial Relations and Disputes Investigation Act. "I am sure that it will be unnecessary for me to speak for more than a few minutes in moving the second reading of this bill, which has been before the House every year since 1948." *Debates*, Jan. 29, 1957, p. 763.

A more useful instrument in the hands of the individual member is the notice of motion. It is simple in form and convenient to use. No real care need be shown in its drafting. It is merely an abstract statement that it is advisable for the Government to do something, or that it "should consider" a proposal. It may deal with any subject of interest to a member and, if drafted with reasonable care, may even advocate the spending of money. There is little possibility that a notice of motion will progress far in the House. A few are passed, but the Government tries to see to it that they are not, because, once passed, they are interpreted by their supporters as binding on the Government. The usual course taken by the Government is to ensure that a notice of motion will never come to a vote at all. It is occasionally possible to obtain Government support for an amended form of a notice of motion, although it is unlikely that the accepted form will bear much resemblance to the original proposal.[42]

Few changes have been made in the rules on notices of motions. In the original rules of the House, notices of motions were given a place on the Order Paper; they were to be taken in their proper order and, if not proceeded with when called, were dropped. In 1906 the House added a new clause which permitted a notice of motion to retain its place on the Order Paper should the Government so desire.[43] The change was not so radical as it would appear to be, for it meant only that, once again, the written rule was being brought into line with the actual practice.

In 1910 the House recognized for the first time that a motion for the production of papers on which no member desired a debate differed fundamentally from a motion by a private member designed to test the opinion of the House on a specific matter. The committee of that year separated the two types of motions and made special provision for passing motions for papers without debate.[44]

[42]Note for instance the change made in a notice of motion in 1957. The original motion read: "That in the opinion of this House the Government should consider the advisability of taking steps to further protect the health of the nation by making the necessary amendments to the Criminal Code to provide penalties against owners or operators of all diesel powered vehicles or railway engines for failure to equip said vehicles with some suitable device to render harmless poisonous gases emitted from the exhaust of such vehicles or engines." The amended motion read: "That in the opinion of this House the Government should consider steps to further protect the health of the nation by continuing research to find ways and means of equipping diesel powered vehicles or railway engines with some suitable device. . . ." *Journals*, Feb. 4, 1957, pp. 114–15.

[43]1867 Rules 19, 24, 25; 1906 Rule 31.

[44]1910 Rule 38. These are known now as notices of motions for the production of papers or starred notices of motions. See *infra*, chap. 8, pp. 160–4.

The committee of 1925 presented a more comprehensive plan for the control of notices of motions. Its report noted that there were only about twelve private members' days each year, that few members could get a hearing, and that one member often had as many as three or four notices of motions on the Order Paper at one time. Moreover, many of the questions raised were technical and useless for general debate. The rule suggested by the committee was entirely new: it would limit a member to one notice of motion on the Order Paper at any time and would provide that it should be dropped after being called twice. In addition, the committee had worked out a scheme for arranging an order of precedence for such motions: those to be debated were to be chosen by lot by the Clerk of the House each day.[45] The House failed to accept this new rule in 1925, but adopted a similar rule in 1927.[46] A few changes were made; for instance, the clause which provided a ballot for precedence was omitted and several members criticized the omission. A private member's motion to alter the new rule was defeated and the rule passed into the standing orders.

The rule today (S.O. 48) stands as passed in 1927. A member may have only one notice of motion on the Order Paper at any time, and if it is not proceeded with after having been called twice from the Chair, it is dropped from the Order Paper. A dropped motion may be reinstated after new notice has been given but it takes its place at the bottom of the Order Paper. Should the motion be again called and not taken up, it is finally dropped.

At the beginning of the 1958 session Mr. Speaker Michener made one alteration in the general procedure relating to motions. On the opening day of this session he held a draw for precedence in debate for those motions which had already been presented to the Clerk. The ballot was held in the presence of the Speaker, Clerk, and the whips from both sides of the House, and the few opportunities during the session for debate on motions were allocated in this way. The practice has been continued since then and has probably become an established part of our procedure.

The gradual erosion of the time reserved for private members has probably come to an end.[47] The forty hours set aside for their exclusive

---

[45]*Journals*, May 29, 1925, p. 359. [46]1927 Rule 52.

[47]The revision committee of 1961 suggested a slight alteration in the time allotted to private members' business. Instead of eight whole days being allowed, forty separate one-hour periods were recommended early in the session. As notices of motions have precedence on a considerable number of these days, it is likely that an increased number of these motions will be debated. This change was made permanent in 1962.

use cannot be considered excessive and do not delay (except to an insignificant degree) the work of the Government. Some improvement could be made within these hours to make them more satisfactory to the members themselves. The ballot for precedence which was first recommended in 1925 and finally adopted in 1958 could be extended, and there could be a fresh ballot for each day on which motions would be called. At present only the motions which have been submitted by opening day have a chance in the draw, and there seems little reason why the ballot system could not be extended to give even the late starters an opportunity for debate. A restriction of the time available for each motion when first raised in the House would ensure that a larger number of motions were debated in a session. A restriction on the length of speeches to ten minutes would encourage a wide participation and the expression of the greatest variety of interests.

A certain unreality, however, pervades the whole subject. So far as most of the members are concerned, and in all likelihood the vast majority of the population, a statement of Mackenzie King will carry conviction. When challenged on the point of whether the private members were being too restricted in their ability to present legislative proposals, he answered: "We have been sent here for the purpose of carrying on the business of the country. The business of the country is not primarily private members' motions, it is the business which the Government brings forward."[48]

[48]*Debates*, Feb. 14, 1939, p. 916.

RULES OF DEBATE

6

THE MAJOR FUNCTION of the House of Commons is to debate. Whether members are extolling their own constituencies in the debate on the Address in Reply to the Speech from the Throne, raising grievances on supply, or applying their knowledge to the effect of legislation on the country as a whole, the House carries on its business by argument back and forth across the floor of its Chamber. But debate cannot be allowed to run on unchecked. The House has been forced to accept rules and traditions which protect it from excesses. Certain formalities must be observed in order to keep debate above the pettiness of personalities and protect those who hold high positions from irresponsible attack. Other customs and rules keep debate flowing freely and keep it properly directed. To accomplish these ends the House has put in the hands of the Chair extensive powers to enforce the rules of debate and maintain order so that the business of the House may go forward with all desirable speed.

Dress Regulations

Members who desire to address the House must rise in their places uncovered.[1] There are no exceptions to the rule: it must be followed even by a member who wishes to raise a point of order during a

---

[1]S.O. 28. Bourinot records that on one occasion John Charlton was permitted to keep his seat because he was not well. Sir John G. Bourinot, *Parliamentary Procedure and Practice in the Dominion of Canada* (4th ed., Toronto, 1916), p. 332 n.

division. This is one of the traditional rules which has little modern significance. The old practice of wearing hats in the House has disappeared, and the occasional member who appears in a hat in the House today does so merely out of a sense of bravado. Several Speakers have enforced other dress regulations in the House, although without any written authority. Members have occasionally attempted to remove their coats in the Chamber in hot weather, and the Chair has frowned on the practice,[2] but now that the Chamber is air-conditioned the point is unimportant.

Order of Speaking

There is no official precedence of speakers laid down in any rule. A limited number of members have special rights accorded them under certain conditions, but these rights relate only to the length of their speeches. The theory of "catching the Speaker's eye" is the same in Canada as it is at Westminster and the practical application of the custom follows much the same pattern. The whips of all parties provide the Speaker with lists of members wishing to speak and he "sees" members from opposite sides of the House in a reasonable rotation.

The House has the power to alter the order of speakers recognized by the Chair. When two members rise together any member of the House may move that one of them "be now heard." The passage of the motion settles the order of debate without delay. If the motion is defeated, the member who was originally recognized has the floor.[3] It is thus impossible to move a succession of these motions and, in effect, prevent a member from speaking. There are a few limitations on the use of this motion: it cannot be debated or amended (S.O. 29), and it must be made before a member has begun to speak. This last limitation is by no means well established, however, for although in 1927 the Speaker refused to accept a motion made after one of the members who had risen at the same time had begun to speak,[4] in 1956 a Chairman of Committee of the Whole did accept a motion after a Minister had begun to speak.[5] In the latter case, no question was raised and it is likely that the Chairman accepted the motion as the easiest course to follow.

[2]*Debates*, June 8, 1925, pp. 3957–8; July 2, 1931, p. 3299; July 12, 1943, pp. 4633–4.
[3]*Ibid.*, May 24, 1956, p. 4310.
[4]*Ibid.*, March 16, 1927, pp. 1281–2.
[5]*Ibid.*, May 24, 1956, p. 4293.

Any unofficial complaint relating to the order of speakers is generally met courteously but firmly by the Chair. Twice in the 1956 pipeline debate the Progressive Conservatives challenged the right of one of their own members to speak. The individual in question was known to be opposed to their stand on the subject and they did not want him to be using the time allotted to their party. On both occasions when the matter was raised the occupant of the Chair was decided in his stand.[6] As a primary point he contended that no official order of speakers existed, and that the member first on his feet had a right to be recognized, subject broadly to the right of both sides of the House to be heard; as a secondary and ostensibly not the deciding factor, the member involved had been granted speaking time by one of the other parties in the House. On the second occasion the Deputy Speaker made every effort to persuade the Conservatives to move the proper motion if they felt that an injustice was being done. The suggestion was not accepted.

Extemporaneous Speech

The tradition of the House that all speeches must be made extemporaneously has been broken continually both in letter and in spirit since Confederation.[7] The Canadian House has no written rule which forbids a member to read his speech, but the tradition has been established over the years. The most substantial basis on which it rests is a resolution passed by the House in 1886 which condemned "the growing length of speeches having the character of elaborately prepared written essays."[8] The custom has also been supported by the rulings of various Speakers.[9]

The physical arrangement of the Chamber in Canada favours those who read their speeches. Each member has a desk on which he can rest his manuscript unobserved, and, if his eyesight is good he can read it where it is, or else bring it closer by building up a small lectern of volumes of Hansard and other reference books. Many members merely hold a manuscript in their hands and read shamelessly from it. The practice of reading speeches has also been aided by the exceptions

[6]*Ibid.*, May 15, 1956, p. 3910; May 18, 1956, p. 4080.
[7]In the 1957 session of the Ontario legislature the Speaker ruled that the use of a teleprompter in the House was proper. This mechanical device has not yet made its appearance in Ottawa.
[8]*Journals*, April 19, 1886, p. 167.
[9]A list of forty-two of these were given by Mr. Speaker Beaudoin in 1956. *Ibid.*, Jan. 31, 1956, pp. 94–5.

which have been made to the application of the rule. The Second World War saw the introduction of a custom which allowed ministers to read statements of Government policy. The House agreed that an accurate expression of Government opinion was necessary and accepted the ruling.[10] The policy continued after the war, but without the support of the Speaker.[11] Mr. Speaker Macdonald, however, carried the exemption one step further and ruled in favour of including in it the Cabinet and Leader of the Opposition and also the leaders of the other parties in the House.[12] Other exceptions have been made by courtesy. Members who speak in a language which is not their own are generally permitted the use of a written text. Maiden speeches may be read as may speeches dealing with technical material and statistics. Any member who speaks on the Address in Reply to the Speech from the Throne, on a motion for supply, or in the budget debate, is also allowed to use a written speech.

The problem of enforcement is formidable. The exceptions are recognized by every member of the House and no back-bencher wishes to alter a custom which is so useful. The Speaker, since he is at one end of the Chamber, cannot see all the offenders himself and must depend on the other members of the House. There is, of course, no lack of members who delight in calling attention to the fact that a boring speech is being read. But a doubt always exists, and the word of the accused member is accepted no matter how obvious the deception may be. Thus a solemn farce is periodically enacted: a member is challenged and the Speaker asks him to refrain from reading his speech if he is in fact doing so; the member answers that he has "extensive notes" and is merely following them closely; this closes the affair. The answers have also been given (and accepted) that a member may be reading his speech but has the subject in mind and wants it on the record in the best possible form (May 20, 1930), and that a member is reading his speech so as to be as brief as possible (Feb. 14, 1951). If it is a particularly blatant offence the Speaker may conclude with a general appeal against the practice of reading, and he has, on occasion, instructed members to consult their notes a little less freely. It is unlikely that the convention can ever be properly enforced. A popular member will always be able to read what he likes, and an unpopular or dull speaker will often be called to order. There is no power in the hands of the Speaker which enables him to challenge a member who is obviously

[10]*Debates*, June 14, 1940, p. 781; Sept. 20, 1942, pp. 730–1.
[11]*Ibid.*, Sept. 11, 1945, p. 66; May 29, 1947, pp. 3567–8.
[12]*Ibid.*, Feb. 20, 1951, pp. 496–7; May 29, 1951, pp. 3494–5.

reading. Above all, the House itself does not, in fact, favour such a limitation. One acting Speaker summed up the situation when called on to rule on such a point: "the House," he said, "and all members thereof, always disapprove of the reading of speeches, except when we do it ourselves."[13]

It is doubtful, of course, whether there is much to be said for the custom of extemporaneous speaking under modern conditions. Many authorities have held that its main purpose is to maintain the free flow of debate, in the hope that members will make an attempt to meet the arguments of the opposing side and try to convince by logical discussion.[14] This view is too idealistic to be taken seriously today. The party system has been developed to such a degree that no member seriously expects to convince either side by a speech. A few minor amendments may be made in a Government bill as a result of opposition pleading but these would be made as readily after one or two short speeches. Major amendments are rarely made, and then only after opposition attack has aroused public opinion against the measure. This form of pressure could as easily be aroused by written speeches as by those delivered extemporaneously.

The Content of Speeches

The content of speeches has caused more confusion in the House than the method of their delivery. The points at issue concern the use of quotations, repetition and relevance, and the language which may be used to refer to members, strangers, and certain protected persons.

USE OF QUOTATIONS

The custom which forbids the use of extensive quotations is closely allied to the custom which prohibits the reading of speeches. It has generally been accepted that a member is at liberty to quote briefly from a newspaper or other document provided it does not contain improper references to the royal family or others in high position, or to members of the House or the actions of the House. The member must be willing to identify the source of his quotation and, if he is a Minister, must be willing to table any public document which he quotes.

Letters and telegrams in particular have given trouble. They are

[13]*Ibid.*, March 14, 1956, p. 2143.
[14]See for instance Sir T. Erskine May, *Treatise on the Law, Privileges, Proceedings and Usage of Parliament* (16th ed., London, 1957), pp. 444–5.

usually short and cannot therefore be forbidden as constituting extensive quotation. Telegrams have, however, been ruled out of order because there is no way of ensuring the authenticity of the signature,[15] but they may be allowed if they are of an inoffensive nature. Letters have been subject to various interpretations. For many years members refused to divulge the names of the writers;[16] more recently, Speakers have ruled that a member must give the name or take full responsibility for the contents himself,[17] and letters which have been read in the House and for which a member would not take responsibility have been expunged from Hansard.[18] It is never in order to read an unsigned letter[19] nor is it in order to read an imaginary letter into the record.[20]

There is no doubt that a Minister must table any public document which he quotes in the House, for the House is entitled to all the information which is used by the Government to influence debate. Only the document actually quoted, however, need be tabled: a request that a complete file be laid before the House has been refused,[21] and a recent attempt to force the production of a letter after a Minister had merely admitted its existence has also been blocked.[22] On this occasion the House rejected the contention of one member that an admission of the existence of a letter could be construed as "citing" the letter in debate.

The application of the rules with regard to quoting has been fairly consistent, although glaring exceptions can be found in most sessions. Long extracts have generally been ruled out of order. Members have occasionally read extract after extract and joined them together with a few sentences of their own. Speakers have agreed that such a speech is improper: the most common ruling is that a member is allowed to read portions of an article and base his argument on the contents; an extensive series of extracts or a single long quotation without further comment is an abuse of the right to quote.

The rule on quotations rests on as shaky a foundation as that against the reading of speeches. The principle that a member should present only his own views to the House is defensible and is not inconsistent with a

[15]*Debates*, May 31, 1928, p. 3604.
[16]*Ibid.*, March 6, 1877, pp. 511–12; May 9, 1904, col. 2786; Feb. 26, 1932, p. 563, etc.
[17]*Ibid.*, May 14, 1936, pp. 2811–12; April 28, 1938, pp. 2371–2; April 17, 1939, p. 2845; April 6, 1943, pp. 1918–19; Feb. 19, 1951, p. 478; Nov. 17, 1953, p. 97, etc.
[18]*Ibid.*, May 14, 1936, pp. 2811–12; April 28, 1938, pp. 2371–2.
[19]*Ibid.*, April 11, 1916, p. 2743; May 16, 1928, p. 3073; Feb. 20, 1959, p. 1261.
[20]*Ibid.*, May 12, 1921, pp. 3260–1.
[21]*Ibid.*, April 17, 1913, cols. 7925–45.
[22]*Ibid.*, April 3, 1957, p. 3008.

speech which is composed of one long quotation. The conventional objection was put forward by one Speaker when he ruled "I cannot imagine anything so improper as that any gentleman, no matter how eminent [who is not a member of the House], should be allowed to take his place in the House by having his opinions or his comments introduced upon what an honourable gentleman might say in his place in the House."[23] The leading offenders against this principle today are not the private members but the Cabinet ministers who call on the civil service to write their speeches. There seems little reason why a private member should not avail himself of any resources he may be able to muster. The only conditions which need be applied are that the member must himself take responsibility for the facts alleged, and if quoting direct, must be willing to identify the source.

A few other commonsense rules have developed. A member cannot quote a debate of the Senate, and this rule cannot be evaded by stating that the remarks were made "in another place,"[24] or by neglecting to mention their origin at all.[25] Members have used such references in debate, but only when the Speaker did not realize their origin. No member may quote from the proceedings of a committee before it has reported to the House.[26] More important for the efficient procedure of the House, a member may not refer to another debate of the same session or quote it, a regulation which applies also to questions in the House.[27] The only exception to this rule is a previous debate on the same subject: thus, at various stages of a bill, references may be made to speeches delivered earlier in the bill's progress. There have been few deviations from this rule.

REPETITION

The rule relating to repetition is extremely difficult to enforce. Standing Order 34 (2) states clearly that the Speaker may call a member to order if he persists in repetition. Unfortunately, the whole system of procedure is based on an assumption of repetition. Not only does every bill go through three readings during which nearly all aspects of the bill may be discussed, but in practice members assume today that the principle of a bill may be debated three times—in Committee of the Whole on the resolution, on second reading, and on clause one in committee stage. The current freedom of debate in Canada also means

23*Ibid.*, April 5, 1877, p. 1190.
24*Ibid.*, April 5, 1889, p. 1050; March 31, 1941, p. 2006.
25*Ibid.*, April 10, 1896, col. 5895; May 3, 1897, cols. 1646–7.
26*Ibid.*, March 31, 1879, p. 839; April 14, 1943, p. 2179.
27*Ibid.*, Jan. 31, 1896, col. 959; March 20, 1896, col. 4304.

that a large number of members speak on each bill. It can safely be said that after a dozen speakers have presented their views on a bill in forty-minute speeches, little more can be said that is not repetitive.

In its most narrow construction the rule against repetition applies to members who repeat the arguments of other members. In a prolonged debate this rule could cause a major problem if it were rigidly enforced. On occasion occupants of the Chair have ruled in this way but little has been accomplished.[28] The most sensible interpretation, and one invoked all too rarely, is that a member may not repeat his own arguments. This prohibition extends over all parts of a debate and is not limited to speeches within any one stage of a bill.[29]

One rule designed to prevent repetition in debate is that which precludes the moving of an amendment for the purpose of anticipating a notice of motion on the Order Paper. It is a rule which has been largely ignored in recent years. The custom now is to move amendments to the Address in Reply and to supply motions in such sweeping terms that they anticipate debate on many notices of motions. In general, the strict letter of the rule has been waived in view of the fact that few notices of motion are called for debate in any session.[30]

The rule which forbids any reference to a matter already settled by the House in the same session has been applied consistently to prevent repetition. In exceptional cases a motion may be made to rescind the decision and the matter may thus be raised again, but this is rarely done and is procedurally unimportant.

RELEVANCE

The rule which requires relevance in debate is also very difficult to enforce and has suffered much the same change. Relevancy has, by common consent, been abandoned completely at certain stages of House procedure. The passage of bills provides good examples. The rule (S.O. 59 (2)) which deals with relevance in committee is clear, and reads "Speeches in Committee of the Whole must be strictly relevant to the item or clause under consideration." In spite of this a Leader of the Opposition has recently found it possible to protest with all seriousness when debating clause one of a bill that "we have not reached the point where it is out of order to talk about the rights of parliament."[31] Debate on any other clause may be, and often is, as irrelevant. Debate in Com-

[28]*Ibid.*, May 11, 1920, p. 2286; June 9, 1955, p. 4609.
[29]*Ibid.*, Feb. 17, 1956, pp. 1289–90; April 19, 1956, p. 3073.
[30]*Ibid.*, Feb. 20, 1956, p. 1379.
[31]*Ibid.*, May 28, 1956, p. 4385.

mittee of Supply also lacks relevance. A member who cannot find a convenient item on which to ask a question merely asks it on any other item which comes along: thus the item in the estimates which deals with the construction of buildings for the Department of External Affairs has involved a discussion of the plight of an individual improperly detained by the United States immigration authorities.[32]

The other annual occasions on which the House ranges far afield are the debates on the Address in Reply to the Speech from the Throne, the budget, and motions for the House to go into Committee of Supply. The first of these is particularly notable, for the original motion on which the debate is based is meaningless. The amendments moved are usually more specific, but as they are merely want of confidence motions great latitude in debate has always been allowed. The same is largely true of debates on motions for supply: debate is usually more restrained, but the breadth of many of the amendments makes nearly any speech a proper one. The budget debate is perhaps more restricted than debates on motions for supply, as it is generally recognized as a debate on financial policy; nevertheless the various aspects of this field are consistently broadened to encompass nearly any problem a member wishes to raise.

Little interest can be aroused in the question of irrelevancy in these annual debates: the rules, which since 1955 have limited their length, make the question unimportant, and pressure for relevancy comes now more from within the party than from the Chair. Relevancy on other occasions, however, needs more serious attention, as it is a constant problem throughout the session. The situation has developed to the point where a leading member of the Opposition can say that a general and irrelevant debate on the first clause of a bill in committee is "a right which the Opposition cherishes."[33] This condition is obviously one which cannot be bettered by the mere passing of rules, for the written rule is already clear. It requires tact on the part of the occupants of the Chair and a sympathetic approach on the part of the members themselves. It can only be hoped that the future pressure of business will make a strict adherence to the rules necessary.

PARLIAMENTARY LANGUAGE

Parliamentary language has changed much since Confederation, and so noticeably in recent years that members have expressed fears that

[32]*Ibid.*, Aug. 2, 1956, pp. 6852–3.
[33]*Ibid.*, May 16, 1956, p. 3992. The statement did not go unchallenged by the Chairman who denied that such a "right" existed.

the House of Commons will become an "afternoon society meeting" rather than a place of debate between "strong men" with "strong opinions" (July 12, 1955). In the nineteenth century it bore no resemblance to a society meeting; rough words were common and were not even questioned. Today the House objects to the statement that the Government "does not want a free Parliament" (Feb. 15, 1956). It is unlikely that this House would have accepted the statement made by a member without challenge on January 25, 1881, that when he "wanted any information from the pocket edition of Judas Iscariot" he would ask for it. Even the old House had its limits. It was unparliamentary to say that a member had come into the world by accident (May 4, 1886), or that he was a parliamentary pugilist and political bully (March 19, 1875). Oddly enough, a member could not be accused of such an apparently innocuous activity as "dodging the question" (April 11, 1877) or that he "suggested a falsehood" (April 17, 1878). A member went unchallenged, however, when he accused a fellow member of having robbed some individuals of money and told him that he should wipe out the infamy that attached to his name (May 10, 1879).

Some words have been given varied rulings. At one time it was improper to refer to a group as *claqueurs* (March 5, 1878) and yet six years later a single member was so labelled and the term went unchallenged (March 26, 1884). The word "cowardly" has also been open to various interpretations. It was ruled out of order on numerous occasions[34] but in the midst of a few debates it was used with impunity.[35] The use of a word "in the parliamentary sense" occasionally brings it within the rules. This device has been used to justify the description of a member as a "bag of wind" (Feb. 15, 1878) and the attitude of another member as being "politically depraved" (May 3, 1887). The same method was used by a member forced to withdraw the statement that a fact was contained "in a ribald, lying, scoundrelly letter emanating from Senator Perley": his withdrawal was the statement that "the Parliamentary thing to say is that the honourable gentleman is a truthful and honourable man and a credit to the Senate" (Aug. 21, 1891).

Modern language has become much more mild. It has been ruled unparliamentary to say that an argument is "pure bunkum" (Feb. 2, 1926), that a bill is being passed by "railroading" (July 13, 1944), or that a Minister is "being trickier than ever" (June 13, 1929). On a few occasions the rules have been relaxed and the House has recaptured

[34]*Ibid.*, March 11, 1885, p. 498; April 28, 1885, p. 1436; June 19, 1895, col. 3001, etc.
[35]*Ibid.*, April 17, 1878, p. 2058; May 4, 1886, p. 1074.

some of its old colour. The pipeline debate and its aftermath in 1956 roused both sides of the House and led to heated exchanges that were not generally challenged.[36] The Government was described as being "despotic," an "arrogant oligarchy," and rapists of the liberties of Parliament. Opposition members labelled various ministers of the Crown "dictator," "Lord High Executioner of Parliament," "pipsqueak," and "Little Lord Fauntleroy." The Government benches responded with "Pocket Mussolini," "official snooper of the Opposition," and "jackass." While no one would seriously contend that any of these terms lend dignity to the proceedings of the House, they ought, at least, to give encouragement to those who think that the House is becoming rather more fastidious in its language than is necessary.

When referring to one another, members are expected to use the customary circumlocutions. This custom has not been developed to the same extent as it has in the United Kingdom and members are referred to only as honourable or right honourable. There has never been any attempt to adopt the use of "gallant" and "learned" to describe officers of the armed forces or members of the Bar, and although examples may be found of the use of "gallant" in reference to a retired officer, the term is not common and not expected. The description "honourable and reverend member" has actually been ruled out of order (April 19, 1899). Politeness has, of course, broken down occasionally. Sir John A. Macdonald was not called to order for his statement that a member was "honourable only by courtesy after tonight" (April 30, 1880). Speakers have, however, ruled out references to members as the "political sewer pipe from Carleton County" (Sept. 14, 1917), the "blatherskite from West Assiniboia" (May 7, 1890), and the "poet of East Assiniboia" (June 19, 1895). In this last case the offending member admitted that his statement was unparliamentary, and added that it "might hardly be considered true." He therefore withdrew "the statement that the honourable gentleman was a poet." Such lapses from good taste are unusual, and the tradition of politeness remains unchallenged.

It has been assumed that those inside the House will be able to look after their own interests in debate, but of course those outside the House cannot do so. It has, therefore, been thought necessary to adopt a standing order to protect certain persons from attack. This rule (S.O.

[36]The most unusual complaint of this debate was that of a front-bench Opposition member who protested that the Leader of the House had referred to the "Tory party" seven times, and accused the Minister of "insulting" them and "using terms which no Cabinet Minister should stoop to use." *Ibid.*, June 7, 1956, p. 4007.

35) covers the royal family, the Governor General or Administrator of the Government, and the Senate.[37] It was first adopted in 1867 and except for a few minor verbal changes has remained unaltered. The prohibitions specifically stated in the rule have been extended by rulings from the Chair to cover a variety of other persons. No set rule can be established, as the protection of other individuals is a matter of taste. Speakers have been consistent in ruling that persons outside the House cannot be protected from the excesses of members; they have, however, been similarly consistent in pointing out such breaches of good taste and requesting that they should not be repeated.

The bench in particular has been protected. It has been ruled to be irregular to refer to any judge in debate except on a substantive motion to remove him.[38] It is not even proper to commend a judge; and when a judge has been employed as a royal commissioner or in a similar capacity, it is proper to criticize the report of the commission in the House, but not its author.[39] The position of a magistrate has not been clearly defined. On May 14, 1919, Mr. Speaker Rhodes ruled that the custom which protects judges "has never been held applicable to magistrates." However, on February 12, 1954, this ruling was reversed by the Deputy Chairman, who decided that magistrates were covered by the rule.

As judges are protected, so also are proceedings which can be alleged to be *sub judice*. This ruling has been used to prevent debate on election cases and on other matters actively before the courts or merely pending;[40] and it has been extended to include bodies which carry out judicial or quasi-judicial functions. The Pension Commission has been ruled to be, at least in part, a judicial body.[41] It was, however, decided on September 19, 1919, that the old Board of Commerce was not a proper court as its members were appointed for a fixed term of years and could be removed for cause by the Governor in Council. Proceedings before the Board of Transport Commissioners may not be debated,[42] but, oddly enough, should a case be appealed from the Board to the Governor General in Council, it then becomes a proper subject for debate; a long ruling was made in 1923 which established that the Governor in Council

[37]This protection would now seem to extend also to lieutenant-governors. *Ibid.*, June 20, 1958, p. 1462; March 12, 1959, p. 1870.
[38]*Ibid.*, May 9, 1888, p. 1301; March 3, 1892, cols. 69–70; March 28, 1893, cols. 3289–91; April 19, 1917, p. 637; July 31, 1942, p. 5072, etc.
[39]*Ibid.*, Jan. 26, 1926, p. 437; July 27, 1942, pp. 4796–7.
[40]*Ibid.*, April 1, 1897, col. 366; June 14, 1897, cols. 3971–2; Feb. 16, 1927, pp. 360–71; June 29, 1942, p. 3745.
[41]*Ibid.*, April 7, 1927, p. 2049.
[42]*Ibid.*, June 18, 1925, p. 4477; June 12, 1951, pp. 3971–5.

was acting in an administrative capacity and such an appeal could not thus be covered by judicial immunity.[43]

The other group generally protected by the House are those of "high official station." The term is not defined and has been used to cover such diverse persons as the Commissioner of Taxation (June 19, 1925), the Prime Minister,[44] ranking officers of the armed services,[45] the United Kingdom High Commissioner in Canada (May 20, 1943), and a Minister of the Crown who was not a member of either House (Nov. 23, 1944). It has not been used to cover provincial legislators: these have on occasion been accused of being "false to their country and not patriots" (Jan. 23, 1908) and "gorillas" (Feb. 25, 1942).

Parliamentary Behaviour

In spite of the multiplicity of rules and traditions which the House has for controlling debate and maintaining its dignity, proceedings in the Commons have not always been dignified. On some occasions the House has degenerated into a mob. Such action was common in the past on the last day of a session, when little if any constructive work was done. Sometimes the same unruly spirits were carried over into the rest of the session, and special occasions such as the day on which the Queen achieved the longest reign in British history (Sept. 23, 1896) were used to excuse riotous conduct. At other times minor distractions were caused by members who threw paper (May 9, 1883) and firecrackers[46] around the House. On at least one occasion a member found a more solid missile, and another member complained that he had been hit during a debate by a blue book thrown from the other side of the House (April 25, 1892).

There is one period at which such irresponsible conduct is always excused. While the bells ring for a division (usually for ten minutes, but often longer), members wander aimlessly around the Chamber, and the House often indulges in singing. No business can be transacted in this period and the result is harmless. The songs have ranged from the

[43]*Ibid.*, April 17, 1923, pp. 1911–14. This has recently been challenged by a Minister, but his suggestion that an appeal to the Cabinet was exempt from discussion as being *sub judice* was neither accepted nor denied by the Chair. *Ibid.*, Jan. 3, 1958, p. 2776.

[44]*Ibid.*, Feb. 17, 1926, p. 1094. At that time Mackenzie King, who had been personally defeated in a general election, was still looking for a seat.

[45]*Ibid.*, April 30, 1942, p. 2002; July 22, 1942, p. 4572.

[46]May 13, 1882. On this occasion a member took care to fix the blame on the members of the House and to exonerate the pages.

National Anthem (March 2, 1926) to a rousing chorus of "Good Night Ladies" as a visiting group of women left the gallery (July 10, 1956). Special songs have been composed: on one occasion (May 24, 1956) a Minister was serenaded by a group of the Opposition[47] and shortly afterwards the Opposition was drowned out by a chorus from the Government benches.[48]

Certain noises and interruptions in debate have always been recognized as parliamentary. The most common of these—a feature of the Canadian House—is caused by members banging the tops of their desks, and it is used to applaud or interrupt. This noise, and other laughs, cheers, and antagonistic remarks are accepted as part of debate and appear in Hansard merely as "hear, hear" or "oh, oh." A few others have been heard and recorded by Hansard. One member who had made himself temporarily unpopular was greeted for a short time by "boo, boo" (May 15, 1956) and another who had delivered a speech on the wastefulness of an army goat mascot was met for months by well-imitated "baas" (July 19, 1956). In general, however, a member is permitted to deliver a speech without any such interruptions. A violent speech occasionally provokes comment; under such conditions the Speaker rarely interferes, and has been known to remark (June 28, 1955) that the remedy is in the hands of the member who is provoking the disturbance.

Enforcement of the Rules of Debate

The rules of debate are, of course, enforced in the House by the Speaker. Should general disorder reach such a pitch as to prevent debate, he is empowered by tradition to suspend the sitting. Should an individual member break the rules, the Speaker informs the House of the offence, warns the member, and gives him an opportunity to make a statement and a retraction.[49] Should the opportunity be refused, the Speaker can impose the traditional sanction of "naming." It is then the duty of the Leader of the House to move the suspension of the member for a

[47]The Minister had tried to get the floor and failed. The song was a gentle reminder that it was one of his Cabinet colleagues who had persuaded him to yield the floor.

[48]The words of this song were even recorded in the *Debates* (June 1, 1956, p. 4553). The song had obviously been prepared well in advance for just such an occasion, and was sung during one of the most violent scenes ever witnessed in the House. It did nothing to lessen the anger of the Opposition.

[49]In 1913 the House accepted Michael Clark's retraction, and although he had been named he was not suspended.

suitable length of time.[50] For a minor offence the period of suspension is the remainder of the sitting of the day, and for a repeated offence, or presumably for a more serious disturbance, the length of suspension is greater.[51] The motion for suspension is put to the House like any other motion and is decided, by a division if necessary, without debate or amendment. If the motion is passed, the member leaves the Chamber either by himself or under the escort of the Sergeant-at-Arms.

When the House is in committee, the Chairman of Committees is, of course, in the Chair to enforce the rules of debate. If disorder, whether individual or general, should occur, he warns the offender or offenders and, if his warning proves ineffectual, makes a report to the House. In committee this report by the Chairman takes the place of "naming" by the Speaker in a regular sitting, and the report to the House must be made before the offence can be dealt with (S.O. 59 (4)). However, if proceedings in Committee of the Whole become unmanageable, the Speaker can resume the Chair without motion or report.

These sanctions have been applied only rarely in Canada. The Speaker has never suspended a sitting of the House for disorder, and only twice—in 1913—has he been forced to resume the Chair to suppress disorder when the House was in committee. Control of individuals has presented more difficulties. The Speaker has threatened members with naming on several occasions[52] but has used it only four times. The first of these was on March 15, 1913, in the midst of the naval bill debate; the Speaker took the Chair to restore order and named a Liberal member, but before the House could take further action the member apologized and the incident was over. Another member had the doubtful distinction of being named twice: on both occasions he persisted in interrupting another member, and, after repeated warnings by the Speaker, was named. On the first occasion (March 24, 1942) he was suspended for the remainder of the sitting; on the second (July 4, 1944), for seven days. The most recent naming occurred in the 1960–1 session when a member refused to retract certain words he had used in debate. The Speaker gave him several opportunities to withdraw his

[50]The contention of Mr. Fleming in 1956 that the motion for his suspension was a "Government motion introduced by the Minister of Finance" is a distortion of the facts (*Debates*, June 4, 1956, p. 4652). It is the responsibility of the Leader of the House to make the motion irrespective of the party to which the offender belongs.

[51]In 1944, for his second offence, L. Lacombe was suspended for seven days. There has never been a suspension for a truly serious offence.

[52]*Debates*, May 9, 1890, c. 4717–18; Sept. 28, 1903, col. 12562; July 12, 1940, p. 1566, etc.

remarks and only named him when he flatly refused to do so. Suspension for the remainder of the sitting followed at once (Feb. 10, 1961).

Twice members have been reported to the House for a breach of the rules in committee and have been suspended. In 1944, an Opposition member refused to withdraw an offensive remark which was ruled to be a reflection on every member of the House. The Chairman's decision was appealed to the House, which upheld the ruling. The Speaker then directed the member to withdraw the words. When he again refused, he was suspended for the remainder of the sitting (July 31, 1944). In 1956 the House suspended another Opposition member who refused to resume his seat in Committee of the Whole in spite of repeated requests from the Chairman. His refusal was reported to the House and he also was suspended for the remainder of the day (May 25, 1956).[53]

The maintenance of order in the Canadian House presents only a small problem. In its normal work the House is often inattentive, but rarely noisy and almost never out of control. On occasion, in the midst of such acrimonious debates as those on the naval bill in 1913 and on the pipeline bill in 1956, an unpopular decision or an unexpected Government or Opposition manœuvre may precipitate a brief outcry. The effect, however, is short lived and the House quickly resumes its work. It is a tribute to the members and to the Speaker that the House has, throughout its history, shown a remarkable respect for the rules and traditions of debate and that the extreme powers with which the Speaker is endowed have been needed so rarely.

[53]In the 1962 session a third member was suspended for a similar offence.

LIMITATION
OF DEBATE

7

THE LAST CHAPTER dealt with the limitations on the content of debate imposed on members by the tradition of centuries. These customs which, as we have seen, were occasionally written into the rules, have never been sufficient to limit the over-all length of debate. It is necessary to turn now to what are generally more modern restrictions placed on members as a result of developing conditions. These new rules have for the most part been aimed at shortening debate and enabling the House to get through more work in less time. By their passage debate has been (or can be) shortened; although it is interesting to note that the members of the House have shown no particular anxiety to see that the debate that is allowed is more productive. It is not the intention here to go into this question, which can be solved only by trial and error in the House, but rather to examine the procedures which are now available to shorten the parliamentary session.

In 1902, while recommending a plan to reform British procedure, Balfour noted that the rules which had in the eighteenth century been designed to "promote a fertilizing and irrigating flow of eloquence" in the House, had in the twentieth century to be altered "to dam up its vast and destructive floods."[1] The House of Commons in Canada has never been faced with the problem of promoting eloquence, but early in its life it began to realize the necessity of stopping the flow of words. It has been slow to do so. In no branch of its procedure has the Canadian House been more loath to follow Great Britain than in instituting these unpopular restrictions. For many years it was unnecessary to im-

[1] J. Redlich, *The Procedure of the House of Commons* (3 vols., London, 1908), I, p. 198.

pose limitations on members: the country was small, and the business transacted by the federal House took little enough time without control. Determined obstruction was met with compromise on the part of the Government or by an appeal to the people. As the country developed, this primitive method of settling differences became cumbersome and more effective methods of ensuring Government control over the House were adopted.

At the present time the House employs four distinct methods to restrict debate.[2] The oldest of these is the simple motion that "the question be now put." The House adopted this motion with its first set of rules in 1867 and it has remained unaltered (S.O. 51). In 1913, the House took its first big step in limiting debate and adopted a closure rule (S.O. 33), which has also remained substantially unchanged. A revision of the rules in 1927 provided a forty-minute time limit (S.O. 31) for nearly all speeches. This was amended in 1955 (S.O. 59 (3)) to allow only thirty minutes for speeches in Committee of the Whole. The revision of 1955 also introduced in the House a series of orders allocating the time for the debate on the Address (S.O. 38), supply motions (S.O. 56), and the budget debate (S.O. 58). The effect of these limitations has been negligible; during the longest session of the House (1960–1) all of them were available, while during the second longest (1903–4) only the previous question was in the rule book.

The Previous Question

The first of these methods—the "previous question"—is the most ineffective.[3] The words of the motion are identical with the British closure motion but the difference is immense. In the United Kingdom the "previous question" is put in a negative form: "That the question be not now put," and is used not to force a vote on a question but rather to delay a decision. When the motion is passed the House proceeds to the next order of business. In Canada, the motion "that this question be *now* put" merely prevents a further amendment to the main motion (S.O. 51). The motion is debatable (S.O. 32 (1)(c)), and on two

[2]This figure does not include such limitations as the standing orders which limit the number of debatable motions, provide three days of the week when no question is put on a motion for supply, set a fixed hour of adjournment, allocate a fixed number of days to private members' business, or otherwise restrict debate. They may be more conveniently dealt with elsewhere.

[3]For the use of the previous question in Canada to delay rather than speed up proceedings see chap. 9, p. 171.

occasions when it has been used it has needed closure in addition to end the debate.[4] The fact that it is debatable and the restrictions surrounding its use make the previous question a little-used instrument.[5] The Government occasionally uses it in an attempt to restrict the length of a debate, but with little effect. In 1955, for instance, the Government moved the previous question on the defence production bill, but it had no effect at all in shortening the debate, and after lengthy discussion and important concessions by the Government, the motion was passed by consent, without even a division.[6]

Little has been done to make the previous question an effective instrument for limiting debate. Should the House wish, a simple change in Standing Order 32, removing the motion from the list of those which are debatable, would be effective. This, of course, would provide the Government with a most efficient form of closure, and place in its hands a weapon which no party would wish to concede to any Government without such protection at least as the rules of the British House provide.[7] Alternatively, a limit could be imposed by standing order on the length of any debate on this motion. An intermediate form of closure of this sort might be useful, although the limitation imposed on the possibility of amendment of the main motion is not likely to commend itself to the opposition parties. It is more probable that the trend over the last ninety years will be continued and that new forms of limitation on debate will be developed to the exclusion of this rule.

Closure

The Canadian House of Commons has never been faced with anything comparable to the obstruction of the Irish nationalists which precipitated the introduction of closure in the British House, nor has it had among

[4]See the debate on the Address in Reply in 1926 and the debate on the Unemployment and Farm Relief Continuance Act in 1932.

[5]It cannot be moved on an amendment, although once an amendment has been voted on, the previous question may be moved on the original motion whether amended or not.

[6]*Debates*, July 11, 1955, p. 5941. In 1943 Mackenzie King defended his use of the previous question on the grounds that he desired not to restrict debate but rather to concentrate it on the main motion. *Ibid.*, July 5, 1943, p. 4347.

[7]In Great Britain a closure motion may be moved in the House only if the Speaker is in the Chair. It may be refused if the Speaker considers it to be an infringement of the rights of the minority. It must also be supported by at least 100 members. (U.K. standing orders 29 and 30).

its members a group dedicated to the destruction of the parliamentary process by the systematic use of obstruction at every opportunity. The only time that this has been a real possibility was in 1867 when the anti-Confederation block of Nova Scotian members might have adopted these tactics to force its will on the Government.[8]

Opposition in Canada has been conducted on different lines. Specific bills have been chosen by the Opposition and all the weight of argument at the party's disposal has been used to force either amendment to the bill or dissolution of the House for an appeal to the people. Most notable in the years preceding the introduction of the closure were the prolonged battles in 1885 on the Macdonald franchise bill, in 1896 on the Manitoba school bill, in 1908 on a Liberal franchise bill, and in 1911 on reciprocity. Two of these struggles resulted in compromise with the Opposition and two in dissolution. It was in the middle of a fifth debate on the naval bill in 1913 that Borden decided to end the problem, as he thought permanently, and introduced closure. It is significant that on all of these occasions, as well as throughout the later history of obstruction in Canada, opposition has come not from a small dissident minority like the Irish nationalists but from the large minority of the official Opposition. This fact undoubtedly delayed the introduction of the closure and has been an important factor in limiting its use since then.

The possibility of introducing closure had been present in the years before 1913. Partisans of all parties could be found to advocate its adoption and similarly violent opposition was occasionally stirred up by the suggestion. Generally, however, feeling in the House was against the closure. In the debate which preceded the establishment of a committee to revise the rules in 1909, one member objected in advance to any limitation on freedom of debate, and another reported that he had heard rumours of closure and asked for elaboration.[9] A few months later, one back-bencher spoke for many others in the House when he criticized a new rule which merely required relevancy in debate in committee: "I do not feel like giving up any privilege or right in the way of obstruction that I have at the present time as a member of the Opposition in any legislation which I consider not to be in the best interest of the country. . . ."[10] The rules committee of the 1909–10

---

[8]In the first federal House of Commons, seventeen of the eighteen Nova Scotian members were avowed anti-Confederates, and were led by Joseph Howe who for some time to come was to agitate at home and in the United Kingdom for the repeal of the union so far as Nova Scotia was concerned.

[9]*Debates*, Dec. 14, 1909, cols. 1442, 1443.

[10]*Ibid.*, April 29, 1910, col. 8376.

session seems to have taken the same attitude. A memorandum containing notes on foreign methods of limiting debate was circulated to the committee, but no recommendations were made in its report.[11]

The reciprocity debate in 1911 and the subsequent dissolution of the House brought matters to a head. Cabinet ministers and the press of the country campaigned for the introduction of a rule to bring an end to obstruction. On April 27 the *Manitoba Free Press* spoke approvingly of the introduction of closure "which will take our Parliament out of the freak class and make it an assembly that can act as well as talk." There seems little doubt that, had the Liberals been returned to power in the election of 1911, strong pressure would have been brought to bear on the Prime Minister to introduce a closure resolution. Sydney Fisher, the last Minister of Agriculture in the Laurier Government, put forward at an election meeting what he stated to be the view of the Government: "If we are returned to power we will pass reciprocity and we will also pass a measure changing the rules so that the business of the country may go briskly forward. Full investigation we believe in, but empty obstruction is a drag on the country."[12]

In the session of 1912–13 the Liberals voted supply and passed all the Government programme without undue delay except the bill introduced by the Conservatives to make a substantial Canadian contribution to the royal navy. In respect of that one bill the Liberals insisted on their right of what Sydney Fisher would undoubtedly have called "full investigation" and what the Conservatives looked on more properly as obstruction. The obstruction of the Opposition culminated in Committee of the Whole when they kept the House in virtually continuous session for two weeks.[13] Before the end of the sitting the debate reached a violent state. Twice the Speaker had to take the Chair to restore order and a leading Liberal was named. Borden consulted Laurier who admitted that the Liberals were obstructing the bill as the Conservatives had obstructed in 1908 and 1911. Borden offered the Liberals all the time they wished for debate and merely asked Laurier to set a date for third reading. The Liberals rejected the plan, and Borden announced to his cabinet that closure had become a necessity.[14]

[11]"Memorandum of information compiled for the use of the Committee on the subject of matters connected with the abbreviation of debate." P.A.C., Laurier Papers, pp. 220881–91.

[12]Speech at Waterloo, Que., quoted in *Debates*, April 9, 1913, cols. 7397–8.

[13]The House sat from 3 P.M. on Monday, March 3, to midnight on Saturday, March 8, and from 3 P.M. on Monday, March 10, to 11:32 P.M. on Saturday, March 15.

[14]Henry Borden, ed., *Robert Laird Borden: His Memoirs* (2 vols., Toronto, 1938), I, pp. 413–15.

With the consent of the Cabinet and the support of the Conservative party caucus, Borden moved the adoption of three new rules.[15] The Prime Minister pointed out in his speech that there were nineteen stages in the passage of a bill on which every member of the House could speak without limit. There were in addition innumerable stages in committee when every member could speak, again at interminable length. Up to 1913, he said, business had been transacted through "closure by consent," that is, after a certain time had been spent in debate, both parties agreed that a vote should be taken.[16] In 1913, however, the Government, although supported in the House by a majority of about forty-five, was helpless in the face of determined obstruction.

When Borden resumed his seat, Sir Wilfrid Laurier and J. D. Hazen, Minister of Marine and Fisheries, rose. The Speaker recognized Sir Wilfrid as Leader of the Opposition, according to normal parliamentary tradition. Another Conservative member rose and moved "that the Minister of Marine and Fisheries . . . be now heard." A division followed, naturally carried by the Government. The speech of the Minister was merely the motion "that this question be now put." This motion for the previous question was debatable, but precluded any amendment to the main motion. Sir Wilfrid Laurier, who later admitted that he had hoped to move an amendment, was thus prevented from further obstruction on the new motion.[17]

The aftermath was inevitable—a bitter debate which could end only in the passage of the new rules. The debate dragged on for two weeks. Great heights of oratory were reached on both sides. The rights of the Government and the Opposition were thoroughly examined, and British parliamentary history was exhaustively reviewed by both sides. At last, with the final appeal of a Liberal member—"we stand for freedom on every count of the indictment; and we have not the shadow of a shade of doubt that the people of Canada stand with us"[18]—both the previous question and the motion for closure passed in the early morning of April 24, 1913.

[15]Of these three, only the closure will be examined here. The other two, dealing with debatable motions and the provision of two days in each week when the House could resolve itself into Committee of Supply without question put, will be considered later.

[16]Borden did not bother to explain or justify the earlier occasions on which this "closure by consent" had failed in the face of obstruction by the Opposition.

[17]Sir Wilfrid Laurier's amendment would have been merely that the new rules be referred for study to the usual committee on revision of the rules. However innocuous this may appear on the surface, the possibility of the closure emerging from such a committee before the end of the session was slight.

[18]*Debates*, April 23, 1913, col. 8453.

The closure rule (S.O. 33) stands today virtually as it passed in 1913:[19]

Immediately before the order of the day for resuming an adjourned debate is called, or if the House be in committee of the whole, or of supply, or of ways and means, any Minister of the Crown who, standing in his place, shall have given notice at a previous sitting of his intention so to do, may move that the debate shall not be further adjourned, or that the further consideration of any resolution or resolutions, clause or clauses, section or sections, preamble or preambles, title or titles, shall be the first business of the committee, and shall not further be postponed; and in either case such question shall be decided without debate or amendment; and if the same shall be resolved in the affirmative, no member shall thereafter speak more than once, or longer than twenty minutes in any such adjourned debate; or if in committee, on any such resolution, clause, section, preamble or title; and if such adjourned debate or postponed consideration shall not have been resumed or concluded before one o'clock in the morning, no member shall rise to speak after that hour, but all such questions as must be decided in order to conclude such adjourned debate or postponed consideration, shall be decided forthwith.

This closure rule is at once more difficult of application and more open to abuse than that in Great Britain. It can be applied only after a motion has been before the House for two days.[20] Notice must be given and a formal motion made and passed before it can go into effect, and even then an extraordinarily long day's debate ensues before the final vote is taken.[21] The moderating power of the Speaker, so important in the British closure, is not brought to bear. The motion for closure is made by a Minister and the Government takes full responsibility for cutting off debate when it sees fit. There is no guarantee parallel to that in the United Kingdom that the rights of the minority shall be protected.

All this is emphasized by the fact that the use of closure in Canada has always been marked by strong feelings and violence of debate. It has been used only as a last resort and has never become a common weapon of any Government. The lack of pressure on the time-table of the House is likely as much responsible for this attitude as any particularly sympathetic approach by the Government. The Canadian House has still

[19]The only alteration of this rule was made in 1955 when it was agreed that the vote should take place at 1 A.M. rather than 2 A.M. as had been originally specified. This was done to correspond with the change in the normal adjournment time from 11 P.M. to 10 P.M.

[20]Normally two days' debate is possible on any motion. It is possible, however, as in 1917, for a motion to be brought before the House late in the evening and notice of closure given at once.

[21]The problem of application is most strikingly shown by the pipeline debate of 1956 when the opposition successfully talked out a closure motion in Committee of the Whole. *Debates*, May 31, 1956, pp. 4498–534.

not reached the point where debate on a substantial number of Government bills must be cut short. On most occasions the Opposition contents itself with a reasonable time of debate and then allows a bill to pass. In the last few years this attitude may have developed through the absence of any real difference in the policies of the two major parties in Canada. Most of the important debates in the House in the past few years have been tactical battles aimed at the next election, rather than divisions on basic policy.

Closure has been used in Canada fifteen times, on various stages of six bills, in the debate on the Address in Reply to the Speech from the Throne, and also in Committee of Supply. Only twice has it been used as often as possible on the one bill—in 1956 on all four stages, and in 1917 on three stages. (This was not a money bill and thus was not based on a resolution.) Mr. Walter E. Harris apparently shocked the opposition parties in the House in 1956 when he stated in a radio broadcast only a week after the end of the pipeline debate that the purpose of closure was "to limit the time available for debate so that a Government could meet a timetable or overcome prolonged obstruction."[22] In fact, Mr. Harris was correct; closure has been used by the Government on three bills to cut off debate long before obstruction could properly be charged to the Opposition. On the other occasions the Government usually met obstruction with the guillotine.

Two bills that were put under closure early to ensure speedy passage were the Canadian Northern acquisition bill and the War-time Elections bill, both of 1917. The first of these bills was read a first time on August 1, and the Government moved second reading on August 14. The House debated second reading for two and a half days and then sent the bill to Committee of the Whole. There it got more extensive examination for four and a half days and was passed by closure. Third reading was a formality and occupied little more than one day, for on Wednesday, August 29, after two hours of debate, the Minister in charge of the bill gave notice of closure. The Opposition questioned the propriety of the motion, and he defended it merely on the ground that Friday was not a good night to hold a division as so many members went home.[23]

One week later the War-time Elections bill was introduced and given first reading. The Government called it for debate on September 8 and the House debated it for nearly three hours. Borden notes in his

[22]Broadcast on Trans-Canada network, June 15, 1956. Reprinted in *Liberal Newsletter*, June 1956.
[23]*Debates*, Aug. 29, 1917, p. 5121.

Memoirs, "it was apparent that it would meet with fierce and protracted resistance,"[24] and at the conclusion of the sitting the Government gave notice of closure. It is easy to accept the description of Sir George Foster, a leading member of the Government, that the "Opposition was bowled over" by this sudden move to restrict debate.[25] The bill thus passed its second reading in less than two days, and the committee stage followed quickly. Again the Government moved the closure. Sir Wilfrid Laurier was unwilling to accept an offer that three days would be allowed for debate in committee on the understanding that third reading would take only one day, and Sir Robert Borden moved to end the debate.[26] Third reading was similarly dealt with in two days.

The most recent use of closure was also intended to enable the Government to pass a bill after only a limited amount of debate.[27] The Government made known the final date on which the provisions of the bill could become effective and the Opposition also made public its intention of blocking the bill if possible. Notice of closure was given at the end of the Minister's speech introducing the resolution. The House spent four days on second reading, eight in Committee of the Whole, and two on third reading. Each stage ended in closure and the bill passed within the set time. The House did not spend more than a small proportion of these sixteen days in debate on the bill itself: the debate revolved more around procedural technicalities and no less than seventy divisions were necessary to pass the bill.

On the other occasions closure has generally been used to pass a few contentious clauses of a bill in Committee of the Whole. It has been used in committee on three occasions, on two of which only a small proportion of the clauses were covered by the closure motion. In 1932, however, all three clauses of the unemployment relief continuance bill were passed after weeks of debate.[28] In 1921, one supply item and an interim supply resolution were both passed with one closure motion after a considerable debate on the former but little on the latter.

The use of closure in 1926 stands alone among all the instances in that it was used to pass the Address in Reply to the Speech from the Throne so that the House could adjourn for a brief holiday before it proceeded with legislation. The Government met the House in January

[24]II, p. 709.
[25]P.A.C., Foster Papers, Diary, Sept. 8, 1917.
[26]A similar offer was made in the pipeline debate of 1956, and was likewise rejected by the opposition. *Debates,* May 30, 1956, pp. 4464–9.
[27]The Northern Ontario pipeline Crown corporation bill.
[28]In this case closure had also been used to pass the motion that the Speaker leave the Chair for the resolution stage of the bill.

without a clear majority and as its first item of business moved a motion of confidence. With this safely passed, the House turned to the Address and debated it for nearly two months. At the end of this time the Government moved the closure so that it could reinforce its small numbers in several by-elections and prepare the work of the session. The debate on this occasion ended before the 2 A.M. deadline.

In 1956 in particular, and on various earlier occasions, the House has questioned the interpretation of the closure rule. Rules and precedents have been cited in great numbers, but few are strictly relevant to the questions raised: closure has been used so rarely in Canada that there is little or no case law connected with it. Up to 1956 little trouble had arisen over the use of closure. It might be disliked, but it was accepted as inevitable. In the pipeline debate, however, the opposition adopted new tactics. Every move of the Government was fought on procedural grounds and closure was opposed in every possible way. This reached its peak on May 31, when a motion for closure made shortly after 2:30 P.M. was talked out by the opposition before it could be voted on.[29]

This procedural obstruction raised problems which cannot easily be solved. One problem arose four times, for the rules do not specify exactly which motions are covered by any one closure motion. The rule merely states that at 1:00 A.M., "all such questions as must be decided in order to conclude such adjourned debate or postponed consideration, shall be decided forthwith." In committee on the resolution preceding a money bill, a strict interpretation of this rule would mean that only the original motion for concurrence in the resolution would be carried. But this leaves the formal subsidiary motions for concurrence in the resolution (after the committee reports to the House), for leave to introduce a bill based on it, and for the first reading of the bill until later days and presumably for three more closure motions. Similarly, on second reading, there is an extra formal motion that the bill be considered in Committee of the Whole; in Committee of the Whole there is a motion ordering the bill to be reported; and on third reading there used to be the final motion that "the bill do now pass and the title be as on the order paper."[30] Naturally, these motions cannot be specifically covered in a closure motion before they are moved. Equally obviously, to accept the position that each requires separate action on the part of the House would render the closure rule completely useless. Up to 1956 this ques-

[29]This feat is a tribute to the ingenuity and perseverance of the opposition as the motion itself is not debatable.
[30]This motion has now been eliminated. *Debates*, May 14, 1958, p. 84.

tion had not been raised: each closure motion moved its bill one full stage nearer to passing. When the Opposition challenged this position in 1956, the Speaker made two rulings.[31] In both cases he followed a commonsense interpretation of the rules, decided in favour of the precedents, and allowed the bill to proceed one full stage on each closure motion.

One point was raised and caused more controversy than any other in the pipeline debate. The standing order reads that "the further consideration of any resolution . . . , clause . . . , section . . . , shall be the first business of the committee, and shall not further be postponed. . . ." In Committee of the Whole on May 24 C. D. Howe introduced the first clause, spoke seven minutes on it, and moved that "further consideration of this clause be postponed." The motion is not debatable and if it had passed would probably have prevented any further discussion of the clause.[32] The Minister moved similar motions for clause two and clause three. At each motion the argument was advanced that the motion was out of order in that no consideration had been given any of the clauses. The arguments generally raged around the meaning of the words "further consideration": the opposition claimed that their meaning was clear and that more than one speech was necessary;[33] the Government held, and the Chair ruled, that by being called, a clause was brought under the consideration of the House.

Certainly these rulings were not popular. The opposition members saw their opportunities to block the bill slipping away with their opportunities to debate and realized that the inevitable end was a third motion for closure. This method of limiting debate had never been used previously. Debate on clauses of a bill had often been short but never limited to one speech. Little can be said against the legal position of the Chairman. His precedents were sound and more directly to the point than were those of the opposition. Again, however, the rule itself is at fault, in being so vague as to permit such debate.[34]

[31]*Journals*, May 15, 1956, pp. 554–6; June 5, 1956, pp. 705–9.

[32]It is unlikely that this clause, which contained only the short title of the bill, would ever have been called again, although this type of postponement does not preclude the possibility of reverting to a clause after the later ones are dealt with.

[33]This ignores, of course, the opposition claims to be allowed to debate the clauses as a matter of justice. Much of the argument rested on this foundation.

[34]One parallel which was not drawn by the Chairman when making his rulings illustrates the foolishness of appealing to a dictionary definition for a ruling in the House. It is the terminology often used when a bill is given second reading by the House and by custom the Speaker leaves the Chair for the House to go into Committee of the Whole. The Chairman takes the Chair,

A final point raised, and in the long run a more important one, was the validity of a ruling regarding the number of clauses which must be called before closure can be applied to a bill in Committee of the Whole. The rule does not specify that a clause must be called before closure can be moved on it. It seems clear, however, that for "postponed consideration" a clause must have been called at least briefly. This view is certainly borne out by the evidence of Arthur Meighen in 1913, when he answered a direct question on the subject by saying that clauses which had not been called "could not possibly come on again. They must be discussed and the discussion postponed before they can be brought up on this last day. . . ."[35] In 1913, 1917 (twice), and 1919 this advice was followed. All clauses on which closure was moved had been discussed and postponed.

In 1932 R. B. Bennett introduced a new precedent when he had a three-clause bill in Committee of the Whole. After a little more than a day's debate he moved closure, although only one clause of the three in the bill had been called in committee. He justified his action in words that his own party was to regret twenty-four years later: "You will observe that the words are 'further consideration'. Last evening it was impossible to separate one clause from another in the discussion since the honourable gentlemen opposite thought it desirable to discuss all three clauses at the same time, notably my honourable friend from Shelburne-Yarmouth. It is clear, therefore, that there having been some consideration of the measure, the words 'further consideration' are correct."[36] A point of order was raised, but it was brushed aside by the Chairman.

In 1956 the Liberals revived this precedent. After six days of debate only four clauses of seven had been called, and progress was slow. The Government, which up to that time had intended calling all the clauses and postponing them, altered its tactics and decided to use a different precedent.[37] The Prime Minister moved closure on the three postponed clauses, the one under consideration, and the three which had not been called. The procedural fight on this motion lasted all day. By 10 P.M. that evening the House had not yet voted on the Prime Minister's motion, and the House was forced to adjourn. The motion was ruled in order the

---

calls clause one, and immediately leaves the Chair again to report to the Speaker that "the Committee of the Whole has considered a certain bill, directed me to report progress and ask leave to sit again." In this case "consideration" and "progress" are achieved merely by the voice of the Chairman.

[35]*Debates*, April 10, 1913, cols. 7537–8.
[36]*Ibid.*, April 1, 1932, p. 1609.
[37]*Ibid.*, May 31, 1956, p. 4503.

next day on the basis of the 1932 precedent and the bill passed Committee of the Whole.[38]

The precedent established in 1932 and strengthened in 1956 is obviously an undesirable one. A system under which only a few clauses of a bill are considered before being passed is neither wise nor sensible. It would, of course, be even less desirable if the rule of relevancy were enforced and discussion on each clause were kept strictly to its provisions. On both these occasions debate ranged over the whole bill although few of the clauses had been called. An attempt was made in the debate of 1956 to draw a distinction between 1932 and 1956 on the basis of the content of the clauses which had been called: in 1932 the one clause considered was the only operative clause in the bill; in 1956 the three main clauses were never called. Distinctions of this sort are dangerous. In some bills the important clauses may easily be defined, whereas in others they may not be nearly so obvious.[39] Certainly no clear rule can be drafted which will differentiate satisfactorily between the contents of various clauses.

The only alternative is to place this power in the hands of the Speaker, and leave to his judgment the question of whether or not all the important clauses of a bill have been properly discussed before closure may be moved. Given the present traditions surrounding the Speakership such a responsibility would be unwelcome. Neither the Opposition nor the Speaker would appreciate the placing of such a power in the hands of an occupant of the Chair about whose impartiality there was the slightest doubt. Any such change in this rule, therefore, must follow a change in the Speakership.

In 1913 Arthur Meighen admitted that the closure rule was not entirely satisfactory. It left in the hands of the Government the power to decide on its own responsibility the proper length of time for any debate in the House. He admitted that many things could be done under the closure rule which would be oppressive but denied that they would be done except by a Government that was both "insane and vicious."[40] The responsibility for deciding on the length of time for debate has always been accepted by the Government. Opposition is extended to the point of obstruction with the contention that nothing but proper

[38]*Journals*, June 1, 1956, pp. 680–1.

[39]This difficulty is shown clearly even in 1956. The opposition held that the last four clauses were the most important, but at the same time stated that the clauses which defined the abbreviations used in the bill and the formal clause which established the pipeline corporation were so important that all debate on later clauses, which covered the financing of the corporation and its duties and its powers with respect to the rest of the pipeline project, was meaningless until the early clauses had been passed.

[40]*Debates*, April 10, 1913, col. 7533.

opposition is being carried on, and notice of closure is met with cries of "gag." The Opposition is certain that were the issues involved placed before the electorate the decision would be against the Government, and it is invariably trying to establish that the Government lacks a "mandate" for its proposals.

On some occasions opposition to the point of forcing dissolution might be justified. The War-time Elections bill of 1917, for instance, which was advanced through all of its stages by closure, has been described by Professor Ward as "frankly biased in its [the Government's] own favour."[41] Professor Ward continues to say that the bill "could hardly fail to return a majority in Parliament for the party which enacted it."[42] The propriety of passing such an act in the final year of the life of a Parliament, and one which had had its life extended for a year by constitutional amendment, may well be questioned. On most bills, however, such an extreme measure as forcing dissolution cannot be defended. There is little reason why an item of Government policy must be submitted to the electorate at the whim of the Opposition. One must assume that so long as the Government can command a majority in the House it ought to be able to pass such legislation as it feels is in the best interests of the country. This assumption is, of course, the justification for a closure rule in whatever form it may exist. The need of the Government to maintain public support for a coming election will act to a large degree as sufficient deterrent to protect both the public and the Opposition from an abuse of the Government's power.

The closure rule in Canada has now arrived at the point where it should be revised. The pipeline debate of 1956 showed the inadequacy of the rule both as a protection to the Opposition and as an aid to the Government. This is a problem which must be faced, but one which no party has cared to touch seriously. Revision committees have assiduously avoided the issue. In the election campaign of 1957 the Leader of the Progressive Conservative party took what might be the first step and pledged his party to repeal of the closure rule.[43]

Complete abolition of closure is highly improbable except for political

[41]N. Ward, *The Canadian House of Commons* (Toronto, 1950), p. 226.

[42]*Ibid.*, p. 227. O. D. Skelton has described this bill as "a stacking of the cards, a gerrymander on a colossal scale, an attempt without parallel except in the tactics of Lenin and Trotsky to ensure the dominance of one party in the state." See his *Life and Letters of Sir Wilfrid Laurier* (2 vols., Toronto, 1921), II, p. 529.

[43]A motion for the repeal of the rule was put on the Order Paper by the Government late in the 1957–8 session. However, the motion was never called for debate and it is doubtful if it was ever meant to be debated. In four sessions since, the motion has not been renewed.

reasons. It is difficult to believe that any Government today would willingly deliver itself into the power of the Opposition so completely. On the other hand, a revision seems inevitable. Several points have come to light in the last few years which might be a guide to its revision. The position of the Speaker, the weakness of the "usual channels," and the uncertainty of application of the rule are predominant. The Speaker, should he ever become in Canada the impartial arbiter he is in Westminster, could be given considerable authority in the rules or in practice over the working of the closure. He could certainly act as a mediator between Government and Opposition were his impartiality beyond question. In the case of lengthy bills, his judgment on important clauses and even on the sufficiency of debate at various stages could be trusted by both sides. This type of reform, however, cannot be achieved at once and is dependent on more widespread changes in attitude in the House.

The "usual channels" in Ottawa are notoriously less efficient than those at Westminster. The whips do relatively little by way of exchanging information or making arrangements for debate. More frankness here could make an immense difference to the conduct of a debate under closure. The uncertainty which overshadows the use of closure in Canada is most undesirable. The opposition generally does not know except through rumour that closure is to be used, until the notice is given in the House. Certainly some of the bitterness of the pipeline debate was caused by the ignorance on the part of the opposition of the plans of the Government. Nothing was gained by the Government's secrecy in this instance. The opposition was dedicated to a blockade of the bill at all its stages and took no pains to disguise its aims. The Government was certain after its first use of closure that it would have to be used again at each future stage. Had a time-table been drawn up and discussed with the opposition even with the assurance that closure would be used to pass the bill by its deadline, much of the opposition's attack on the Government would have been blunted. Concessions could have been made to allow more time for any stage the opposition desired to debate more fully and closure would have been used with the knowledge, if not the approbation, of the opposition to enforce a limit on debate at each stage.

Should the Canadian Commons find it impossible to achieve reform along these lines, a formal amendment of the rules might be feasible. The most satisfactory reform would probably be to establish a minimum time limit for each stage of a bill. After the allotted time had expired, the Government would be free, as now, to apply closure.

This at least would remove the danger of abuse by the Government. A generous allowance could be made for each stage and the opposition would be assured of at least that length of time, while the Government would not be relieved of the necessity of answering to the electorate at the next dissolution for its decision to use the rule.

The problem is not a simple one, and in a country which has a relatively unbroken record of complete freedom of debate it becomes even more complex. It is unlikely that the opposition will submit quietly to a further restriction on its power of obstruction, although the pipeline debate may make the opposition parties more willing to accept alterations to ensure further control over the Government. The question will become more important in the years to come. Although the Canadian House has never had a small obstructive group, there is no reason to believe that one might not appear. It could be an ultra-nationalist French-Canadian group or a small protest party from the Maritimes or the West. Should one appear and make its presence felt as Parnell and his Irish party did at Westminster, the Canadian Parliament could rapidly become unmanageable.

More urgent, the growing pressure of parliamentary work makes some change desirable. The Canadian House has not yet reconciled itself to sitting for more than a fraction of the year. Until it does so, the ever-increasing amount of work which the modern state imposes on a Government must be completed in the same time as the House has always spent. It is this which leads to pressure of time in a session today. It is to be hoped that, to some degree at least, a new and more equitable closure rule can be passed which will answer the question fairly, and reconcile the legitimate demands of the Government to have its legislation passed with the legitimate rights of the minority to adequate discussion of all these measures.

Length of Speeches

One month after the first Parliament of the new Canadian federation met in 1867, a private member (D. A. Macdonald) expressed the fear that should a Hansard report be made of proceedings in the House, the practice of the Confederation debates might be continued and the new House be the scene of speeches of "unnatural" length. He concluded with the hope "that some check would be put upon those gentlemen who are eternally on their legs."[44] The idea was not a new one. Although

[44]*Debates*, Dec. 12, 1867, p. 63.

the Province of Canada had not had any limit on the length of speeches, both Nova Scotia and New Brunswick had found such a rule to be necessary.[45]

Macdonald's fears were fully justified. Few members could resist the complete freedom of debate. The custom of the time condoned the practice and both the Cabinet and back-benchers took full advantage of the opportunities offered. It is impossible to say which member holds the record for the longest speech ever delivered in the Canadian House, but the record was certainly established by the turn of the century. Edward Blake, Clifford Sifton, and Sir Charles Hibbert Tupper all seem to have been leading contenders for the honour. Four hours was nothing to Blake, and in July 1885 he spoke for three-quarters of a twelve-hour sitting. Sifton in 1899 spoke all day in a sitting which lasted a little under nine hours, equalling the feat which Tupper had accomplished some five days earlier. Three months later Tupper again spoke for a full day on the administration of the Yukon, and occupied another forty columns of Hansard the next day.[46]

In 1885 a member suggested that Hansard be used to restrict debate rather than encourage it, and moved an amendment which would have required Hansard to print only the first hour of a member's speech, and only the first ten minutes in committee. The amendment was negatived after little comment.[47] The next year, however, a private member made a formal protest. He moved a resolution:

that the growing practice in the Canadian House of Commons of delivering speeches of great length having the character of carefully and elaborately prepared written essays, and indulging in voluminous and often irrelevant written extracts is destructive of legitimate and pertinent debate upon public questions, is a waste of valuable time, unreasonably lengthens the sessions of Parliament, threatens by increased bulk and cost to lead to the abolition of the official Report of the debates, encourages a discursive and diffuse style of public speaking, is a marked contrast to the practice in regard to debate that prevails in the British House of Commons, and tends to repel the public from a careful and intelligent consideration of the proceedings of Parliament.[48]

He recommended the mild cure of a limit on the leaders of Government and Opposition of two hours and on other members one and one-half hours. After three days of debate speeches could be limited

---

[45]N.S. Rule 14; N.B. Rule 15.

[46]For Blake, *Debates*, May 8, 1872, cols. 431–47; June 17, 1885, pp. 2600–19; July 6, 1885, pp. 3075–111. For Sifton, *ibid.*, April 4, 1899, cols. 805–88. For Tupper, *ibid.*, March 30, 1899, cols. 701–801; June 27 and June 28, 1899, cols. 5945–6046 and 6053–91.

[47]*Ibid.*, July 14, 1885, pp. 3369–70.   [48]*Ibid.*, April 19, 1886, p. 789.

further, and after five days, by the consent of three-quarters of the House, no member should have more than fifteen minutes. But even this generous allowance was too little and the resolution was amended out of existence.[49] This same member persisted in his views in spite of his rebuff by the House. In 1899 he moved another resolution similar to his earlier one, and repeated it in the two succeeding years.[50] The whole House seems to have agreed that speeches were too long, and that a limit should be applied to save time, but while members agreed with the principle, they were unwilling to support any practical proposals to that effect, and the motions were withdrawn.

Over the next twenty-five years the problem remained unsolved. It survived two major revisions of the rules and several suggestions for reform from private members.[51] One member even went so far as to characterize the existing system of long and frequent speeches as a "public and private nuisance."[52] Finally, the revision committee of 1925 took the first effective step and recommended a forty-minute limit on most speeches in the House or in Committee of the Whole.[53] However, the House never considered the report of the 1925 committee and the adoption of the forty-minute rule was postponed for two years until the 1927 committee made an identical recommendation.[54]

Rule 37 adopted in 1927 read: "No Member, except the Prime Minister and the Leader of the Opposition or a Minister moving a Government Order or the member speaking in reply immediately after such Minister or a member making a motion of 'no confidence' in the Government and a Minister replying thereto shall speak for more than forty minutes at a time in any debate." The House did not accept the rule without a certain amount of bitterness. Most of one day was spent debating the merits of the suggestion. It was attacked because it gave special privileges to a small group of members—the Prime Minister, the Leader of the Opposition, and a few ministers and private members. The representatives of the minor opposition parties[55] resented the opportunities afforded the Leader of the Opposition and suggestions were made that equal rights be given to the leaders of other opposition groups. A member even suggested that the right of unlimited

[49]The resolution was amended so that only the principle (quoted above) was left. The clauses which would have imposed a limit on debate were rejected.

[50]*Debates*, May 8, 1899, cols. 2755–73; March 28, 1900, cols. 2763–83; Feb. 12, 1901, cols. 73–7.

[51]*Ibid.*, July 10, 1906, col. 7618; July 18, 1908, cols. 13537–40; Jan. 25, 1909, cols. 129–31; Sept. 29, 1919, pp. 646–54.

[52]*Ibid.*, Sept. 29, 1919, p. 646.

[53]*Journals*, May 29, 1925, p. 355.   [54]*Ibid.*, March 22, 1927, p. 329.

[55]At this time, chiefly the United Farmers of Alberta and the Progressives.

reply could be abused through collusion between the Government and a subservient member. A. W. Neill spoke for the opposition to the rule when he summed up his remarks with the statement: "This is a reactionary thing which I have never heard of before in Parliament. We are going back instead of forward. We are going to take away from the common people the right of expressing themselves in Parliament. In the past people have gone to great length and have shed blood to get the right of free speech."[56] The support for the motion was most succinctly expressed by Agnes Macphail when she said: "We suffer more in this House from long speeches than from any other cause."[57] Modifications were proposed to soften the blow—fifty minutes instead of forty and the inclusion of the other opposition leaders in the exempted class—but the House did not see fit to approve them, and the rule passed as proposed.

The forty-minute rule has never been the panacea which its inventors hoped. In particular, it has been ineffective in Committee of the Whole. With the Speaker in the Chair each member is limited to one forty-minute speech on each motion debated[58] but in Committee a member may speak as many times as he chooses, and should a member wish to obstruct, this exception, in practice, makes the forty-minute rule unworkable.

In 1944 a committee on revision of the rules recommended a fundamental change. It suggested in its report that no member in any Committee of the Whole should be allowed to speak more than once on any clause or for more than twenty minutes on that one occasion. The right of a member to ask questions, particularly in Committee of Supply, was not to be impaired. R. B. Hanson, the Leader of the Opposition, noted at the time that the committee was unanimous in its support of this suggestion[59] but the recommendation was shelved with the rest of the report. In 1947, Gordon Graydon suggested that speaking time be cut in half[60] and in the same year Mr. Speaker Fauteux made the same recommendation. He went further, however, and proposed that speeches in the House be limited to twenty minutes after the first two days of debate, and to only ten minutes should a member decide to read his speech.[61] Two later committees of revision recommended changes as well. The committee of 1948 agreed that no member should speak longer than twenty minutes in Committee of the Whole, but did not,

[56]*Debates*, March 18, 1927, p. 1355.   [57]*Ibid.*, p. 1356.
[58]S.O. 37. A reply is allowed under very limited conditions, but this does not affect the general principle.
[59]*Debates*, March 7, 1944, p. 1245.
[60]*Ibid.*, June 25, 1947, p. 4617.
[61]*Journals*, Dec. 5, 1947, p. 29.

like the 1944 committee, suggest limiting the number of speeches a member could make.[62] The 1951 committee proposed an experiment for one session: speeches in the House could be limited to thirty minutes, except the speeches of the same few persons mentioned in the standing order.[63] Mr. Fleming made it plain at the time that this portion of the report, while it had passed the committee, had done so only on division. Neither the 1948 nor the 1951 report was accepted. Since then a few individuals have suggested changes at various times. On at least three occasions Mr. Knowles made known his support of a reduction of all speeches to thirty minutes.[64] In 1955, Mr. Hodgson supported this view and Mr. Schneider advocated a reduction to twenty minutes.[65]

This support from private members may have encouraged the committee of revision of 1955 to suggest a change. At any rate it recommended that although speeches in the House should not be affected, speeches in Committee of the Whole should be restricted to thirty minutes. The House accepted this recommendation (S.O. 59(3)). It was, however, only a compromise. The Government had proposed to the committee a new rule, modelled on the recommendation made by Mr. Speaker Fauteux in 1947, that speeches in the House should be limited to thirty minutes for the first two days of debate and to twenty minutes thereafter. This was opposed on the grounds that there should not be a division of members into two distinct groups with differing rights in debate.[66] On this point the Conservative members of the committee seem to have been victorious and the suggested reduction was eliminated before the report reached the House.[67]

Allocation of Time in Standing Orders

The latest, and as yet relatively untried, method of limiting debate is by the simple expedient of allocating time in the standing orders for specific debates. The committee of revision of 1955 made this suggestion

[62]*Ibid.*, June 25, 1948, p. 680.   [63]*Debates*, Dec. 13, 1951, p. 1858.
[64]*Ibid.*, April 7, 1952, p. 1188; Jan. 11, 1955, p. 92; Jan. 14, 1955, p. 182.
[65]*Ibid.*, Jan. 28, p. 664, and Feb. 3, p. 829.   [66]*Ibid.*, July 1, 1955, p. 5562.
[67]Throughout the sittings of the committee and in the House during the debate on the report, the C.C.F. reiterated its support of a thirty-minute rule in the House, and Mr. Knowles stated that Mr. Fulton, the leading Conservative on the committee, had been unalterably opposed to this reduction. See statements of Mr. Knowles, *ibid.*, July 1, 1955, p. 5568, and Mr. Coldwell, *ibid.*, July 12, 1955, pp. 5986–7. The Social Credit party also seemed willing to have a further limit on the allowance of time. See statements of Mr. Quelch, *ibid.*, July 1, 1955, p. 5571, and Mr. Hansell, *ibid.*, July 12, 1955, pp. 5992–3.
In 1962 speeches were limited to thirty minutes on the Address and the budget, twenty on private members' business.

and the House adopted it and also further restrictions in 1962. Only three major debates were affected: the debate on the Address in Reply to the Speech from the Throne was limited to a maximum of ten (now eight) sitting days;[68] the first six motions for the House to resolve itself into Committee of Supply to a maximum of two days each; and the debate on the budget to a maximum of eight (now six) sitting days. For all of these, the standing orders also set the time of divisions on amendments and sub-amendments.

The origin of this type of regulation might logically be said to stem from the opinion of Joseph Howe, who in 1867 said of the debate on the Address in Reply: "As a public man of some experience [I think] discussion on this speech is a mere waste of time."[69] Had this feeling become general there is little doubt that part, at least, of the revision of 1955 could have been effected seventy-five years earlier. In some years, indeed, as few as four speakers made remarks on the Address,[70] but the private members began to recognize the possibilities of this debate. Occasionally the debate was prolonged, as in 1896 and 1897 when over twenty spoke, or as in 1899 when nearly eighty speeches were made. In 1910 the flood was let loose in earnest, and with minor exceptions the debate on the Address became a tedious chore to be endured each session. The debate became the great forum for back-bench members who regaled the House with stories of the tremendous importance of individual constituencies, as well as their problems. The situation continued to worsen and members and strangers alike began to talk of reform.

In 1943 Brooke Claxton mentioned the possibility of some form of limitation and in the same year the Clerk of the House wrote in the preface to his *Rules and Forms* that a committee of the House should examine the possibility of establishing a set number of days for the Address debate. A committee set up to revise the rules the next year also considered the problem. This committee, oddly enough, recognized the fact that certain debates were "protracted" but refused to recommend any remedial action. It suggested that consultation between parties should be used instead of rules. The Leader of the Opposition adopted a similar attitude in 1946 when he expressed his willingness to commit his party to a voluntary scheme to limit the debate on the Address. Two private members proposed another limit the next year and suggested

[68]On most of these days the sittings are lengthened by two hours by a special rule (S.O. 2(2)), under which the House meets at 11 A.M.
[69]*Debates*, Nov. 8, 1867, p. 3.
[70]1879, 1882, 1884, 1887, 1889, 1890, 1892, 1901.

that the debate on the Address should be restricted to the leaders of the various parties in the House or their substitutes. A former member writing in the press shortly after recommended a limit on both the number of days and the length of speeches.[71]

Throughout this period of discontent, various committees on procedure met and even occasionally reported to the House. No attempt was made to settle the problem. The first definite proposal was put forward in a private member's motion in 1952 when Mr. Cleaver moved that the standing orders be amended to provide (among other things) "for the fixation in standing orders of a time limit on debate on the Address in Reply to the Speech from the Throne and the debate on the Budget, after the expiration of which periods of time the motion and all underlying amendments would be put by Mr. Speaker. . . ."[72] The House debated the suggestion and referred it to a committee which never reported.

By this time, however, the Government had begun to show an interest in the proposal, and Mr. Walter E. Harris was willing to admit in the press that "most" members would like to see a time limit on debates.[73] Less than a year later, an outside expert on the rules, E. R. Hopkins, presented a definite scheme, outlining specific proposals for an allowance of eight days on the debate on the Throne Speech and on the budget at the end of which time all outstanding votes would take place. He also recommended that morning sittings be used to make the best use of the eight days available for these limited debates.[74]

Finally in 1962 the committee on procedure reported a new standing order (S.O. 38) to the House. The debate on the Address in Reply to the Speech from the Throne was shortened to eight days in addition to the day on which the Address is moved. The House meets at 11 A.M. on these days,[75] thus extending each day by two hours and, in effect, giving the House nearly three extra debating days. No further restriction is made on the number of amendments which may be moved. On the

[71]*Debates*, Feb. 9, 1943, p. 293. A. Beauchesne, *Rules and Forms of the House of Commons of Canada* (3rd ed., Toronto, 1943), p. vii. *Debates*, March 7, 1944, p. 1239; March 18, 1946, p. 35; Feb. 4, 1947, pp. 86, 102. R. J. Deachman in *Saturday Night*, April 19, 1947.

[72]*Debates*, April 7, 1952, p. 1178.

[73]*Saturday Night*, May 31, 1952.

[74]E. R. Hopkins, "Streamlining Parliament," *Canadian Banker*, Spring 1953, pp. 37–48. The similarity of the proposals suggested by Mr. Hopkins in this article to the suggestions of the Government laid before the revision committees of the next two years would indicate that this article reflected, to some extent, Government thinking on the subject at this time.

[75]Except Wednesdays. S.O. 2(2).

sixth allotted day, should a sub-amendment have been moved, the House must divide on it. This, of course, allows the fourth party (if any) an opportunity to move another sub-amendment, which may then be debated until the ninth day. On that day all outstanding amendments are voted on. The question is put on every other question relating to the main motion immediately before the adjournment on the tenth day.

The 1962 rule has not yet been tested at the time of writing, but the 1955 rule did prove efficient. The Address was moved on January 11. The next day, the first appointed for resuming the debate, the Conservative party moved an amendment and the C.C.F. a sub-amendment. The debate continued from day to day until January 19, the sixth day, when the House negatived the C.C.F. sub-amendment. Early the next day, the Social Credit party moved a new sub-amendment, and the debate carried on for three more days. On the ninth day the House disposed of both the Social Credit and Conservative amendment, and on the tenth day adopted the Address without a division, ordered it to be engrossed, and be presented to the Governor General "by such members of the House as are of the honourable the Privy Council." Few members suffered under the new procedure: over one hundred spoke on the motion or on the amendments. This number is smaller than in several sessions previously, but was sufficient to satisfy most members. Nearly two-thirds of the opposition members spoke and one-third of the Government members.

The 1962 rule which limits the budget debate (S.O. 58) is very similar to that which limits the Address. Six days only are allowed on the order for resuming the adjourned debate. On the second of these days the House votes on any sub-amendment, and on the fourth, divides on the main amendment.[76] On the sixth the House passes the main motion and resolves itself immediately into Committee of Ways and Means. This rule in its 1955 form worked with success in the 1956 session. The House debated a C.C.F. sub-amendment until the fifth day and a Conservative amendment until the seventh. Only about one-quarter of the members of the House spoke, but the budget debate has never been as popular as the Address or supply as a vehicle for the expression of constituency problems. Once again, following the normal custom, the opposition parties occupied a disproportionate amount of time.

The new standing order which relates to supply motions (S.O. 56) is

[76]Under S.O. 45 only one amendment and one sub-amendment may be moved to a motion for the Speaker to leave the Chair. Thus no further amendment of the motion is possible between the second and fourth days.

much more complicated in both form and application than either of the other orders that allocate time. The first six motions in a session for the Speaker to leave the Chair so that the House can resolve itself into Committee of Supply are declared debatable.[77] These motions must stand as the first order of the day on Monday. If the debate on the motion is not completed on Monday, the debate becomes the first order of the day on Tuesday. Except when there is an allowance for unexpired time, no supply debate may take more than two sitting days.

Should the House pass the motion for the Speaker to leave the Chair before the expiry of two sitting days, the unused time may be added to the debate on any subsequent supply motion. The concluding portions of such an extended debate may be called on any Government day. Amendments to these motions are voted on at fixed times, normally at 8:15 P.M. on the second day of the debate. However, if any unused time is carried forward, the amendments are voted on at the beginning of the two-hour period before the expiry of the time carried forward from the previous debates. At 10 P.M. on the second day, or at the end of the unexpired time carried forward, the Speaker puts the question on the main motion. The standing order also provides that should the main motion be superseded by the adoption of an amendment, another motion for the Speaker to leave the Chair may be made at once and the debate will proceed as an extension of the debate concluded by the adoption of the amendment.[78]

To understand the operation of this standing order, it is really necessary to study an example. In the session of 1956 the House used the rule for the first time. The first supply debate covered two full days. On Monday the Government moved for the Speaker to leave the Chair and the Opposition moved an amendment. On Tuesday at 8:15 P.M. the House negatived the amendment and at 10 P.M. passed the main motion without a division.[79]

Two weeks later the Government moved the second supply motion, and it was followed by an amendment and a sub-amendment. The House negatived both of these on division at 8:15 P.M. on Tuesday and passed the main motion by consent at 9:50 P.M.[80]

[77]These motions must be distinguished from those made on Wednesday, Thursday, and Friday for the same purpose. Under section 1 of S.O. 56, on these days the Speaker leaves the Chair without question put. For the difference between these two apparently similar motions see chap. 12, p. 215.

[78]Thus, if this motion is made before 8:15 P.M. on Tuesday it may be amended. Should it be made as the result of a vote on an amendment at the time specified in the standing order, it would not be subject to amendment.

[79]Journals, Feb. 6–7, 1956, pp. 129–33.

[80]Ibid., Feb. 20–1, 1956, pp. 181–6.

The House felt the effect of this early entry into supply when the third motion was made. Again the opposition moved an amendment and a sub-amendment. For the first time, however, the House voted on them according to the alternative method as there was a ten-minute surplus carried over from the previous debate. Thus the House defeated these two amendments at 8:10 P.M. rather than 8:15 P.M.[81] on Tuesday and the debate continued to 10 P.M. on the main motion.[82]

The fourth supply motion was allotted two days and ten minutes as the third one had been, since the unexpired ten minutes had not yet been used. Again the House voted on the amendments at 8:10 P.M. on Tuesday, and at 8:45 P.M. the House went into supply.[83]

The Government moved for the fifth time to go into supply, with a possible debating time of two days, one hour, and twenty-five minutes.[84] The House voted on the amendments at 9:25 P.M.[85] The debate adjourned for royal assent[86] and was continued on Wednesday. The motion passed on Wednesday afternoon leaving a surplus of six minutes.[87]

On the sixth and final motion the House defeated the single amendment at 8:06 P.M. on Tuesday and the debate was adjourned at the customary 10 P.M. On the Wednesday the House solemnly debated for six minutes and then divided on the main motion.[88]

The consensus in the House at the end of the session seems to have been that the new rule worked with commendable success. The Government scattered the supply motions well, and ample opportunity was offered to the opposition to move amendments. In addition to formal amendments the rule provides for nearly two hours on each motion for a discussion of grievances. This, of course, may be abused when the time for such grievances is limited. A transparent attempt to prevent a member from raising a grievance was made on July 10, 1956, when

[81]The computation of this time is mathematically simple. The unexpired time from the previous debates (ten minutes) is added to the regular 10 P.M. adjournment. Subtracting from this the two-hour period specified in the standing order, the House voted on the amendments at 8:10 P.M.

[82]*Journals*, March 12–13, 1956, pp. 276–82.

[83]*Ibid.*, April 30–May 1, 1956, pp. 456–62.

[84]Ten minutes of unexpired time from the second motion plus one hour and fifteen minutes from the fourth.

[85]Computed from the ten o'clock adjournment plus one hour and twenty-five minutes unexpired time (11:25) less two hours.

[86]This precedent by which extra time is allowed should the debate be interrupted in any way might easily become a problem. Should the question period or any item of routine proceedings take an unusual length of time, the opposition might easily claim compensation of the same sort.

[87]*Journals*, June 25–7, 1956, pp. 778–825.

[88]*Ibid.*, July 9–11, 1956, pp. 858–85.

several members debated an innocuous question for no other reason than to block a discussion on the action of the Speaker: by tradition a new grievance cannot be raised while members still wish to debate an earlier one, and Mr. Knowles found himself forced to wait for the end of a discussion of free air transportation for members of Parliament before he could raise a new issue.

Similarly there will undoubtedly be a tendency to arrange the time of speeches so as to leave one side of the House or the other in an unfavourable position. Again in the 1956 session a member made a strong attack on the Government to which the Prime Minister replied. His reply left only six minutes for the Conservatives, and the party used it to deliver a similar attack. The Conservative member who spoke concluded at the end of what he estimated was six minutes in the hope that the Government would be unable to reply. In fact, on this occasion, the Leader of the House managed to make a two-sentence speech in reply to the attack, to the annoyance of the Opposition.[89]

The only surprising development from the session was that the unexpired time of the House was generally measured in minutes rather than hours. The alternative method of voting on amendments was designed to take care of a considerable allowance of extra time and not to force the House to divide before the normal 8:15 P.M. set in the standing orders.[90] Some of the minor problems raised may be attributed to a desire on the part of members to experiment with a new rule. It is difficult to believe that a ten-minute surplus in a two-day debate on one occasion and a six-minute surplus on another can be pure chance.

Effect of Limits on Debate

The result of these four limits on unrestrained free speech in the House has been negligible. No one of them has achieved any significant shortening of the session, and it seems unlikely that such a result can be achieved under present conditions. It has often been said that no attempt should be made to limit members merely for the object of

[89]One point which was settled in the 1956 session is that in debates of limited time the clerks at the Table act as official time-keepers for the Speaker. No other accounting will be recognized. On this occasion Mr. Fleming's desk-mate was keeping time with a stop-watch to ensure that there would be no time left. His accounting, however, did not agree with that of the Clerk, and was not accepted. *Debates*, July 11, 1956, p. 5864.

[90]On three occasions out of six in the 1956 session, the House voted on amendments before 8:15 P.M. Only once did the rule retard the time of the division.

sitting for a shorter time each year. But there is no reason why the same length of time should not produce more fruitful results. For this end, an attempt must be made to direct the energies of the House into more productive channels, and to ensure some balance between those items of business which arise early in the session and those which are introduced near the end. Too often today a few bills are debated at great length in the first months of the session whereas vastly more important measures slip through in the last few days without proper scrutiny. The blame may be apportioned to both sides of the House. The Government is always willing to leave unpopular bills to the end of the session in the hope that the opposition will not look too closely at them or, at least, will not debate them for any prolonged time. The opposition, on the other hand, is willing to dissipate its energies on matters of little interest through much of the session until the hot weather of summer makes its back-benchers restive and extensive debate unpopular, if not impossible.

The efforts to restrict debate outlined in this chapter will doubtless be extended. It is unlikely that the previous question will ever be used in an effective way, but further limits on the length of speeches is certain. The forty minutes now allowed might easily be cut to thirty without the loss of anything but mere verbiage, and a further reduction could be made in Committee of the Whole. It would also be desirable to accompany the latter reduction by the improvement recommended in 1944— that a member could speak only once on any clause in committee.

Committee of Supply is also a fruitful area for reform. Sooner or later constituency interests should give way to efficiency and the House should set an over-all time limit for supply. The Opposition must then be given the opportunity to indicate which departments will be called first, and some agreement must be reached to ensure that consideration will be given to the smaller parties in the House with regional and specialized interests. The gradual development of the Committee on Estimates may make progress along these lines easier. Several departments are now sent to this committee each year and other departments have been considered by other standing committees. These can be studied thoroughly in committee and need not be discussed further in the House. The opposition must show restraint in the House if this system is to work at all, but with a set number of days allotted for Committee of Supply, experience will soon provide the background for effective, if shorter, examination of Government spending.

Procedure in the Canadian House of Commons is just emerging from what Lord Campion has termed the "slimming" stage at which time the number of opportunities for debate is severely limited, and is now progressing to the next, or "squeezing" stage.[91] This portion of development is characterized by orders for allocating time under which important controversial bills are subjected to a planned and clearly established series of closures. The Canadian House has made a small start in this direction by limiting the sessional debates under standing orders. This might well be developed to cover the debates on major bills during the session. No amendment to the standing orders would be needed, although an arrangement similar to that in Britain would be an advantage, and would probably make the process easier. Even today if the Government, before embarking on a bill involving a major item of policy, would, in agreement with the other parties in the House, draw up a schedule of time for debate, much time could be saved and much confusion eliminated. Even on controversial bills where agreement is not possible, and closure becomes a necessity, a prior announcement of the time available for each stage would minimize Opposition charges of dictatorship.

No matter what changes were made and what protection given the Opposition in the rules, no appreciable improvement would be possible until a measure of confidence in the new system had been built up on both sides of the House. The House could not put virtually unlimited power in the hands of the Government until the Opposition was certain that it would be allowed a reasonable length of time for debate no matter what deadlines the Government wished to set for any bill. The Government would be willing to restrict its powers under a new set of rules only if it could be sure that the Opposition would not abuse its position and attempt to block the business of the House by the use of technicalities. The trial period would be difficult and would be a challenge to both sides of the House, but an experiment of this sort must be attempted if the House is to avoid an even more stringent set of rules controlled by the Government alone.

[91]Lord Campion, "Parliamentary Procedure, Old and New" in Lord Campion, ed., *Parliament: A Survey* (London, 1952), p. 156.

INFORMATION FOR THE HOUSE

8

PRIVATE MEMBERS OF THE HOUSE, and particularly Opposition members, are constantly searching for information. Statistics may not be available in a usable form and other facts may be hidden in Government files. The attitude of the Government to a proposal put forward by a province or municipality may seem unsatisfactory to the local member who may, as a result, want to get the full story of the negotiations involved. On other occasions he may merely want to show up the inadequacy of Government action in a particular field. Whatever his motive a member of Parliament is forever on the hunt for facts. He obtains some in debate in the House. More specific information relating to Government expenditures is available in Committee of Supply. But neither of these sources is adequate to provide a member with the information he wants at the time he wants it. He cannot wait for the House to go into committee to get information on which to base further questions in Committee of Supply or other Committee of the Whole. The House has, therefore, over the years, developed procedures by which members of all parties may receive answers to questions and copies of documents. Requests for specific information are made by questions asked orally in the House or printed in the Order Paper. Papers are tabled in the House as returns. The Government, either in response to a request from a member or on its own initiative, also periodically makes statements of policy in the House before the business of the day is begun.

Questions

Questions in the House are, of course, the most interesting method of obtaining information. Sir Ivor Jennings has referred to questions in the British House as being the "cocktails before the oratorical feast."[1] The question period has certainly been so regarded in Canada for many years. At no other time in the parliamentary day is the House so full: committees do not meet until after the question period, and the galleries are always occupied. It is predominantly private members' time and even more predominantly Opposition time. Questions of all sorts are asked and are followed by supplementary questions. There is no limit on the length of this question period and it comes to an end only when the Opposition has exhausted its imagination and can, for the moment, think of no more questions to ask. These questions, which make up the major portion of the Canadian question period, are oral questions "asked on the orders of the day." The system used is simple. After the daily routine of the House is completed, the Speaker calls for the "orders of the day." At this point, any member may rise and ask an oral question. The conventions and restrictions which surround this custom will be examined later.

In addition to these oral questions asked almost every day, the Canadian House also recognizes the written question for written answer and the written question for oral answer (the "starred question" so called because of the asterisk marking it on the Order Paper). In fact, in 1867 only the written question was officially recognized by the rules of the House of Commons, which copied an old rule from the Province of Canada and allowed members to present written questions to ministers about public affairs, and to other members about matters which related to the business of the House.[2] A few minor limitations were imposed which followed the British practice of the day.[3] One rule required two days' notice for any question and another provided space on the Order Paper for "questions put by members." When the required notice had been given, therefore, a member's question was printed on the Order Paper,[4] and when questions were called from the Chair the member

[1]In his *Parliament* (Cambridge, 1939), p. 109.
[2]1867 Rule 29.
[3]Sir T. Erskine May, *Treatise on the Law, Privileges, Proceedings and Usage of Parliament* (6th ed., London, 1864), p. 302.
[4]1867 Rules 31, 19. On three days a week questions were likely to be asked. On the other two, questions were placed after Government business and so would not be reached.

rose and read his question, the Minister responsible answered the question orally, and the matter dropped.

The distinctive Canadian practice of asking oral questions "on orders of the day" grew at the same time, but it was not founded on the written rules. Three weeks after the new House of Commons met in 1867, a member asked the chairman of a committee whether it was proposed to establish a Hansard report of proceedings in the House.[5] The habit of oral questioning, thus started, continued until in 1878 a Speaker could say that it was "customary for honourable members to ask the Government for any special information between the various calls from the Chair for the day. . . ." He questioned the right of any member to do this and attempted to limit the content of the questions.[6]

The practice of asking questions in both forms—written and oral—proved to be popular and abuses soon grew. Speakers faced the usual problems regarding the form and content of questions. In addition, friction arose over which questions were to be asked on the orders of the day. No firm decisions seem to have been made. Speakers attempted to control the members, but the rules were so loosely drawn that little could be accomplished. In 1896, however, the House began to number the questions on the Order Paper.[7] It then became possible to ask a question without reading it, and inordinately long questions became more popular. The solution to this particular problem was in the hands of the House, and occasionally it took action to protect itself. In 1900, for instance, one member gave notice of a question nine pages long which related to the expense account of a Government employee, and to his chagrin several members asked him to read his question when it was called from the Chair. He objected to this procedure, but on the insistence of the Prime Minister the Speaker ruled that the proper method of putting a question was to read it in full. The member gamely began to read. After four sections, when the principle had been firmly established, the question was put in the customary manner. The statement of the Prime Minister on this occasion that "the system of spreading on the paper matters that can be found in the blue books has grown to an abuse" was indicative of changes to come.[8]

The revision of 1906 radically altered the rule which related to

[5]*Debates*, Nov. 29, 1867, p. 50.
[6]*Ibid.*, March 20, 1878, pp. 1269–70.
[7]*Ibid.*, Sept. 16, 1896, cols. 1303–4.
[8]*Ibid.*, March 21, 1900, col. 2372. The question began, "Is the following a correct statement of the expenses of J. Perrault when Chief Commissioner of the Philadelphia Exhibition?" and nine pages of itemized expenses followed. *Ibid.*, March 21, 1900, cols. 2378–96.

written questions. A small change was made in the old rule and hence-forth the answers as well as the questions were to be matters on which "no argument or opinion is to be offered, nor any facts stated, except so far as may be necessary to explain the same."[9] The comment of a member that ministers had used the answers to questions as vehicles of propaganda and argument would indicate that abuse of the question period had not been entirely one-sided.[10] More important, a new section was added to the rule. At the request of the Government, any question which, in the opinion of the Speaker, required a lengthy reply, could be transferred to the heading "notices of motions" on the Order Paper.[11] It would then become a debatable motion. Since few of these could, in fact, ever be debated by the House the members soon abandoned the long and involved questions which had become popular in the preceding years, and this provision which still appears in the rules (S.O. 39 (4)) has been used only rarely.[12]

By 1910 the question period needed reform again, and two sections were added to the rule on written questions. There were now four ways of dealing with a question. The little-used provision mentioned above by which the Speaker could transform a question into a notice of motion was preserved. The second, merely an elaboration of the rule, allowed a Minister to decide if any question would best be answered in the form of a return. Should he so decide, and have no objection to tabling such a return, his statement to that effect would be accepted as an order of the House for the production of the required papers at an indefinite time in the future. The third and fourth methods of dealing with questions were created by dividing written questions into two types according to the kind of answer that was wanted. When a member wished an oral answer he could mark his question with an asterisk and the Minister was to answer it orally in the House. Should the member not mark his question, the Minister was merely to hand in (at once) a written answer to the Clerk to be printed in Hansard. There is no doubt that the addition of an asterisk was intended to make an oral answer obligatory on a Minister. When the change was being discussed in 1910 the Leader of the Opposition defended this particular rule with the assurance that "any member of this House who desires to have a question answered orally may retain that right by simply making a mark on it."[13] There was some uneasiness at the time over the new rules. One member claimed that they would limit the use of the oral

9 1906 Rule 36 (1).
10 *Debates*, July 10, 1906, col. 7602.
11 1906 Rule 36 (2).
12 *Debates*, Feb. 16, 1923, pp. 343–4.
13 *Ibid.*, April 29, 1910, col. 8369.

question and answer and that most members listened "with a good deal of interest" to the oral answers which were given in the House. "It is one of the educative ways by which members keep themselves familiar with the work of the House going on from day to day. . . . I know for my own part I have often listened eagerly to the answers that are given to questions in the House." However, the Leader of the Opposition stated what was probably the opinion of many in the House when he remarked that "so far as answers to questions in this House are concerned, I am bound to say that I have never been able to understand the answers to ten per cent of them."[14] The amendment carried on a division.

From 1910 to 1955 most of the attention was focused on a different problem. Oral questions asked on the orders of the day gradually assumed a greater importance in the work of the House than was originally contemplated, and in those forty-five years much discussion and several suggested amendments to the rules were directed toward curbing the more obvious excesses of this procedure and toward bringing oral questions within the rules of the House. The time available for such questions, their content, and how much prior notice was to be given were all considered.

In 1944 a committee made the first definite suggestion which was intended to bring more certainty into the oral question period. It drafted a new rule which would recognize officially the existence of oral questions on the orders of the day. Questions of an "urgent character" could be asked provided copies were sent to the Minister and the Clerk at least one hour before the meeting of the House. The answer to the question was to be oral and no more than three supplementaries were to be allowed.[15] The suggestion seemed to command general support but died with the rest of the committee's report.

In 1947 Mr. Speaker Fauteux also dealt with questions in his report. His suggestion was more simple than that of 1944. Oral questions were to be given a place on the Order Paper on four days each week immediately after routine proceedings. A period of one hour was allowed for routine and questions combined. He also recommended restrictions on the content of oral questions and a limit of three supplementaries. In a memorandum to the committee which studied the Speaker's report, the Clerk of the House recommended the recognition of oral questions, but suggested that one day's notice should be given.[16] In its report, the committee did not accept the Clerk's idea in its entirety, but rather

[14]*Ibid.*, April 29, 1910, col. 8369.
[15]*Journals*, March 3, 1944, p. 151.
[16]*The Table*, XVII, 1948, p. 239.

recommended a rule in the same terms as that of the committee of 1944 with the significant exception of the provision requiring notice. This was omitted entirely.[17]

The interest of the House in oral questions asked on the orders of the day did not entail a lack of interest in the other types of questions. The regular question period also came under observation and complaints were made by members who believed that the Government was using its right to answer a question by tabling a return as a device for burying information. The returns when brought down were merely listed as presented in the *Votes and Proceedings* and only one copy was available in the sessional papers office.[18] Even if the Minister answered the question when called, all he need do was deposit the answer with the Clerk, for printing. The member who asked the question was given a copy, but had no opportunity to pursue the answer with supplementaries. Members were also known to complain that even when oral answers were given the Chair discouraged supplementary questions.[19]

The starred question first introduced in 1910 fared even worse. The "right" to an oral answer which seemed so certain to the Leader of the Opposition in 1910 proved illusory. In fact the private member was never able to enforce this right and ministers answered these questions orally or in writing at their own discretion. In the sessions immediately preceding the 1955 change in the rules this right seems to have been briefly regained. On one occasion at least, the Speaker ruled that a starred question had to be answered orally and in 1955 five different ministers drew attention to the fact that questions were starred when they gave oral answers.[20]

The committee of 1955 attempted to provide a new approach to the question period. It left unchanged the general regulations which related to the content of written questions but removed them from the Order Paper as part of the daily business of the House. They were still printed on the Order Paper and when the minister was prepared to answer he handed in a written answer to Hansard to be printed. At the same time the committee made an attempt to limit the use of questions on the orders of the day, not by formal rule, but by providing an alternative— the starred question, whose unsatisfactory history has already been described. Starred questions were given a special place on the Order Paper on one day of the week. No member was allowed more than

[17]*Journals*, June 25, 1948, p. 680.
[18]*Debates*, March 8, 1923, pp. 938–40; April 13, 1939, pp. 2730–1; Feb. 26, 1943, pp. 734–5; March 1, 1943, pp. 774–5.
[19]*Ibid.*, May 28, 1943, p. 3126.
[20]*Ibid.*, Feb. 22, 1954, p. 2298; March 2, 1955, pp. 1643–4, 1645; March 16, 1955, p. 2071; July 14, 1955, p. 6107; July 16, 1955, p. 6247.

three on the Order Paper at one time, and routine proceedings plus starred questions were limited in length to one hour. Supplementary questions were not asked immediately but were postponed until the orders of the day were called.

The House in 1962 reverted to the pre-1955 question period. Questions again appear on the Order Paper as part of the business of the House and they may again be marked with an asterisk for oral answer. Questions on the orders of the day were not touched.

It is hard to understand why the House decided to reverse the process of reform in this way. The old question period for written questions was time-consuming and unprofitable. We have seen how unsatisfactory the starred question was up to 1955. The question period was not perfected in 1955, but the answer should have been further change and not reversion to old rules.

Limitations on Questions

Questions in the House are subject to many limitations. These are, generally speaking, not contained in the written rule which governs questions, but are part of the vast unwritten law of Parliament. There are conditions under which oral questions may not be asked at all. On three occasions in each session when "Notices of Motions" stand first on the day's business, the Speaker does not call for the "orders of the day" and questions are, therefore, not reached. Even more rarely, the House may pass a motion to proceed to the orders of the day. Here the House is deemed to be embarked on its daily business without the usual call from the Chair, and again questions may not be asked. At other times the Speaker may prevent an occasional question from being asked. The most obvious, and the most common reason for ruling a question out of order is that it contains an assertion of fact which cannot be proved and is liable to lead to debate. In early days the Speaker was quick to reject any portion of a question which appeared to transgress this rule. In some cases the facts alleged seem to be relatively innocuous. A member who inquired into the disposition of old iron rails to an obscure railway in New Brunswick was ruled out of order because he added the assertion that the railway would become "one of the most important feeders which the Intercolonial can possibly have."[21] Another question containing the more serious accusation that a member of the House was an annexationist was likewise ruled out.[22] On some occasions only the form of the question has been at fault. In 1897 a question was

[21]*Ibid.*, Feb. 27, 1878, p. 569.   [22]*Ibid.*, March 1, 1888, p. 44.

asked whether a certain promise made by the Prime Minister to an individual was to be fulfilled. The Speaker ruled it out of order, but obligingly explained that if the question were rephrased to ask whether the stated promise had been made it would be in order.[23] One form of question has been regularly forbidden: it is put as the second part of a question which asks whether the Government has any intention of taking certain action, and merely adds "if not, why not?" Such questions are obviously designed to provoke debate and not to elicit information and have been ruled out of order consistently.[24]

Speakers have developed from this a general regulation that a question must not be based on a newspaper article. Such a question usually proceeds along these lines: an editorial or news report is provided and the general question is posed: "What comment does the Government have on this?" or "What action does the Government propose to take?" The Speaker in 1897 made a salutary ruling that such questions should not be asked unless the member involved had made an attempt at least to check their accuracy personally.[25] More recently such questions have been banned by the Speaker.

Limits have also been placed on questions on the general grounds of propriety. Beauchesne lists forty specific restrictions which he gathered from many authorities.[26] Among these he cites discourteous references to a friendly foreign country, the internal affairs of foreign countries, and the royal family as being beyond the bound of proper questions. References to legal proceedings are certainly prohibited.[27] Similarly, questions may not be based on extracts from the debates of the Senate.[28] Most important, a question may not reflect on the character of a member or of a previous Government.[29]

The Speaker is, of course, the arbiter on all points of order relating to questions. He has the unquestioned right to amend or reject any question either before it is printed on the Order Paper or as it is asked. Sometimes only a few words are removed as in 1900 when certain words implying judgment and casting aspersions were ruled to be improper.[30]

[23]*Ibid.*, June 7, 1897, col. 3506.
[24]*Ibid.*, March 5, 1930, p. 293; Jan. 25, 1935, p. 189.
[25]*Ibid.*, June 14, 1897, cols. 3974–6. Also March 15, 1943, pp. 1233–4; May 7, 1956, pp. 3619–20.
[26]In his *Rules and Forms of the House of Commons of Canada* (4th ed., Toronto, 1958), pp. 147–9.
[27]*Debates*, June 14, 1897, cols. 3971–2; June 29, 1942, p. 3745.
[28]*Ibid.*, April 2, 1900, col. 3048.
[29]*Ibid.*, July 4, 1892, col. 4499; Feb. 7, 1912, col. 2580; May 3, 1899, col. 2484.
[30]The question contained references to the "wrongful retention of a cheque" and "illegally retaining money." *Ibid.*, March 29, 1900, cols. 2833–4.

A whole question has also been removed from the "Notices of Motions and Questions" on the grounds that it was offensive.[31] Several times the second part of a question has been removed as being likely to precipitate debate, although members complained bitterly about the "amputated and mutilated" questions which finally appeared on the Order Paper.[32]

Should a member himself wish to have his question dropped, he may do so in one of two ways. He may withdraw his question by writing a note to the Clerk of the House or he may state his wish to do so from his place in the House.[33] Leave is granted automatically in either case. The Government does, however, have the right to answer the question even if the member withdraws it.[34]

Supplementary Questions

Supplementary questions are not mentioned in any rule, although they are now an accepted part of the question period. Until recently they were strictly limited. As early as 1895 the Speaker ruled that supplementary questions should not be allowed in Canada; he admitted the British practice, but denied that it had ever been followed in this country. Another Speaker ruled that supplementaries could be put only by consent. Nearly twenty years later Mr. Speaker Glen remarked in passing that supplementaries "should be prohibited" and in 1943 he ruled that such extra questions were out of order. Since then supplementaries have been asked in great profusion without comment. They are, however, still under the direct control of the Speaker and he will, on occasion, limit them to a reasonable number.[35]

Protection from Questions

A few general regulations have been developed to protect the House against an unreasonable abuse of the question period. The Government is given only a minimum of protection, but ministers may be questioned only on such public matters as they have under their control; a question which relates to a Minister's relations with his constituency, for instance,

31*Ibid.*, May 20, 1931, pp. 1789–91.
32*Ibid.*, March 5, 1930, p. 293; Jan. 25, 1935, p. 189; Jan. 23, 1935, p. 119.
33*Ibid.*, Jan. 13, 1910, col. 1799; March 26, 1942, pp. 1644–5.
34*Ibid.*, Jan. 13, 1910, cols. 1800–1.
35*Ibid.*, May 31, 1895, col. 1882; June 26, 1924, p. 3707; Feb. 25, 1942, p. 821; May 28, 1943, p. 3126; May 7, 1956, p. 3619.

cannot be asked.[36] More important, a Minister may refuse to answer any question without advancing a reason; there is no limit to this privilege except the political necessity of appearing to be free and open with the House.[37] In particular, a Minister may not be asked for his opinion on a point of law, or on a question of Government policy, and he may refuse to answer any question for reasons of security or on grounds of public policy.[38] The Speaker will enforce the claim of a Minister that he has answered a question in spite of the protestations of a member that an adequate answer has not been given.[39] The refusal of a Minister to answer a question may not be made the subject of another question or be raised as a matter of privilege.

The same general rules apply also to questions to private members, but in their case the rules eliminate virtually all questions. The most common, and, indeed, almost the only proper question to put to a private member refers to a committee of the House of which he is the chairman.[40] A question which relates to a member's intention to introduce legislation has been ruled out.[41]

The Speaker is more strictly protected than any other member. No questions may be addressed to the Chair in any manner, though at his own discretion the Speaker may make a statement relating to a matter raised in the House.[42] On most occasions, however, he merely rules the question out of order and informs the member involved that the information is available privately.[43]

The growth of public corporations in Canada has produced a few of the problems in question period which have become so important in the United Kingdom. There is still no clear practice surrounding questions addressed to public corporations. In spite of the growth of Crown companies which have now entered into many branches of industry, members of Parliament have showed remarkable restraint in their quest for information. Any attempt to obtain detailed information relating to

[36]*Ibid.*, March 6, 1957, p. 1924; Feb. 20, 1957, p. 1464.

[37]*Ibid.*, April 4, 1935, p. 2400. On one occasion the Speaker ordered an answer to be expunged from Hansard as irrelevant to the question and ordered that an answer be given should the question be asked again. Presumably, however, the Government could still refuse to answer for reasons of public policy. *Ibid.*, April 6, 1925, pp. 1916–17.

[38]*Ibid.*, March 30, 1928, p. 1849.

[39]*Ibid.*, April 12, 1897, cols. 788–9; April 29, 1942, p. 1974; July 13, 1955, p. 6039.

[40]*Ibid.*, Nov. 29, 1867, p. 50; May 28, 1920, p. 2843; April 11, 1956, p. 2822; Jan. 7, 1958, pp. 2937–8, etc.

[41]*Ibid.*, May 16, 1955, p. 3787.

[42]*Ibid.*, Jan. 19, 1956, p. 303; Oct. 18, 1957, pp. 131–2.

[43]*Ibid.*, Feb. 15, 1932, p. 182; May 21, 1951, p. 3218; April 30, 1954, p. 4276; Aug. 3, 1956, pp. 6921–2; Dec. 12, 1960, p. 703.

the operation of these companies has been met with a blank refusal on the part of the Government. Questions which deal with the "internal business" of the corporations have often been held to be outside the scope of the Government's knowledge and not answerable. In addition, ministers to whom questions are addressed on the subject of public corporations take no responsibility for the answers presented. They are merely the agents through whom messages pass between the corporation and the House. When the Prime Minister refused to accept a question in 1932 he noted that in order to answer the question he would write to the Canadian National Railways and they would merely reply that it was not in the public interest to give the information requested. Three years later another Minister refused a similar question to the Canadian National Railways on the grounds that he had no information on the matter.[44] To emphasize this position of the Minister, answers are often prefaced with the remark that "the corporation advises."

The most general objection made by corporations to answering questions in the House is that their competitive position may be influenced by making such information public. This is particularly true of the Canadian Broadcasting Corporation and the Canadian National Railways, both of which are in direct competition with private industry. Thus questions which ask for the price of railway stock or performers' salaries have been refused.[45] A corporation may also give an evasive answer or claim that the excessive clerical costs of preparing an answer make it unwilling to do so.[46] There have even been refusals on the part of the Government to pass on questions to the corporations. In 1935 the Government refused to give information on the administration of the Bank of Canada; the Minister announced that he would give such information as was in the Government's possession, but no more.[47] The Minister of Finance made a similar answer in 1956 when questioned on the size of directors' fees for the bank; his answer began with the statement "not of Government record," and continued with an extract from the by-laws of the bank and a statement by the Governor before a House committee two years previously.[48] The question remained largely unanswered.

In spite of the limits imposed by the question period, it is not impossible for a member to get information about the public corporations.

[44]*Ibid.*, Feb. 15, 1932, p. 181; April 8, 1935, p. 2500.
[45]*Ibid.*, March 21, 1956, p. 2482; Feb. 15, 1957, p. 1363; Feb. 2, 1959, p. 615; Feb. 6, 1961, p. 1793.
[46]*Ibid.*, Feb. 16, 1939, p. 995; May 2, 1956, p. 3513; Jan. 13, 1954, pp. 1065–7; March 3, 1959, p. 1581; March 11, 1959, p. 1855.
[47]*Ibid.*, March 25, 1935, p. 2041.
[48]*Ibid.*, May 4, 1956, p. 3609.

Although the Government has been unwilling to answer detailed questions in the House, it has been quite willing to allow the same questions to be asked directly of the officers of the corporations in committee. The House has had a sessional committee on railways nearly every session for over thirty-five years, and has had also a number of special committees on broadcasting. These committees are free to question the responsible officials themselves, and although the corporations maintain a reticence on some matters, many detailed questions are answered here which would undoubtedly be refused in the House. A Minister, while refusing to answer a question in the House, may even offer to establish a committee with the power to demand from the corporation itself the information requested. This was suggested in the case of the Canadian Broadcasting Corporation and Polymer Corporation. Answers have also been refused in the House when such a committee was sitting on the grounds that the committee was the proper place to obtain the information.[49]

The Need for Reform

There is little doubt that the question period of the Canadian House will have to be studied carefully in the near future with a view to its early reform. The amendments of 1955 laid the groundwork for future changes, but the sessions since 1957 have demonstrated the necessity of another revision of the rules.[50] In these sessions the Opposition took full advantage of the laxity of the question procedure and extended the question period to absurd lengths. On many days oral questions, which normally occupy fifteen or twenty minutes, were extended over an hour. No subject was too large or small to be touched. Egg prices and prison paroles, Indians and hotels, box car allocations and water diversions were all mentioned. The comment of one newspaper that "if the Opposition back-benchers have not been able to come up with any $64 question they have apparently decided that 64 different $1 questions will do the trick just as well" was an accurate reflection of the situation.[51]

[49]Ibid., Feb. 16, 1938, p. 507; March 9, 1949, p. 1300; Oct. 1, 1945, pp. 600–1; July 18, 1946, pp. 3554–7.

[50]The revision committee of 1961 for unexplained reasons recommended for one session trial complete reversion to the pre-1955 question period. The new starred question disappeared and the old practice of answering all written questions in the House was revived. Journals, Sept. 26, 1961, pp. 949–50. This change has now become permanent.

[51]Montreal Gazette, Feb. 8, 1957.

The result of this practice was not happy. Ministers tended more and more to become annoyed with the opposition, and generally to give less and less information. Occasionally this ministerial attitude even gave rise to little lectures by Opposition spokesmen on courtesy in answering questions.[52] Such a conclusion is not satisfactory. There is little to be said for a question period which on one side is noteworthy for a virtual absence of rules except the patience of the Speaker and on the other by a growing disinclination on the part of the ministers to disclose any information no matter how trivial.[53]

Part of the difficulty lies in the attitude to questions which is revealed in the rules. Questions are recognized by the rules of the House, and by the authorities on procedure, for one purpose only—that of eliciting information. Many of the questions on the Order Paper undoubtedly have this object in view. This is, however, the most limited and least valuable use of the parliamentary question. There is little doubt that a letter or telephone call to a Minister would produce factual information more quickly than would a question in the House. The rules, of course, ignore the real purpose of most questions. Over the years they have become the principal weapon in the hands of the opposition parties. There is little hope in their minds that they will get a major amendment accepted in the House or otherwise alter Government policy significantly. They may, however, harass the Government and demonstrate its deficiencies to the electorate. For this the oral parliamentary question is unequalled. The question itself must be short but each answer as it comes from the Minister can be dissected and its weaknesses exposed. A line of argument can be followed to a conclusion, whether that conclusion be a revelation by the Government of all the significant facts, or perhaps, even more revealing, a refusal to disclose them.

The opposition parties in Canada have taken full advantage of the political aspect of the question period. The prevalence of the oral question on the orders of the day has, of course, affected the whole procedure. There is little subtlety in any of the questions asked. They cannot be read by the Speaker or the Clerk before they are put, and so have a much higher political content than do their British counterparts. In this way the Canadian member has developed a type of bludgeon question which compares most unfavourably with the question of a

[52]*Debates*, March 27, 1957, p. 2735; April 5, 1957, p. 3136.

[53]This attitude on the part of the Government has not been limited to one party. In 1957–8 the Conservatives, who had begun the abnormally long question period while they were in Opposition, objected most strenuously to the Liberals' following the same course. There has been a recent tendency to limit oral questions asked each day but little has yet been accomplished.

member at Westminster. A large number of these Canadian questions even have a recognizable form. The member who asks the question begins: "in view of the fact that . . ." or "would the Minister care to comment on the report that . . ." and continues with a highly biased statement from an often unknown source. The only adequate reply under the circumstances is that the Minister cannot agree with the premises advanced by the member and that therefore the question is irrelevant. But often the Minister attempts a more lengthy answer. He denies the allegations, gives his "true" version of the facts and a few, strongly political, remarks on them. Such exchanges have few, if any, redeeming features and serve partisan purposes primarily, their original objective of acquiring information having been subordinated.

All the changes necessary to improve the Canadian question period could be made within the framework of the present rules; they would be few and slight, representing alterations in detail rather than in principle. Questions on the orders of the day could be eliminated except in cases of urgent national importance; their admissibility could be decided by the Speaker, whose acceptance could be a prerequisite of their being asked in the House; and, as at present, notice would be sent to the Minister whenever possible. In place of the present informal oral question period, the starred question could be raised to the status it now has in Westminster. Four or five times a week starred questions could be asked, followed at once by supplementaries. Written questions have great advantages for all concerned: they can be properly drafted to provide such information or hide such traps as the questioner has in mind; they must conform to the rules or they will not be accepted for the Order Paper; not least important, perhaps, they guarantee adequate notice for the Minister. These advantages, combined with the spontaneity of an adequate supplementary question period should satisfy all but the excessively partisan members.

Should this revision be too sudden and too drastic for the House, a change along the lines recommended in 1944 would accomplish nearly as much. Questions on the orders of the day could be asked only after notice to the Minister and to the Clerk of the House. The number of supplementaries should probably be left, as it is today, in the hands of the Speaker to limit as his judgment dictates.

Any change in the question period would undoubtedly not be popular with the opposition parties: the opportunities today are too great and the restraints too few to be abandoned for a plan which requires attention to detail and more skilful drafting. But a revision of the rules relating to questions ought really to be a challenge to them. A well-worded question carefully followed up with supplementaries can be an infinitely more effective weapon than an awkward attack launched on a sudden inspiration in the House. It is impossible to believe that the opposition members in Canada are incapable of taking advantage of the opportunity offered and that the resultant question period would offer inadequate possibilities for what Professor Corry has called "trying to skewer the Minister." [54] One could even hope that in time the question period in Ottawa might reach the stature of its model in Westminster and prove more useful than it is today.

The Tabling of Papers

Although questions are an interesting exercise in political provocation, much information cannot be asked for or obtained in this way. It has been seen that the question period has been altered over the years to allow the Government to provide answers of a long and complicated nature in the form of returns. Other papers provided for the use of the House are also tabled with the Clerk as returns. No paper may be presented to the House except on some parliamentary authority: by message from the Governor General, in pursuance of a statute which requires its production, or in answer to an order of the House or an address to the Governor General.[55] The last method is used to obtain copies of correspondence or other exceptional papers required by a member. When the papers desired are within the immediate control of a department, an order of the House issues for their production. Other papers, such as correspondence between the federal government and national, provincial, and municipal authorities, or corporations, or individuals outside the government service are produced only after the House has passed "an humble Address to His Excellency the Governor General praying that he will cause to be laid before this House" the documents required. This division has always been indistinct and

[54]J. A. Corry, *Democratic Government and Politics* (2nd ed., Toronto, 1951), p. 214.

[55]In practice this regulation is relaxed if a Minister agrees in debate to table some specific documents. He will then deposit them with the Clerk of the House as if they had been formally ordered. Most departmental annual reports are tabled by the appropriate Minister "by command of His Excellency the Governor General." The estimates are sent direct to the House by His Excellency. Royal commission reports are also tabled "by command." Many statutes require that yearly accounts be submitted to the House showing receipts and expenditures from special funds, etc. The capital budgets of most Crown corporations are also submitted to the House under the Financial Administration Act.

makes no difference so far as the rules and practice of the House are concerned.[56]

When the House orders a return of any sort a formal order issues over the signature of the Clerk. This is transmitted to the Secretary of State who communicates with the departments involved. The returns, when made, are sent through the Secretary of State to the Clerk of the House, and are tabled in the name of the responsible Minister. Should more than one department be affected, the Secretary of State collects the material from all the necessary departments and the return is tabled in his own name. Under Standing Order 82, a prorogation does not nullify an order for a return, and lengthy returns are often brought down in the next session.[57] A dissolution, however, kills all outstanding orders for returns.

In the early days of the House motions for papers were treated in the same way as other private members' motions. They were called only on private members' days and had priority only according to the date on which they were put on the Order Paper. The system was not satisfactory. The House normally did not expect to debate them, and yet they might never be reached as their passage was blocked by other resolutions for debate. The House developed a custom by which motions for papers were called by consent and passed in a block. The arrangement worked adequately and no real pressure built up in favour of reform, though a few members objected. As early as 1876 a member suggested that notices of motions might well be divided into those which were intended for debate and those on which no debate was desired. In 1909 another private member suggested that when a motion for papers was made, and the Government agreed to produce them, no debate should be allowed.[58]

Little interest and no antagonism, therefore, was aroused in 1910, when a new and more effective method of obtaining papers was introduced. Any member who wished to move for papers without debate marked his notice with an asterisk. The House altered its order of business slightly by giving the new "Notices of Motions for the Production of Papers" precedence over the usual "Notices of Motions." Thus in 1910, motions for papers would be reached, and dealt with, regularly on Monday, Wednesday, and (for the first four weeks only) on Thursday. As the new rule came from the revision committee of

[56]Up to the session of 1876 all papers ordered for presentation by the House were requested by address. From that year on the British practice was adopted.

[57]The rule was first passed in 1906 (1906 Rule 33).

[58]*Debates*, March 29, 1876, p. 907; Nov. 15, 1909, cols. 82–6.

1910 it also provided that all motions for papers would be disposed of at once. The committee expected that most of these motions would be passed without question, but if the Government wished to debate any such motion, it would be transferred at once to the old heading of "Notices of Motions" and would wait its turn for debate there. The House made only one change in the rule before accepting it. Some members pointed out that the provision for transferring a motion for papers to the debatable class was unduly restrictive. The House finally agreed that the wording should be amended to allow a request from any member to force the change.[59]

This rule has remained largely unchanged to this day. A slight improvement was suggested in 1944 when Gordon Graydon asked if the Speaker could not dispense with the reading of motions for papers, as all were printed on the Order Paper and every member had a copy.[60] The House has now adopted this practice and unless a vote is necessary, the motions are called only by number. The revision of 1955 made slight alterations in the standing order. Since 1910 motions for papers had had a place on the Order Paper only by virtue of a rule (Rule 38) which placed them before "Notices of Motions." They did not appear in the order of business at all. The amendment of 1955 listed them formally in the daily agenda of business, and divorced them entirely from "Notices of Motions." The new rule also guarantees that motions for papers will be reached on Monday and Wednesday throughout the session.

Most motions for papers are granted without hesitation. The Minister himself takes the initiative when he decides that a question should be made into an order for a return. At other times, his assent is a formality. Some motions are passed with reservations. By custom, provincial governments are informed when correspondence with them is requested. Should they raise objections to the production of papers the House would doubtless not insist. Similarly, privileged and confidential communications are excluded from a general request for papers.

Some papers are never produced. For instance, correspondence within a department or between ministers is always privileged.[61] These papers are rarely demanded, and if a member makes such a motion the Government asserts that the public interest prevents their production. The Opposition has little choice but to accept the statement. Its

[59]*Ibid.*, April 29, 1910, col. 8371.
[60]*Ibid.*, May 29, 1944, p. 3327.
[61]The position of the public corporation is still far from clear. Generally, however, the same restrictions are applied to motions for papers as are applied to questions.

only recourse is to divide the House on the motion. The argument has been put forward that any motion for papers must be passed unless it can be claimed, to the satisfaction of the mover, that the public interest prohibits their production.[62] This point of view, however, ignores the form in which a motion for papers is made. No individual, and no party or group in the House is competent under the rules to order the production of papers. An order of the House issues either direct or by address to the Governor General. The House must, therefore, decide if it desires the papers. It is obvious then, that each member must decide for himself whether the papers asked for should be produced, and must vote accordingly. By custom this process has been developed into a straight party division. The Government refuses certain papers and the Opposition votes for their production.

There is another little-used way of dealing with motions for papers. Any member may ask that the motion for papers be transferred to notices of motions for debate.[63] Under this rule, no motion is made for the transfer and no debate is possible on the request.[64] This means that the motion will drop to the bottom of the list of motions for debate and will never be reached.[65] This means of avoiding a decision on a motion for papers has been used only rarely: in 1922; 1926, when no less than ten motions for papers were transferred; 1938; and 1956.[66] On this last occasion, however, a revision of the rules had altered the circumstances slightly. Until then, debatable notices of motions remained on the Order Paper until the end of the session and could be called on private members' days. When the number of private members' days was limited by standing order in 1956, another rule was added under which debatable notices of motions were removed from the Order Paper after private members' days had expired (S.O. 15(4)). This meant that for a large part of the session, a request to transfer a motion for papers to notices of motions actually transferred the motion to a section of the Order Paper which not only would not be reached, but also in fact no longer existed. The Speaker met this anomaly in 1956 with an *ad hoc* ruling which authorized the printing on the Order Paper of two

[62]*Debates*, April 3, 1957, pp. 3011–14.

[63]Even the sponsor of the notice of motion may ask that it be so transferred and debated. *Ibid.*, June 18, 1958, pp. 1390–3.

[64]S.O. 47: ". . . but if on any such motion a debate be desired, . . . it will be transferred by the Clerk to the order of 'Notices of Motions'."

[65]In a normal session perhaps six notices of motions are called for debate. As there will be thirty or forty such notices on the Order Paper those at the end will never be reached.

[66]*Debates*, April 19, 1922, p. 942; *Journals*, March 15, 1926, p. 138; June 13, 1938, pp. 442–4; March 21, 1956, pp. 322–9.

transferred motions for papers in spite of the standing order to the contrary.[67]

These expedients are not indicative of any reluctance on the part of the Government to furnish information to members. In the 1956 session, for instance, members gave notice of ninety-nine motions for papers: of these one died on the Order Paper at prorogation, two became debatable notices of motions, five were refused by the Government, and the remaining ninety-one were passed. The situation, therefore, does not appear serious. Many papers asked for and refused are confidential and could not properly be produced under any system. A few other papers refused are needed for purely political reasons. It must also be kept in mind that should the Government refuse to produce papers to which the Opposition felt entitled, the question period could then be used with great effect to procure much of the same information.

Ministerial Statements

The least important access to information that a member can avail himself of is the ministerial statement made either on "Motions" or on the "Orders of the Day." For many years the Government has been allowed by custom to make statements of new or altered policy at the opening of the daily proceedings. These announcements usually relate to matters of general interest and urgency and the practice is accepted today as a useful vehicle by which Government policy may be made known to the House when no other proceeding offers a suitable opportunity. These announcements are not made by the consent of the House, nor are they recognized by any rule; but at least one Speaker has ruled that the practice is one of such long standing that a Minister may make such a statement by right.[68] This right may not be exercised without restraint, for although there is no set limit on the length or content of the statements, a Minister who persisted in long and argumentative recitals would soon find himself in trouble with the Opposition.[69]

The rights of the Opposition in this matter have also gradually

[67]*Journals*, April 12, 1956, pp. 389–93. The committee of revision in 1961 suggested a trial solution to this problem for one session. On alternate Thursdays for the whole of the session these debatable notices of motions for papers were given priority in debate between 5 P.M. and 6 P.M. Thus debate could be assured on them at any stage of the session. This is now permanent (S.O. 15).

[68]*Debates*, June 15, 1955, p. 4812.

[69]*Ibid.*, Oct. 23, 1957, pp. 305–12.

developed and become more clear. Early ministerial statements were followed by a few questions asked largely for the purpose of clearing up doubtful points of fact. These questions occasionally got out of hand and as early as 1891 a Speaker appealed to the House to support him in an effort to suppress the practice of conducting long discussions at such a time.[70] Later Speakers appear to have had little difficulty and although from time to time they referred briefly to the "custom" which allowed only questions, they made no formal ruling. Mr. Speaker Macdonald extended the practice during his occupancy of the Chair and by 1951 the House had accepted a new "practice" by which each one of the leaders of the opposition parties was allowed to comment briefly on the statement made. Mr. Speaker Beaudoin extended the custom still further in 1954 and ruled that each party would henceforward be allowed one comment on any ministerial statement. The change was made to allow the party spokesman on a specific subject to represent his party should he so wish. The House has followed this practice since.

There is little doubt that the opportunities which are offered to a private member for obtaining information are adequate. No unnecessary barriers are placed in his way should he wish to help a constituent or amass factual information for his own use in debate. Statements of policy are infrequent, but generally informative. Documents and statistics are supplied in answer to motions for papers and questions. Most important, the ministry and civil service are only too anxious to give sympathetic hearing to his constituents' problems. A member's only difficulty arises in his quest for political material, but his success or lack of success in his hunt for such material is of little interest here.

[70]*Ibid.*, June 18, 1891, col. 1013.

MOTIONS AND AMENDMENTS

9

THE HOUSE CONDUCTS ALL ITS BUSINESS by the use of motions. These vary greatly from the relatively unimportant routine motions which begin each session to the motion for second reading of an important Government bill. The rules which govern motions subdivide them even further: some motions may not be debated and some may not be amended; many require notice before they can be moved. The nature of motions also varies. A division is generally made between substantive motions and subsidiary motions. Broadly speaking, a substantive motion stands by itself and is not dependent on any other action of the House; a motion to censure the Speaker, for instance, comes within this definition. Subsidiary motions are more common and include a large number of interdependent motions; the succession of motions used to advance a bill are of this type, as are amendments. These definitions are not entirely satisfactory ones, as many exceptions have to be made to both.

Several rules of the House refer directly to motions. Standing Order 43 provides that all motions must be in writing and seconded before they are put from the Chair, and that they must be put in both official languages. Another rule allows a reply to the member who moves certain motions. Notice is required for some motions under a third rule. Several other rules deal only with such specific motions as adjournment motions and motions for the House to go into Committee of Supply and of Ways and Means. Amendments to motions are similarly covered in a number of rules.

Standing Order 43

The first portion of Standing Order 43, which requires a motion to be in writing and seconded before being put from the Chair, is generally followed closely. The Speaker does not usually see fit to demand that a Minister who moves second reading of a Government bill put his motion in writing, but should an amendment be moved the original motion and the amendment are formally set out by the staff of the House for the use of the Speaker. Amendments are invariably required in written form, for the protection of the member who moves them as well as for the convenience of the Speaker. Seconders are usually provided in much the same way. When a Government order is called, the Minister in charge stands as the mover and his desk-mate is usually named as seconder. A private member who moves a motion or an amendment is expected to provide the name of a seconder. This other member may be a purely formal nomination and on occasion the seconder has even been known to vote against his own motion.[1]

The second portion of this rule, which requires the question to be put in both languages, is not followed closely in practice. Questions are normally put to the House in English only, although any member may request that they be read in French also. A Speaker who is not conversant with both languages may have the question read by the Clerk in one language after he reads it himself in the other.

Right of Reply

The general rule of the Canadian House is that no member may speak twice on any question (S.O. 37(1)) but this strict rule has always been modified slightly to allow a limited number of members the right of a reply. As passed in 1867 the rule allowed a reply to a member who moved a substantive motion but not to a member who moved an order of the day. In practice this meant that even a Minister who moved second reading of a Government bill had no opportunity to rebut the critics of the bill before it was submitted to the House for a vote. This unusual situation was corrected in 1906, when the House revised the rule so that a member who moved second reading was permitted a reply. The committee of 1925 suggested that the rule be brought up to date: one section, for instance, still gave the right of reply to the mover of an adjournment during a debate although the

[1]*Debates*, June 10, 1887, p. 876.

motion itself had not been debatable since 1913. The 1925 committee redrafted the other sections of the rule in the form they bear today, the committee of 1927 concurred in most of these recommendations, and the House adopted them.

The rule has remained as accepted in 1927, despite two attempts at alteration. In 1944 the revision committee advocated the addition of a Minister who introduced a Government measure and a member who moved second reading of a bill to the list of those to whom a reply should be allowed. These members had been included in the rule passed in 1906 but had been omitted (apparently by mistake) when the rule was redrafted in 1927. The Minister for years had been able to answer criticisms, but permission was always dependent on unanimous consent. The amendment was to remedy this situation. The Clerk of the House made the same recommendation in his memorandum to the revision committee of 1948.[2] Nothing has been done with either suggestion. Despite this, the right of reply on second reading has apparently been conceded by the House: no question is ever raised today when a Minister rises to reply, and actually it is far more likely that a Minister who does not reply will be attacked in the House for showing a lack of interest in Opposition criticism.

Notice of Motions

Standing Order 41 requires forty-eight hours' notice before certain motions may be put to the House—a motion for leave to present a bill, resolution, or address, for the appointment of a committee, and for placing a question on the Order Paper. Shorter notice is possible for a motion for closure (S.O. 33) and for taking a private members' Monday for a supply motion (S.O. 56). Notice is also required for the appointment of a special committee of more than fifteen members (S.O. 67).

Once a bill is in the hands of the House, no further notice is required. In practice, however, informal notice is always given. The House knows which days of the week are reserved for private members. On these days the order of business is strictly regulated by the Order Paper (S.O. 18). There is, then, no doubt about which bills or resolutions will be called. The Government has the advantage of greater flexibility, for it is permitted by the rules to call its business in such order as it sees fit. A custom has, however, grown up in the House of announcing Government business in advance. The form of the announcement is not invariable—

[2]*The Table*, XVII, 1948, p. 239.

it may range from a brief statement of the Leader's hopes for the next day to a detailed agenda, obviously prepared with the co-operation of the opposition, of the business for several days. The Government does not bind itself in any way by this announcement but generally does not deviate from it except with the consent of the opposition.

The rules which require notice are tempered by custom, which relaxes the strict letter of the law. It has become the practice, for instance, to move concurrence in most committee reports without the formality of notice: the House grants unanimous consent and passes them at once. Other similar motions are often made without notice by consent of the House with the result that the business of the Commons goes on with a minimum of formality and delay.

Debatable Motions

At the time of Confederation the great majority of motions made in the House were debatable; only a few, such as the first reading of a bill, were non-debatable either by rule or custom. Over the years the House added a few more motions to the non-debatable list. After 1906 a motion to hear a member could not be debated, and in the same year the House adopted a new form of limited adjournment motion. Finally in 1910, when motions for papers were separated from private members' notices of motions, the House agreed that motions for papers would henceforth be decided without debate.

The great change was made in 1913. When the Prime Minister introduced the closure in the Canadian House he accompanied it with a rule (Rule 17A) which limited severely the number of debatable motions, and which undermined the freedom of speech of members far more effectively than did the closure. The rule listed the motions which could be debated and then in a sweeping clause declared that "all other motions shall be decided without debate or amendment." In the flurry of debate on the "gag" the House largely ignored this rule. A few members attacked it, but their remarks lack conviction. The impression left by the debate on this section of the rules is that both sides recognized the necessity for some change of this sort. The greatest problem was the poor draftsmanship of the new rule. Several suggestions were made at the time about motions which obviously should be debatable (an amendment to third reading of a bill, for instance) but which were not covered by the rule.

The revision committee of 1927 clarified some of the provisions of this rule, enumerating several motions whose status had been doubtful and on which debate had proceeded only by consent; these included motions for second reading of a bill, consideration of Senate amendments, a conference with the Senate, the appointment of a committee, and suspension of a rule of the House. All these were made debatable without question. It is perhaps indicative of the general acceptance of the principle involved that the debate on this portion of the committee's report was negligible. In 1948 a committee recommended another change in the rule—that the motion for the Speaker to leave the Chair for the House to go into committee on a resolution preceding a money bill should be non-debatable.[3] The House did not accept the committee's report, but in 1953 the motion was made non-debatable by Speaker's ruling.[4] The list of non-debatable motions grew again in 1955 when the House added the motions for the Speaker to leave the Chair and for leave to introduce a bill.[5] The House made no changes at that time which were not dependent on changes in other standing orders.

The rule today is far from satisfactory. Each session provides an opportunity for an exercise of the ingenuity of the Opposition in presenting a case for the propriety of debate on certain motions, and an opportunity for the Speaker or Chairman to show tact and firmness when ruling these debates to be out of order. Thus in 1955 the Speaker ruled that a motion to refer estimates to the Committee on Estimates was not debatable. In 1956 he gave the same decision on motions to instruct the Committee of the Whole and for the suspension of a member for the remainder of the day. There seems little hope that the rule will ever be properly clarified. Members can always be found to argue that special circumstances or a citation in Beauchesne ought to be used to modify the strict letter of the law. The problem, however, is not serious and except in the most extreme cases a decision from the Chair is taken in good part by all sections of the House.

Dilatory Motions

One series of motions have no object except to delay progress by superseding the question under discussion. The most common of these dilatory motions is a motion to adjourn the debate or to adjourn the House. If the House is in committee, the motion is that the committee rise and report progress. All these questions are decided without debate. Should

---

[3]*Journals*, June 25, 1948, p. 680.   [4]*Ibid.*, March 26, 1953, pp. 419–21.
[5]*Ibid.*, July 12, 1955, pp. 881–945. There are a few exceptions to this general prohibition specified in other standing orders.

any of these motions pass, debate in the House or committee will, of course, end at once. It is unusual for these motions to pass when moved by the opposition, but even if defeated they may accomplish their purpose of delaying progress. They cannot be debated, but a division occupies half an hour at least and will thus block progress for that length of time. The only restriction on this use of adjournment motions is that some other proceeding of the House must intervene before another similar motion may be moved. An opposition cannot, therefore, fill a whole day by moving a succession of these motions.

Another dilatory motion is that which requires the House to leave one subject which is under debate and pass on to another. There are three forms in which this can be used. First, when a motion is being debated under "routine proceedings" a motion is in order to proceed to the "orders of the day." If this is passed the motion originally being debated is shelved for the day and the House passes on to the next section of the Order Paper. This motion was used for instance in 1956 when the Government wished to postpone debate on a motion to censure the Speaker so that its own bill could go forward more rapidly.[6] The second form that this procedure may take is a motion to proceed to a specific item of business on the Order Paper. A private member, however, cannot move that the House proceed to a particular Government order. The Government is, under the rules, entitled to call its business in such rotation as it sees fit and it is not within the power of a private member to dictate what this order shall be. A third motion, to proceed to some other portion of the Order Paper, is also in order; if, for example, the House is engaged in public bills, it is possible to move to proceed to Government orders. However, such a motion would be unusual today as private members' days are limited and the Government is unlikely to use its majority to limit the time of private members still further.

The "previous question" may also be used as a dilatory motion. Its chief function is to limit debate, as it does when it is passed. If, however, the previous question is negatived by the House, the motion under debate is superseded and disappears temporarily from the Order Paper. If the previous question is moved and negatived on a bill, the bill is merely passed over temporarily. It is not removed from the Order Paper.[7]

[6]*Debates*, June 5, 1956, pp. 4688–9.

[7]This use of the previous question is unusual in Canada. It was used in 1869 on a private member's motion relating to Irish church disestablishment. The Prime Minister moved the previous question and then voted against his own motion. *Journals*, May 31, 1869, pp. 163–4. For the use of the previous question to limit debate, see *supra*, chap. 7.

The Adjournment

A motion for the adjournment of the House appears in several different guises. We have already seen how it can be employed as a time-wasting device by the opposition, but this is not its most common use. It can also be moved by the Government to end a sitting at the end of the day or interrupt a sitting under extraordinary circumstances, and to allow time for a debate when no other procedure is available. It may also be used by the opposition to precipitate a debate on some specific urgent problem.

From 1867 to 1906 motions to adjourn either the debate or the House were debatable, and the House regularly used them to provide time for discussions which otherwise would have been out of order. There was only one drawback to the system, and one which became evident early in the history of the House—there was no way in which these debates could be controlled. Members moved the adjournment for different reasons: to discuss a specific topic which could not otherwise be raised; to begin a debate on an unsatisfactory answer to a question; or in the middle of a debate, to enable a member to make a second speech on the matter under discussion. The possibilities were endless, and a custom grew up which Speakers, who repeatedly deplored its inconvenience, were powerless to end.[8] Both parties suffered: in 1895 a Conservative Minister of Finance and Leader of the House complained of the abuse of the adjournment, and five years later it was a Liberal Prime Minister who noted the abuse and appealed to the then Conservative Opposition to limit it.[9]

The revision committee of 1906 removed this problem, by providing that the majority of adjournment motions should be decided without debate, and in 1913 adjournment motions were formally listed among those on which no debate was allowed.[10] The only exceptions to this general rule are adjournments moved for the purpose of debating matters of urgent public importance. These have a history of their own and are discussed separately below.

ADJOURNMENTS TO END A SITTING

The automatic adjournment of the House has rendered obsolete the use of a motion for the adjournment of the House at the end of the

[8]*Debates*, March 8, 1877, p. 568; Feb. 27, 1893, cols. 1319–20.
[9]*Ibid.*, May 17, 1895, cols. 1275–80; May 21, 1900, col. 5740.
[10]The revision of 1906 did not specifically state that adjournment motions could not be debated, but by providing a substitute, implied this. The 1913 rule settled the question permanently.

day.[11] However, when the House completes its business for the day a few minutes early, a motion to adjourn is not unusual. On rare occasions it may also seem desirable to interrupt a sitting in the middle of the day. For instance, should a member die while the House is sitting, the Leader of the House (with the support of the opposition) at once moves the adjournment.

ADJOURNMENT DEBATES BY AGREEMENT

Under certain circumstances a motion to adjourn has been used as a peg on which to hang a debate that the House as a whole wants to be conducted but which has no connection with any business before the House. This method has been used for instance to have a general debate on foreign policy.[12] At the end of the day the motion lapses and the House adjourns automatically as usual. These debates can be carried on only by consent, as in this form the motion to adjourn is not debatable under the rules.

ADJOURNMENT DEBATES UNDER STANDING ORDER 26

The revision committee of 1906 made most adjournment motions non-debatable, but at the same time it provided a substitute. The new procedure which was introduced was copied from the British House and was passed virtually in its present form (S.O. 26). The only debatable adjournment motion is defined as one which is moved to discuss "a definite matter of urgent public importance." The rule itself is hedged about with restrictions about how the motion may be moved, and Speakers' decisions have imposed further limitations on the subjects which may be discussed. Leave to move this form of adjournment can be asked only after routine proceedings and before the orders of the day are called. The member who wishes to make the motion hands a written statement of his motion to the Speaker. If the Speaker decides it is urgent and in order, the member asks leave of the House to proceed, and he may do so if twenty members support his motion. If more than five but less than twenty members support the motion, the question of leave is put directly to the House and may be settled by a division.[13]

The House debated the new rule at length in 1906. Some members felt it was too restrictive, and one expressed the view that it was derogatory to the dignity of the House that a member should be obliged to

[11]See *supra*, chap. 5.
[12]*Debates*, Jan. 29, 1954, pp. 1584–1622.
[13]This was done in 1931. Although only thirteen members rose at first to give their consent to proceed, 147 voted in the division to allow the motion. *Journals*, May 19, 1931, p. 217.

"hawk around a petition to get the signatures of twenty Members."[14] The belief was widespread that an individual member was the best judge of the urgency of the situation which led him to make his motion.

The history of this rule has never been happy. In its early application the House abused it as it had the earlier adjournment motions, and members raised many matters which could never be classed as of "urgent public importance." The proposed outlet of a canal, the drainage and sanitation of a river, a particular railway connection in Ontario, and the rules of the National Rifle Association of Great Britain were all discussed.[15] Throughout this period the exact position of the Speaker was in doubt, and his powers under the rule were not further defined until 1927 when an amendment to the rule gave him specific authority to decide on the urgency of the matter to be debated.[16]

The power of the Speaker to decide questions of urgency without an appeal on this decision to the House was first established in 1932, when Mr. Speaker Black refused an appeal to the House on his decision that an adjournment motion was not urgent. He did, however, allow an appeal on his decision that there was no appeal.[17] His decision has been indifferently followed since 1932. His successor in the Chair, Mr. Bowman, allowed three such appeals in one session, and other similar appeals have been allowed.[18] In general, however, the tendency has been increasingly to affirm Mr. Speaker Black's ruling of 1932 and the House has accepted his interpretation.[19]

The use of Standing Order 26 to debate matters of interest to the House and (if possible) embarrassment to the Government has never been very great, as succeeding Speakers have interpreted the rule narrowly. A matter of "urgent public importance" has been interpreted to mean a matter which, if the normal rules of the House are followed, cannot be debated at an early enough time to comply with the public interest. Thus if the matter can properly be raised on a motion for supply, and a day has been set for such a debate in the near future, the claim of urgency is not allowed. The subject to be raised must, moreover, be a specific one and within the power of the federal government to

[14]*Debates*, July 10, 1906, col. 7608.

[15]*Journals*, Feb. 25, 1907, p. 205; April 14, 1909, p. 293; Dec. 4, 1907, p. 28; March 2, 1910, p. 283; Feb. 26, 1912, p. 244.

[16]*Ibid.*, March 22, 1927, p. 335.

[17]*Debates*, Feb. 19, 1932, pp. 360–5.

[18]*Ibid.*, March 27, 1935, pp. 2145–52; May 22, 1935, pp. 2970–3; June 13, 1935, pp. 3585–9. See also July 5, 1955, pp. 5681–6.

[19]On the last occasions on which the ruling was made the House did not even question the propriety of the ruling. *Ibid.*, May 7, 1956, p. 3714; Jan. 16, 1961, p. 1063; Feb. 15, 1961, p. 2068.

remedy: a question which lies within the orbit of a provincial or municipal government cannot be discussed. The Speaker, in considering the question of "anticipation," also considers the probable length of time between the motion and the normal debate in which the matter could be discussed. Such power in the hands of the Speaker effectively prevents the abuse of the rule by individual members who could put motions on the Order Paper to block debate without having any intention of proceeding.

Several reforms have been suggested for this adjournment rule in the past fifteen years, but so far none of them has been accepted. The committee of revision in 1944 recommended generally that the rule should be brought into line with the practice of the House, by defining the powers of the Speaker more clearly. The House, however, found it impossible to agree on what powers should be given to the Speaker under any new rule. Mr. Speaker Fauteux made a more definite recommendation in 1947. He outlined the growth of the parallel rule in the United Kingdom and suggested a major change in the Canadian practice. He advocated an amendment which would postpone debate on an adjournment motion until 8 P.M. The motion could then be debated until the House rose as usual. Such an arrangement would minimize the disruption of the business of the House and would give ample opportunity for the presentation of the problem.[20] The same suggestion was made a few months later by the Clerk in a memorandum to a committee of revision.[21]

Motions for the adjournment under Standing Order 26 have thus become a negligible factor in the procedure of the Canadian House. The same question has aroused considerable controversy in the British House and in a speech on his motion which expressed "regret" over a ruling by the Speaker, Mr. Wedgwood Benn made at least one good point.[22] He contended that these motions are one of the few opportunities for a private member to be heard on a subject chosen by himself and not by either front-bench. The situation is not quite identical in Canada. In Ottawa, it is true that a private member is not able to control the amendments moved to supply motions or at other similar times. The rule of relevancy, however, is loosely enough applied, and the amendments moved by the opposition are often so vaguely worded that it is possible to make extended remarks at frequent intervals. The question period also allows members ample scope for questions and supplementaries on nearly any subject. The question of a relaxation

[20]*Journals*, Dec. 5, 1947, pp. 20–2.   [21]*The Table*, XVII, 1948, p. 238.
[22]*H. of C. Debates* (U.K.), July 29, 1957, cols. 880–9.

of the rule has never been seriously raised in Canada, but should the present trend toward Government control and toward further limitations on the time for debates continue, the back-bencher will increasingly be forced into the position of Mr. Wedgwood Benn of "grubbing for food in the House." When this point is reached the Canadian member should, and undoubtedly will, attempt to reassert his long-ignored rights.

ADJOURNMENT OF THE DEBATE

When the fixed adjournment hour rendered obsolete the daily motion for adjourning the House it also virtually eliminated motions for the adjournment of the debate. When the House rises for the day, debate is automatically interrupted without the necessity of a motion. This does not, of course, mean that a motion to adjourn the debate cannot be moved either as a dilatory motion to hold up progress, or by consent to enable the House to pass on to some other business. Its most common use today is not, strictly speaking, recognized by the rules. It is customary for a member to move such an adjournment when the House rises to establish a priority in debate for himself on the next occasion when the bill is before the House. This device is also used by the party whips on behalf of the Cabinet or opposition leaders.

Amendments

There are few general principles which govern all amendments in the Canadian House. Basic to the whole question of amendments is the obvious truth that a motion which cannot be debated cannot be amended. The mechanical impossibility of amending a motion when there is no way in which a member can get to his feet to speak automatically exempts a large number of motions from the possibility of amendment. There still remain, however, the most important motions with which the House must deal, and ample opportunity is allowed the Opposition to make its opinions known in a relatively clear and concise form.

Amendments in Canada are always put directly to the House, and the House votes first on the amendment and then on the main motion.[23] Only two amendments may be before the House at any time, and on these occasions the House divides first on the sub-amendment. There

[23]The question is always put directly on an amendment. There is no Canadian equivalent to the British motion "that the words proposed to be left out stand part of the question."

is no limit on the number of amendments which may be moved successively to any normal motion;[24] as soon as one is defeated or adopted, another may be moved.

The rules which govern the content of amendments are largely those dictated by commonsense. An amendment to a motion can do one of three things: it can remove words, add words, or replace certain words by others. Within these broad limits other rules, of course, apply. All amendments must be relevant. This rule is strictly applied and has been broadened to apply also to the conventions which surround the passage of bills. Thus amendments in the details of a bill on a motion for second reading are not deemed to be relevant, as they must be made in Committee of the Whole. Equally, amendments to a bill which is designed to continue a bill in force and amend it only in minor details, must be relevant to the bill under consideration; they may not apply to the parent bill which is not directly before the House. Relevancy is most strictly applied in Committee of the Whole, where amendments must be directly related to the clause under discussion. Once that clause has been passed, it is irregular to amend it at a later stage.

Each stage through which a bill passes in the House, therefore, has its own particular types of amendments which may be moved. When second reading is moved it is improper, for instance, to add words to the motion by amendment. It is quite posible, however, to move that certain words be left out and others substituted. These new words are occasionally an expression of principle at variance with that expressed in the bill, or more often, the formal wish that the bill be read "this day six months." Few problems arise in Committee of the Whole. As the bill is considered clause by clause there is no opportunity to move amendments that are not relevant and there is little tendency to move amendments related to the principle of the bill. On third reading it is not possible to move an amendment directly opposed to the principle of a bill. The House at this stage may postpone third reading or it may refer the bill back to Committee of the Whole to be amended in certain particulars. Should a bill be so altered in its passage that an amendment of its title would seem to be desirable, the change may be made on a final motion "that the bill do now pass and the title be as on the Order Paper."[25]

[24]Exceptions to this general rule are contained in the standing order which limits the number of amendments to motions for Committee of Supply or of Ways and Means. Only one amendment and one sub-amendment may be moved to each of these motions (S.O. 45).

[25]This final motion has now been abandoned for most bills. In the unusual event that an amendment to a title should be necessary, the motion would probably be briefly revived. *Debates*, May 14, 1958, p. 84.

The general rules of debate also dictate some of the restrictions on amendments. It is improper to present an amendment which repeats any question already decided by the House in the same session. This means also that the same amendment cannot be offered twice on the same bill. It means further than an amendment offered on the Address in Reply or on a supply motion may disqualify a later amendment to a bill.[26] This is a rule which raises serious problems for the Chair and involves rulings which are rarely popular in the House. It is, however, a most necessary rule and one which protects the House against needless repetition. Further protection is given by the principle that no amendment may anticipate any item already on the Order Paper; this rule is most often applied to eliminate amendments to motions for supply or the Address in Reply. On many occasions the grievances which are mentioned in these amendments are also the subject of private members' motions or even of Government legislation.

It is necessary that an amendment actually amend the bill or motion on which it is based. A negative amendment is not in order as the same result may be achieved through an adverse vote on the motion. If the attempt is made by a motion for the deletion of a vital clause or section of a bill, the move is obvious and will be ruled out. The "expanded negative" is more difficult to define, and the line which divides it from a perfectly proper expression of a principle opposed to that of the bill is one which the Speaker often finds difficult to draw.[27] It is also irregular to move a sub-amendment which strikes out all the words of the amendment. Such a change should be moved as a separate motion after the House has disposed of the first amendment.

Some other matters must be decided by direct motion after notice and cannot be introduced as amendments. It is impossible for instance for a member to move an amendment which extends the order of reference of a committee. Neither can an amendment set up a committee to consider a bill which is under consideration.

The principles which relate to the introduction of money bills by private members apply also to amendments. It is beyond the power of any private member to increase the expenditure of the Government.[28]

---

[26]This provision has been applied with decreasing frequency in recent years.

[27]It is impossible to explain logically why an expanded negative is out of order whereas an amendment to read a bill a second time "this day six months" is in order. The only difference is that the improper expanded negative generally puts forward a positive expression of opposition opinion.

[28]A private member may not introduce a bill even to reduce taxes. He may, however, move to amend a Government tax bill to reduce the rate of taxes and similar items. *Debates*, Dec. 12, 1957, p. 2287.

These provisions have always been strictly applied. Some amendments offered would directly and obviously increase expenditure, such as one moved in 1948 which called for an increase in benefits under the Prairie Farm Assistance Act,[29] but often rulings are more difficult. An amendment which simply extends the time for making unemployment insurance claims may possibly impose a burden on the Government and has been ruled out of order.[30] Similarly an amendment merely to redefine terms used in a bill may have the same effect.[31]

Money amendments are further circumscribed by the tradition that the destination of a grant may not be changed, nor may an amendment alter the conditions laid down in the Governor General's recommendation which precedes any money bill. A change in the destination may be expressed directly as a reduction of a specific amount in one item which is to be transferred to another item in the estimates. It may be more indirect, and merely suggest a use to which a portion of a sum of money might be put. Both forms of amendment are out of order. The prohibition against alterations in the royal recommendation takes in a wide territory as well. In a debate on a bill to provide a majority ownership by the government in the Bank of Canada it was ruled improper to move an amendment in favour of complete government ownership.[32] It is also out of order to suggest that money should be raised by a compulsory loan from certain specified groups instead of by a general loan, or to amend a resolution to provide that a portion of a loan should be raised by the printing of money by the Government.[33] As in the case of most amendments, the ruling of the Speaker or Chairman must be based in each instance on factors peculiar to the time. Few rules may safely be drawn except in the most general terms.

A few amendments which deal with money are in order. In Committee of Supply a member may move the reduction of any item. He may not move that it should be struck out as to do so would be a negative amendment, but a reduction of any vote to one dollar accomplishes the same end. If a member can establish his motion to be an abstract proposition barren of results it will normally be accepted as it cannot bind the Government to take action and thereby spend money.[34] It is also possible for a member to move an amendment which, if put into effect, would place a financial burden on the country. Such an amend-

[29]*Journals*, April 23, 1948, p. 387.
[30]*Debates*, Jan. 13, 1955, p. 146.
[31]*Journals*, Aug. 1, 1946, p. 569.
[32]*Debates*, June 1, 1936, p. 3286.
[33]*Ibid.*, May 6, 1943, p. 2468; *Journals*, April 11, 1939, p. 325.
[34]*Debates*, April 29, 1874, p. 60; Feb. 18, 1876, pp. 125 ff.

ment has been ruled in order on the ground that the proposal was modified by the clause "with the assent of Parliament."[35] The Speaker ruled that such an amendment would be of no effect without further action by Parliament and thus was in order.

Amendments moved to the Address in Reply to the Speech from the Throne and to debatable motions for the Speaker to leave the Chair for the House to resolve itself into Committee of Supply or of Ways and Means are judged by different standards. All of the set debates in the session are looked on primarily as opposition debates and every facility is accorded the leaders of the opposition parties and their back-benchers to express themselves on the general aspects of Government policy. It is assumed that these debates are simply motions of confidence and amendments are proposed which deal with broad problems on which the Government and opposition differ. The rule of relevancy is ignored. In the debate on the Address in Reply in particular, an amendment may be a straight assertion of want of confidence or may be a reasoned amendment of considerable length. It is increasingly assumed that no debate which takes place on these amendments will prejudice future debates on any item on the Order Paper. Some amendments in fact are drawn up in such sweeping terms that virtually any problem can be discussed relevantly. The rules over the years have been relaxed on these few occasions and the general regulations have been slackened by consent.

The whole field of motions and amendments is thus one of the most confusing in parliamentary procedure. No other portion of procedure is as constantly under observation. There is a steady stream of rulings and Speakers' comments on the content and form of motions. Few rules can or should be drafted to control the situation, for each motion and each amendment must stand on its own and must be judged, not so much on the bare words it contains, but more in relation to its sur-roundings, to decisions the House has taken, and to business which is on the Order Paper. In this situation the success of the few rules which the House has written depends entirely on the good sense and good judgment of the occupant of the Chair.

[35]*Ibid.*, June 4, 1900, col. 6576.

DIVISIONS

10

ALL DEBATE BASED ON MOTIONS inevitably ends with a vote. The Fathers of Confederation well understood this principle and the British North America Act (s. 49) provides that "questions arising in the House of Commons shall be decided by a Majority of Voices other than that of the Speaker, and when the Voices are equal, but not otherwise, the Speaker shall have a Vote."

Putting the Question

The method of reaching a decision is of interest as it is one of the most obvious Canadian variations from British practice. When debate in the House on a question has concluded and no member appears to want the floor, the Speaker asks the assembled members, "Is the House ready for the question?" Should no member rise to speak he proceeds to put the question, that is, he reads the main motion followed by any amendments and takes the sense of the House on the last of these by asking those for and against the question to say "yea" and "nay." Both sides generally roar out their answers with great good humour, the minority in particular exerting itself to make a loud noise. The Speaker announces his interpretation of the voices, which is rarely accepted by the losers.[1] At least five members rise to demand a recorded division and the bells

---

[1]Should the Speaker not be able to tell from the voices whether the yeas or nays are the greater he will himself call in the members without being asked. *Debates*, May 15, 1928, p. 3040.

ring to call in the members who are engaged in other work within the Parliament buildings.[2]

No time limit is set for this part of the procedure. Ten minutes or less is generally sufficient for summoning the members but it is not unusual for the bells to ring for fifteen or twenty minutes. When the Government and Opposition whips are satisfied that all the available members have arrived, they enter the House together, bow to the Speaker, and take their seats. They are followed by the Sergeant-at-Arms who also bows to the Speaker to indicate that the doors of the House are closed.

Recording the Vote

The Speaker then puts the question again and calls on those in favour of the motion (or amendment) to rise. As the members rise one after another by parties, beginning with the party leaders,[3] their names are called by the Second Clerk Assistant. The Clerk of the House keeps the official record of the division on a sheet on which the names of all the members have been printed in alphabetical order; he repeats each name as it is called and records the vote. At the same time the Clerk Assistant maintains a numerical count of the division so that there will be no delay in announcing the result once the counting has been done. When those in favour have been counted, the Speaker calls on those opposed to rise and the division proceeds as before. When all the votes have been recorded the Clerk announces the result to the Speaker, who then declares the fate of the motion being considered.[4]

In Committee of the Whole the method of voting is even more simple. The question, "Shall the clause carry?" is put by the Chairman. Should it be obvious that a division is desired the committee is counted at once. The members rise in rows and are counted by a clerk, but no record is kept of the names of those who vote: the Clerk just gives the numbers to the Chairman and he communicates the result to the committee.

[2]Should members wish a recorded vote, it must be asked at this time. A recorded division cannot be demanded after the motion has been declared carried or lost. *Ibid.*, May 10, 1920, p. 2242.

[3]On non-controversial matters such as divorce and other private bills, the party leaders take their turns in their rows.

[4]There has been little change in the method of voting since 1867. A change in the wearing apparel of members has led to one alteration in procedure—it is no longer the custom for a member to tip his hat to indicate his vote; he now must rise and nod to the Clerk.

The Casting Vote

The Speaker and the Chairman in Canada have only a casting vote in any division. Standing Order 10 grants this casting vote and adds that any reasons the Speaker or Chairman may give for so voting will be entered in the *Journals*. Whenever possible he votes so that the question which is being decided will be kept before the House.[5] This principle is not so clear in its application as it might seem, and Speakers have not been consistent in their reasoning on it. Twice the House has split evenly on amendments to bills to postpone consideration for a period of months. On the first occasion the Speaker said that "as he meant to keep the bill before the House" he would vote in favour of the "hoist," and on the second he used the same argument to vote against it. The principle seems also to have been abandoned in 1930 when the Speaker voted against second reading of a bill for no stated reason.[6] In Committee of the Whole, commonsense seems to dictate the policy on this matter. At least twice the Chairman has voted against amendments in committee on the grounds that they could be moved again on third reading.[7] A Government motion, however, to delete a clause, has been accepted, and a motion to rise and report progress refused.[8]

Short Cuts

By custom, certain short cuts have been developed in the House. In law, each question submitted to the House must be dealt with separately. If, however, the members are ready for the question on two motions at the same time the bells are often not rung more than once. The whips indicate that they consider their members to have been called in, and the second division follows the first. More important, the majority of questions decided in every session are settled informally by consent. The Speaker puts the question and a low murmur of "agreed, agreed" indicates general approval. Should any group in the House be opposed to the motion but at the same time unwilling to force a recorded vote, they cry "on division" to register their protest, and the *Journals* record the motion as so carried.[9]

[5]*Debates*, April 15, 1920, p. 1265; March 26, 1928, p. 1681.
[6]*Ibid.*, May 6, 1870, col. 1401; Feb. 28, 1889, p. 368; March 11, 1930, p. 503.
[7]*Ibid.*, April 15, 1920, p. 1265; March 26, 1928, p. 1681.
[8]*Ibid.*, June 23, 1922, p. 3474; June 20, 1904, col. 5164.
[9]For example, this method is used by the opponents of divorce bills to mark their disagreement. For some years the Leader of the House made the protest on

Previous Customs

One old custom has fallen into disuse. There used to be a general agreement in the House that in a series of divisions only one formal vote should be taken. The remainder of the divisions were then recorded with the same names listed as on the first. An immense amount of time and effort was thus saved. In 1882, for instance, twenty-five amendments were moved to the motion for third reading of Macdonald's famous gerrymander bill. All but one were negatived on recorded divisions although the House, in fact, voted only once.[10] In 1955 the Speaker suggested that the old practice might be revived, and that the vote on a motion might be recorded as the vote on the amendment reversed. However, a member objected, and the House divided a second time.[11]

Another unwritten rule which has fallen into disuse is the one which enables any member to have a division list read by the Clerk after he has announced the result to the Speaker. This right, which was designed to give members an opportunity of detecting irregularities in the list, has been used only rarely.[12] Three general categories of irregular voting may be found: members who should have voted in a specific way and have not done so; members who have abstained from a division and should declare their votes; and members who have voted when they should not have done so.

Compulsory Voting

There is no rule in Canada which requires a member to vote in any given way on any motion. The question has been raised on several occasions, and Speakers have been unanimous in their decisions. The most common demand has been that a member who has asked for a recorded division on a question must vote with the minority. In spite of British precedents, on at least four occasions Speakers have ruled that the standing orders merely state that any five members of the House may demand a recorded vote, and that this request does not

behalf of his fellow Roman Catholics, who disagreed with the principle of divorce. Lately, the C.C.F. party has made the same protest on the grounds of opposition to the principle of parliamentary divorce.

[10]*Debates*, May 12, 1882, p. 1479.
[11]*Ibid.*, Feb. 24, 1955, pp. 1493–4.
[12]*Ibid.*, May 6, 1878, pp. 2478, 2459; June 4, 1900, col. 6607; Sept. 1, 1903, col. 10409.

imply any conviction on either side of the question under discussion.[13] Similarly, a member who moves the previous question need not vote against his motion, and even a seconder may vote against the motion he has seconded.[14]

For the first sixty years of the life of the House, members were compelled to vote whenever they were in the House during a division. There was no rule of the House to cover the point, but such unprovided cases were settled according to the British practice of 1867, which was that members in the House could be, and were, compelled to vote.[15] The British House amended its rule on this point in 1906, but even so the Canadian practice, which was still tied to the British rules of 1867, did not change. The Canadian House applied the old rule with vigour. Only a pair or a claim of personal interest could save a member, and even if he was paired he often could escape only by a declaration of how he would have voted if he had been free to do so.

In 1927, Rule 1 of the House was amended (S.O. 1) to make the Commons dependent on the current British practice in unprovided cases. After that session, therefore, members could not properly be forced to vote in Canada, but Speakers' rulings confused the situation. In 1928 Rodolphe Lemieux ruled first that members must vote if in the House and later that they were free to abstain if they so wished; the year after he admitted that there was a "rarely enforced" custom in Canada which compelled a member to vote, but refused to enforce it.[16] Matters came to a head in 1931 when several independent members refused to vote in a division and narrowly escaped being named for disobeying an order of the Chair. One week later, one of the members moved an amendment to the rules, which would have made it unnecessary to vote in any division.[17] The Prime Minister moved an amendment which would have made voting compulsory, and a committee was set

[13]*Ibid.*, March 22, 1875, p. 860; May 6, 1878, p. 2459; May 30, 1887, p. 624; Nov. 30, 1909, col. 781. It is not unusual to have the Government ask that the yeas and nays be called. Such a request is merely a friendly attempt to embarrass an Opposition which has been attacking a measure, the principle of which it does not dare to oppose. *Ibid.*, May 26, 1954, p. 5114; April 19, 1956, p. 3099; Feb. 8, 1957, p. 1125, etc. It may also be used by the Opposition to embarrass the Government by forcing a recorded vote on a measure which does not command the full support of its back-benchers. *Ibid.*, March 4, 1959, pp. 1609–11.

[14]*Ibid.*, March 13, 1879, pp. 407–8; June 10, 1887, p. 876. On this second occasion the member stated that he had been the seconder by courtesy only.

[15]1918 Rule 1.

[16]*Debates*, March 27, 1928, p. 1755; May 26, 1928, p. 3420; Feb. 19, 1929, pp. 265–7. His first ruling was rather indecisive, because although he upheld the principle of compulsory voting, he excused a member from its application.

[17]*Ibid.*, April 28, 1931, p. 1035.

up "to consider jointly with Mr. Speaker the amending of the Standing Orders of the House governing the procedure to be followed in taking a division."

This committee produced one of the most unusual reports ever presented to the House. In spite of its own origins, it interpreted its terms of reference in such a narrow way that it studied only the mechanics of taking a division. It did not consider the question of compulsory voting at all; it simply considered other possible ways of dividing the House. A brief interchange in the House during the debate on the adoption of the report illustrates the surprise of some members at least:

> *Mr. Marcil*: Did the committee give consideration to the question of members voting or abstaining from voting or was that not considered?
> *Sir George Perley*: That was not included in the reference.
> *Mr. Beaubien*: But that was the reason for the appointment of the committee.
> *Sir George Perley*: That question was not contained in the terms of reference at all.[18]

The committee finally recommended only that an extra clerk should keep a numerical tally of those voting in a division so that the House should not have to wait for the Clerk to count up his list of names. As has already been mentioned, this practice is now followed, but the list kept by the Clerk is the official record which rules in the case of discrepancy. The question of compulsory voting has, however, remained unsettled. The most recent suggestion was in 1948 when the Clerk of the House advised that voting should be made obligatory.[19] The suggestion has not been adopted and members now vote or refrain from voting as conscience dictates.[20]

The Disallowing of Votes

Occasionally it is necessary to strike out the vote of a member who has participated in a division. The rules surrounding this practice are not clear. The most common reason for such an alteration is that a member was not in his seat during the vote. Standing Order 12 (2), which is applicable in this case, reads: "When Mr. Speaker is putting a question,

[18]*Ibid.*, June 26, 1931, p. 3077.
[19]*The Table*, XVII, 1948, p. 237.
[20]Note the statement of one member in 1955 that he would be present in the House during a division and "as a matter of deliberate policy I shall refrain from voting." *Debates*, Jan. 21, 1955, p. 411. Also the statement of Mr. Speaker Beaudoin, *ibid.*, July 11, 1956, p. 5865.

no member shall enter, walk out of, or across the House, or make any noise or disturbance." This has been interpreted as meaning that a member must be in his own seat should he wish to vote, and must remain in his seat until the vote is complete and the result announced. However, this interpretation has not been strictly observed and rulings can be found on both sides: twice at least members have been allowed to wander around the House during a division without having their votes expunged; but as recently as 1956 a member had his name struck off a division list when he had not the time to reach his seat in the House.[21]

Closely allied to the striking out of a member's vote are the occasions on which a member has not heard the question put, and has been refused a vote. Generally, a member who has not heard the question put cannot have his vote recorded, and he must be within the precincts of the House to hear the question: it is not sufficient for him to hear it put while he is in a gallery or behind the curtains.[22] The ruling which seems to be most generally applied is the one first made in 1891 when the Speaker decided that only those who had heard the question read in its entirety in either of the official languages[23] would be permitted to vote.[24] When a doubt arises on this point, the Speaker asks the member affected if he heard the question put; if the member's answer is in the negative his vote is not allowed. This rule leads to many interesting sights in the House during divisions. Members who arrive late may often be seen sliding unobtrusively from seat to seat as the division progresses, until they reach their own desks. Members have even been seen crawling into the House on all fours below the level of the desks while the Clerk is calling the names. Should a member be discovered in this embarrassing position he is not only exposed to a friendly chaffing from both sides of the House but is also not allowed to vote.

Should a member himself wish to change a vote he has cast, the precedents are not entirely clear, but in general it is accepted that once a vote is recorded it cannot be changed. Occasionally a request that a vote be changed has been recorded in the *Journals* or in Hansard

[21]*Ibid.*, Jan. 27, 1881, p. 724; Feb. 20, 1889, p. 247; April 18, 1956, p. 3037.

[22]*Ibid.*, Dec. 10, 1867, p. 84; April 30, 1880, p. 1901; April 19, 1888, p. 941; March 13, 1884, pp. 821–2; March 31, 1924, p. 889.

[23]The question is not normally put in French although on request it is put in both languages. This ruling provides the interesting possibility that a member who heard the question read in French could vote, although he might not understand a word of the motion.

[24]*Ibid.*, Aug. 26, 1891, cols. 4455–62. In 1910 the vote of the Solicitor General was challenged and disallowed, although he had heard most of the question put in French and had sent for a copy of it. *Ibid.*, April 27, 1910, cols. 8167–8.

although the division lists remain unaltered.[25] The House as a whole, however, may change its division lists by unanimous consent or by formal motion.[26]

Pairs

Through all the rules and customs which govern divisions runs the modifying influence of the "pair." This practice is widely followed by members who wish to be absent from the House for either a short or long period of time. Pairs may be arranged by the whips and formally registered or they may be made quite informally by two members.[27] Whichever way they are made the Speaker has consistently refused to accord them any formal recognition, although the House itself considers them binding.[28] The death of a member dissolves a pair.[29] The first pair was recorded less than three weeks after the new Parliament of Canada met in 1867.[30] Since then the custom has become common and at times has reached absurd proportions. On one division in 1946, for instance, no fewer than 124 members were officially paired.[31] It is, of course, most convenient for the Ontario and Quebec members who are thus able to spend long weekends at home. Although the western and maritime members have voiced bitter objections to this weekend exodus nothing is done about it and the pairing system helps to perpetuate it. One interesting feature of the parliaments between 1949 and 1957 was the effect of an overwhelming Government majority on the pairing system. In these years it fell into disuse. With a majority in the House

[25]*Journals*, June 1, 1872, p. 195; *Debates*, March 31, 1924, p. 889; July 1, 1924, pp. 3890–1.

[26]*Debates*, March 19, 1890, cols. 2227–8; March 26, 1930, p. 962.

[27]In 1882 one member objected to a statement that he was paired and stated that it was not in the "pairs book." *Ibid.*, April 5, 1882, p. 779. But note the statement of Mr. C. G. Power: "I am paired in a species of gentlemen's agreement with the honourable member for East Hamilton. I consider that the agreement I made with the honourable member for East Hamilton concerns myself and him alone and nobody else." *Ibid.*, Feb. 19, 1929, p. 266.

[28]Before 1927, when members could be compelled to vote, the House accepted a pair as an excuse for not voting, although Speakers often noted that such arrangements were not recognized by the rules.

[29]On May 9, 1890, two members agreed to a sessional pair; one of them died three days later, and on May 13 the other voted in the House. *Debates*, May 13, 1890, col. 4835.

[30]*Ibid.*, Dec. 10, 1867, p. 86.

[31]*Ibid.*, May 24, 1946, pp. 1874–5. On this division only ninety-three members voted in the House. The remaining twenty-eight may have abstained or may have arranged unofficial pairs.

of nearly a hundred members the Government did not need to consider its safety very closely, and as a result there was a marked absence of announced pairs, although absenteeism remained high.[32]

The use of the pair has necessitated the development of an extensive code of procedure to cover the practice. Pairs may be noted in the House immediately after the result of a division has been announced by the Speaker. Any member who wishes may stand in his place and state the way he would have voted had he not been so restricted.[33] Any part of this announcement may be omitted by the member if he so wishes. There is also no certainty about the questions covered by pairs. Presumably the area covered depends partly on individual arrangements, but the definition of one private member would probably be acceptable to most of the House: his pair was "to count upon any matter intro-duced by the Government or any member on its behalf or upon any matter introduced by the Opposition or any member on its behalf."[34] Pairs, therefore, are not normally valid on votes on private and public bills, or on private members' motions. They are also not valid in com-mittees and only intermittently in Committee of the Whole.[35]

Pairs depend entirely on the honesty of the members involved. The Speaker makes no effort to enforce the custom: he can only ask a member if he wishes to vote, and the decision of the member is final.[36] A vote inadvertently cast, which breaks a pair, cannot be rescinded except with the unanimous consent of the House,[37] which has been granted only a few times and refused at others.[38] The most notable

[32]The result of this carelessness was demonstrated on one occasion in the session of 1957 when on a surprise vote on Monday morning the Government escaped defeat by a mere eleven votes although it had a majority in the House of nearly a hundred.

[33]This announcement may even be made the vehicle for propaganda as in the case of Mr. Stewart who in a vote under closure announced that he was paired "with Madame Defarge who presided at the guillotine" (*Debates*, May 24, 1956, p. 4286) or Mr. Dufresne who stated "I did not vote. My pair was absent from the House. I was paired with Democracy." (*Ibid.*, June 5, 1956, p. 4690.)

[34]*Ibid.*, Feb. 8, 1926, p. 811.

[35]The sessional pair of the Prime Minister and the Leader of the Opposition in 1932 covered Committee of the Whole as well as the House (*ibid.*, Feb. 22, 1932, p. 385). But note the Chairman's statement in 1917 (*ibid.*, July 19, 1917, p. 3574) and the objection of members to the practice of announcing pairs in committee (*ibid.*, March 8, 1935, p. 1541).

[36]*Ibid.*, May 9, 1887, p. 358; Sept. 23, 1896, cols. 1849–50.

[37]*Ibid.*, May 4, 1934, p. 2806.

[38]Granted: *ibid.*, May 18, 1888, p. 1548; Feb. 10, 1890, col. 399; Dec. 6, 1909, col. 1098; April 17, 1916, p. 2954, etc. Refused: *ibid.*, May 10, 1887, p. 360; March 13, 1912, cols. 4983–4; Sept. 10, 1917, p. 5566; April 19, 1918, p. 964, etc.

example of a broken pair is that of Mr. Bird in 1926;[39] his vote in an important division defeated the Government—the only occasion in Canadian Parliamentary history when a Government has dissolved the House as a result of a defeat on the floor. To prevent embarrassing mistakes the whips keep a close watch over pairs during divisions, and should a pair be broken, they try to make some arrangement to correct the mistake. The whip himself may sacrifice his vote to even the score or he may allow another member to break a pair so that the result will be unaltered.[40]

Personal Pecuniary Interest

Standing Order 11 reads "No member is entitled to vote upon any question in which he has a direct pecuniary interest, and the vote of any member so interested will be disallowed." This rule has remained as passed in 1867 and expresses the opposition of the House to members' participating in divisions in which they have a personal pecuniary interest. The intricacies of this rule have been derived largely from British practice. The Canadian House has shown little interest in the question and few decisions have been made.[41]

There is no doubt that the interest that is objected to must be strictly personal and not an interest which is shared by the rest of the country, otherwise few items of Government policy would be unaffected. Western farmers vote to guarantee bank loans to themselves, eastern manufacturers vote themselves protective tariffs, and all members vote for increased pay for parliamentarians. But the interest of a member in a bill on which he has acted for a fee is definitely covered by the rule. And the vote of a member who acted as counsel for a company involved in a private bill has been questioned and not allowed.[42]

When doubt arises over the interest of a member, several courses are open. Should he himself acknowledge the interest, he may ask that he be excused by the House,[43] and if his vote is cast, it may be withdrawn.[44] A formal challenge of a vote by another member of the House must be

[39]*Ibid.*, July 1, 1926, p. 5311.

[40]*Ibid.*, May 9, 1887, p. 359; May 31, 1926, p. 3915.

[41]The principles cited by Bourinot are largely copied from May's *Parliamentary Practice* and are backed only by British precedents. Sir John G. Bourinot, *Parliamentary Procedure and Practice in the Dominion of Canada* (4th ed., Toronto, 1916), pp. 385–90.

[42]*Debates*, March 14, 1884, p. 857.

[43]*Ibid.*, Feb. 20, 1884, p. 454; May 3, 1886, p. 1011; Feb. 11, 1890, col. 460.

[44]*Ibid.*, April 29, 1889, pp. 1653–4.

done by a substantive motion that the vote be struck off the division list. This procedure was established in Canada in 1900 when the votes of three members were challenged. At that time the Speaker ruled that he himself had no authority to alter the division lists, and that the only remedy was in the hands of the House: any member could make a motion to disallow a vote, the accused member should be heard, and the House could make its decision.[45] This practice is presumably now the accepted one, although it has never been used, and, indeed, on the one occasion on which action of this sort was threatened, serious doubts were cast on the whole procedure. In 1956 a member of the House challenged the vote of another member on second reading of a Government bill. He stated his case and concluded by saying that he had a motion which he would move at the appropriate time. The member who was challenged denied the interest claimed. Feeling in the House was quite firmly against taking any action. The Leader of the Opposition protested that this method gave little or no opportunity for the House to evaluate the charges and suggested that the matter be referred to the Committee on Privileges and Elections. Another member noted that all the precedents referred only to private bills and suggested that similar action on a Government bill should not be taken hastily.[46] The matter was dropped by consent, and even the request of the accused member that the question be referred to the Committee on Privileges was insufficient to revive it.[47]

Improvements

Although divisions are basic to the procedure of the House, and much conflicting practice has grown up around them, the House has shown little interest in any proposals to alter the rules or customs relating to them. Members seem content with the leisurely and rather tiresome methods which have been in use since 1867. As we have seen, suggestions to make voting compulsory have not been popular and certainly none of the arguments advanced by its supporters have much validity. In addition, any move to compulsory voting runs directly contrary to the spirit of pairing which is obviously popular with the House.

Other suggestions have been made which would reduce the time occupied by divisions. This is a laudable aim, but one difficult to

[45]*Ibid.*, July 10, 1900, cols. 9688–9.
[46]*Ibid.*, May 22, 1956, pp. 4240–6.
[47]*Ibid.*, May 23, 1956, p. 4250.

achieve. One obvious improvement would be to limit by standing order the ringing of the division bells. Today they rarely ring for less than ten minutes and often for longer, so that few divisions can be completed in less than thirty minutes. In contrast, members at Westminster have six minutes to reach the lobbies and the whole division is completed in ten.[48] Six minutes would be too stringent an allowance for Canadian members, for they all have offices and are likely to be in them at the far end of the building, but an outer limit of perhaps ten minutes could be allowed to gather them in the Chamber.

If nothing else, this change would eliminate the present undesirable system by which the whips of the two major parties decide the length of time the bells will ring. The obvious possibility of abuse of this power was clearly demonstrated in the 1957 session. On one occasion the two whips were voting on the same side of the question and cut the ringing time to only two or three minutes, with the result that several members were unable to reach the House in time to vote.[49] On at least one other occasion a surprise division on a Monday morning caught the Government without a majority in the House: the Government whip kept the bells ringing for nearly twenty minutes while a majority was found.[50]

Little can be done to speed the actual voting; American systems of registering votes by machine have been examined and rejected. And in any case it is only at times of extreme stress that the problem becomes acute. When necessary, a division can be extended to remarkable length by having a member rise to be counted only at the last possible minute as the Clerk calling the names is about to pass on to the next member, but the practice is so unusual that it is of little importance. In practice divisions in a normal session are uncommon enough that the few extra minutes spent voting in each one does not cause even an unreasonable waste of time. The attitude of recent committees, which have not recommended any change in the method of taking divisions, is likely to be continued in the future, and this procedure of the Canadian House will be perpetuated in its present distinctive form.

[48]E. Taylor, *The House of Commons at Work* (Harmondsworth, 1951), p. 115.

[49]*Debates*, March 19, 1957, p. 2481.

[50]Many similar stories are told of division bells ringing for even longer periods while members were roused from their beds, taken off trains, or brought in from local hockey games. See W. G. Weir, "Minding Parliament's Business," *Queen's Quarterly*, Winter 1957, pp. 503–8.

COMMITTEES

11

THE HOUSE OF COMMONS OF CANADA EMPLOYS five recognizable types of committee. They are committees of the Whole House, standing committees, special committees, sessional committees, and joint committees. The distinctions between these are often blurred by the intermingling of their functions but a division may be made by an examination of their method of appointment, their life span, and their personnel. Among them, these committees legislate, investigate, administer, and to a limited degree control. Few of them are recognizable to one familiar with British procedure, and the committee system as a whole provides an interesting and distinctively Canadian flavour to the Canadian legislative system.

The three committees of the Whole House are the most important by far. They are also the only group of the five whose composition and functions closely follow those of their British counterparts. As Committee of the Whole the House debates the resolutions which precede money bills, and also the details of bills after second reading. This committee may also be used to consider a few minor items of business such as reports from committees appointed to revise the rules. As Committee of Supply the House is concerned with departmental estimates. The Government's proposed expenditures for the coming year are discussed item by item and are finally passed after lengthy debate. Committee of Ways and Means is used to consider the raising of money required to finance the nation's business in the next year. It also approves the payment of such amounts as are made necessary by grants voted in Committee of Supply.[1]

[1]Committee of Supply and Committee of Ways and Means are discussed in detail in the next chapter.

The standing committees of the House are appointed each session under the authority of the standing orders. They remain in existence until prorogation and may be called on to perform any function. They consider bills and estimates and occasionally conduct investigations. Special committees, as their name suggests, perform merely *ad hoc* functions. They are appointed to do a specific job and cease to exist when they present their final reports to the House. There has been a tendency in Canada to appoint special committees on certain subjects for a number of sessions, and these sessional committees, which are recognized by custom and not by rule, have a greater degree of permanence than special committees although they may not be set up every session. Of all the varieties of committees, the joint committees of the House and the Senate are the least important. There are three joint standing committees which are chiefly administrative, and other joint committees are set up periodically to consider matters of general interest but of little urgency.[2]

Standing Committees

The appointment of standing committees has not always been governed by the standing orders of the House. For nearly forty years, standing committees were established by a separate motion each year. The Commons passed a motion which named its committees and gave them power to call witnesses and report from time to time. It then passed another motion to set up a striking committee to prepare lists of members to serve on the committees previously established. This striking committee performed only nominal duties and was able to present its report almost immediately, because then, as now, the lists were actually prepared by the party whips, and the striking committee merely ratified their decisions. The House accepted the report without question and the standing committees of the House were formed.

The House of Commons has always had specialized committees. The first list contained the following names of standing committees: Banking and Commerce; Contingencies; Expiring Laws; Immigration and Colonization; Miscellaneous Private Bills; Printing; Privileges and Elections; Public Accounts; Railways, Canals and Telegraph Lines; and Standing Orders. The Immigration Committee became the Com-

[2]These joint committees must be distinguished from the occasional conferences used to settle differences between the two Houses. For these see chap. 13, p. 236.

mittee on Agriculture and Colonization in 1887, and the Committee on Contingencies became separated from the standing committees and became the Committee on Internal Economy established under statute,[3] but the rest of the committees were appointed year after year.

The revision of the rules in 1906 brought a change in the method of setting up the committees. For the first time the names of the committees of the House ceased to depend on practice or the whims of the House, and were established under the standing orders. The striking committee was ordered to report "with all convenient speed" lists of members to compose the standing committees which were named. The new rule made virtually no change in practice but merely established on a permanent footing which committees were to be set up each year.[4]

The list of committees has not remained constant. There has been a continuous pressure over the years for the establishment of new ones. In 1909 the Government accepted suggestions from the Opposition and set up three new committees, on Marine and Fisheries, Mines and Minerals, and Forests, Waterways and Waterpower. Fifteen years later the Government again submitted to Opposition demands and added a Standing Committee on Industrial and International Relations and at the same time the Committee on Forests, Waterways and Waterpower was amalgamated with the Committee on Mines and Minerals to form the Committee on Mines, Forests and Waters. After the Second World War the House agreed to split the Committee on Industrial and International Relations into two separate committees: the Committee on Industrial Relations and the Committee on External Affairs. The most recent changes were made in 1958 when the House approved the establishment of two new committees: one on Estimates and one on Veterans Affairs.[5] There are now, therefore, seventeen standing committees of the House.[6]

The size of committees and their quorums has always proved to be a problem in the Canadian House. In the early years their size was decided on by the striking committee, which, as has already been

[3]31 Vict., c. 27. Now part of the House of Commons Act, *R.S.C.* (1952), c. 143.
[4]The Committee on Expiring Laws disappeared and provision was made for a Joint Standing Committee on the Library.
[5]*Debates*, Feb. 19, 1909, cols. 1319–20; March 27, 1924, p. 729; Sept. 18, 1945, p. 52; May 30, 1958, pp. 679–703.
[6]The standing committees of the House now are: Agriculture and Colonization; Banking and Commerce; Debates; Estimates; External Affairs; Industrial Relations; Library (Joint); Marine and Fisheries; Mines, Forests and Waters; Miscellaneous Private Bills; Printing (Joint); Privileges and Elections; Public Accounts; Railways, Canals and Telegraph Lines; Restaurant (Joint); Standing Orders; Veterans Affairs.

mentioned, took its cue from the party whips. In general the committees were large, ranging, for instance in 1872, from twenty-four members to fifty-eight. No quorums, in the usual sense of the word, were established: according to the rules, a majority constituted a quorum.[7] The size of the committees rose steadily, and five years later, although the smallest committee remained at twenty-four, the largest had grown to ninety-nine. By that time the striking committee was suggesting reduced quorums for some committees in its report to the House, but apparently without a consistent policy: a committee of sixty was given a quorum of seven, while a committee of fifty-one was given a quorum of nine. Other committees were left to work with the majority quorum provided in the standing orders.

The trend continued year by year. By 1887 two committees had over a hundred members and one of them had reached 147. Their quorums remained at the same small numbers first recommended by the striking committee ten years before, although these were by now absurdly small in relation to the new size of the committees. Those few committees which were left by the striking committee with the relatively large quorums required under the rules solved their problems anew each year and returned regularly to the House for a reduction: in 1895, for instance, the Committee on Railways, Canals and Telegraph Lines applied to have its quorum reduced from eighty-four to twenty-five as it found it impossible to sit.[8] Although the revision of 1906 improved the committees to some extent, it did nothing to control their size. In the session after the revision, one committee reached nearly 200 members and two others had passed 125. Even this size combined with a small quorum did not mean that the committees could meet. In 1911 one committee of 134 members had to ask the House to cut its quorum from twenty-one to eleven.[9]

The session of 1910–11 marked the peak in the size of committees, and in the next session the Prime Minister suggested that the numbers on standing committees could be reduced.[10] The striking committee obligingly reported a noticeably smaller number of names that year, and for nearly fifteen years the committees remained at this reduced size. In 1925 the question of size arose again. A private member moved that the numbers on committees be reduced to promote efficiency.[11]

[7]1867 Rule 80. [8]*Debates*, June 28, 1895, cols. 3545–56.
[9]*Ibid.*, Feb. 15, 1911, cols. 3599–605.
[10]*Ibid.*, Nov. 16, 1911, cols. 10–11.
[11]*Ibid.*, March 11, 1925, pp. 1034–41.

His motion was referred to the revision committee which was set up in the same session, and it recommended drastic reductions, pointing out that the House had always considered fifteen to be the maximum size of a special committee,[12] and that thirty should be an adequate maximum for a standing committee. It suggested also that the committees which had no routine work to do should not be appointed until a bill appeared to go before them.

The revision of 1927 achieved some of these reforms. The size of standing committees and their quorums were written into the rules. The size was decreased and the quorums raised. The effect of the new rule was to cut the committees roughly in half. Agriculture and Colonization remained one of the largest, with sixty members, but the revision committee agreed that it dealt mostly with non-controversial matters and that a large membership was suitable. The three committees which handled most of the private bills were also left with a large membership as regular attendance was not expected or necessary. The remainder of the committees were reduced to a membership of thirty-five or less. The standing committees of the House have remained at this size to the present day. Members and committees have suggested at various times that they should be reduced in size still further, but until some general change in policy is effected which will give the standing committees a new part to play in the procedure of the House any major revision is pointless.

Membership on the standing committees has always been allocated informally to the various parties in proportion to their membership in the House, and a Government majority on every committee is guaranteed by the fact that the striking committee which prepares the lists of members to serve consists generally of two ministers, the chief Government whip, and only two representatives of the opposition parties.[13] Within the parties there is an attempt to preserve sectional representation also. The attempt is futile, of course, in a party with only a small number of members, but the Government and major opposition parties generally succeed in their efforts. In some of the standing committees an effort is also made to appoint members who have an interest in the problems to be studied. Thus the Agriculture Committee in a normal

[12]The size of special committees has always been limited to fifteen under the standing orders: 1867 Rule 79 and S.O. 67 (1).

[13]In 1926 and 1957 the Government did not have a majority in the House, so it had only a minority representation on the striking committee in those years and was therefore given only a minority in proportion to its House membership on the standing committees.

session has a large proportion of western members while Marine and Fisheries has many representatives from both the east and the west coast.

The chairmen of all Canadian standing committees are Government appointments. The early practice was to have the committees meet soon after their establishment to elect their own chairman. The election, however, was not left to chance or to the committee itself. A letter from the Minister of Finance to the Prime Minister in 1906 points up the practice well.[14] Fielding began by noting that the two committees which were "usually organized by the Minister of Finance" were to meet in a few days' time and asked the Prime Minister to arrange that "in the case of each committee one of the Ministers on the committee attends and moves the appointment of the Chairman." He proceeded to discuss the possible nominations and made his own suggestions.

This practice died out and a new one took its place. Soon after the striking committee had reported to the House, a notice was circulated to all the members of the House over the signature of the Chief Clerk of Committees which announced the meeting of an "organizational committee" to elect chairmen for the standing committees. Only a small proportion of the members attended the meeting, and virtually no members of the opposition. By agreement and tradition the post of chairman of the organizational committee fell to the chief Government whip who called for nominations for chairmen of the standing committees. Generally only one name was suggested for each and the election was a mere formality. Humorous alternative nominations were occasionally made: one minister who had recently been in trouble over his improper amendments to Hansard was nominated as chairman of the committee to supervise the publication of the *Debates*, and even opposition members were sometimes nominated for the posts. But these nominations were never taken seriously and often not even a vote was taken on them.

It was admitted by all that the organizational committee had no legal existence and the mass election of chairmen was merely a device to save time and trouble. The whole procedure was informal. Generally motions were seconded (it was accepted that the mover and seconder must be members of the committee concerned) and the committee voted if, as occasionally happened, another nomination was made. The nominations were approved by the Government but a pretence was maintained and the actual nominations were made by various members of the committees themselves. The list was, however,

[14]Fielding to Laurier, March 17, 1906, P.A.C., Laurier Papers, pp. 108292–3.

known to many in advance and the elections provided no surprises.[15] The standing committees themselves generally accepted the conclusions of this meeting without question and the chairman at the first meeting of his committee thanked the committee for his election.[16]

This rather quaint tradition has given way in recent years to a reversion to the old method. The general meeting for the election of chairmen has been abandoned and the House now allows each committee to elect its own presiding officer at its first meeting. It is well to remember, of course, that the Government has a majority on every committee so that the final result is no different. The Government nominee is still elected, but the controlling hand is a little less obvious.[17]

Special Committees

The special committees of the House are similar in appearance to the standing committees. They differ chiefly in that they are appointed for one specific purpose and have no existence after they make their final report. They are appointed by motion in the House, elect their chairmen, consider bills or investigate specific problems, report to the House, and disappear. They have been widely used in Canada as investigatory bodies for non-controversial subjects. Such matters as the work of the Federal District Commission, veterans' legislation and, of course, House of Commons procedure all go to such committees.

The rule, Standing Order 67, which regulated the appointment of special committees in 1867 remains much the same today. No special committee may have more than fifteen members, and leave to exceed this number may only be requested after notice, but in practice the House regularly makes exceptions to this rule and appoints special committees of a larger size. A majority of the members of the committee are necessary for a quorum unless the House has otherwise ordered, but the quorum is usually reduced for committees that have more than fifteen members. Two changes have been made since 1867. In 1955 the House removed from the rule a clause which stipulated that no

[15]The chairman of the meeting was even known to correct an erroneous nomination which a member made by mistake.

[16]Committees have refused to accept the election of a chairman in this way. Some members of the Public Accounts Committee in 1951 refused to recognize the chairman elected by this meeting and went through the formality of electing him themselves.

[17]In the case of the Public Accounts Committee where an Opposition member is now elected to the chair, presumably the Government and Opposition reach agreement on a satisfactory candidate before the committee meets.

member who declared himself against the principle of the bill or other matter committed should be eligible for appointment to the committee. The other amendment made in 1927 was only slightly more important. The rule in 1867 had provided that a member who moved for the appointment of a committee could name its members unless five members of the House objected, and that in such an eventuality the House itself would nominate the committee. The Clerk called the names of all the members alphabetically and each nominated one person to serve; those with the greatest number of votes were elected. This curious method of appointment was used only three times,[18] and the House abolished it in 1927.

Once a special committee is established, its procedure and practice follow closely those of the standing committees. Sectional and professional representation is usually to be found, particularly on a committee such as that on Veterans Affairs; no party would think of nominating anyone but a veteran to this committee. The chairman is elected by the committee itself, but is always acceptable to the Government.

Sessional Committees

The sessional committee is a development of the special committee: it is a special committee which is appointed over a series of years. It may be a committee which is appointed every year like the Committee on Railways and Shipping. More likely it is a committee which is appointed with only a fair degree of regularity and comes to occupy a recognized place in the committee organization, such as the Committee on Broadcasting. The curious thing about the term "sessional committee," however, is that the House uses it to apply only to the Committee on Railways and Shipping; other committees which are appointed every year or fairly regularly over a period of years are recognized as being sessional committees, but they are still referred to as special committees.

There is no difference in the establishment or procedure of these committees from that of special committees except that their personnel is apt to be more stable. After a few sessions a sessional committee is likely to have a high proportion of members who are conversant with the problems which are to be studied. There is no reason why these sessional committees should not become standing committees in any major reorganization of the committee system.

[18]*Journals*, April 8, 1873, p. 137; March 20, 1876, pp. 173–4; March 9, 1877, p. 118.

Joint Committees

A joint committee may be either a standing committee or a special committee. Printing has always been considered to be a matter of common interest for the two chambers and a joint standing committee on the subject has existed since Confederation. The administration of the Library of Parliament has also been entrusted for many years to a joint standing committee. More recently, the parliamentary restaurant has come under the supervision of a joint standing committee although it is a committee not authorized by the standing orders.

The same striking committee which nominates members to the standing committees of the House also nominates Commons members to the joint standing committees. The House approves the nominations and sends a message to the Senate to make known its decision. One limit has been placed on the numbers appointed. Under Standing Order 65 (2) adopted in 1927 the number of members and senators on any joint committee must always be in proportion to the size of the two Houses, but this rule is regularly ignored. The Speaker of the House serves on both the library and the restaurant committees, but does so in the guise of an administrator; where the internal affairs of the House are concerned he ranks as a Minister, and these committees are nominally appointed to assist him in his administration.

Interesting procedural problems are raised by the appointment of joint committees. Two chairmen are elected and a system of double quorums is necessary. The procedure is confusing, but because joint committees are rarely used for important business the need for clarification is not continually before the House and so has not been regarded as urgent. Indeed, the need for reform does not seem to have touched the joint standing committees which have carried on without trouble since Confederation. The special joint committees have not been so satisfied and the Special Joint Committee on Capital and Corporal Punishment and Lotteries pointed out in its final report that "the rules, standing orders, procedures and practices of both Houses relating to Special Joint Committees are in need of re-examination and revision to effect greater efficiency, uniformity and clarity."[19]

Powers of Committees

The work of committees is varied, and covers widely divergent fields. But whatever their objects, their life span, or their personnel, all com-

[19]*Ibid.*, July 31, 1956, p. 970.

mittees have one thing in common: they cannot consider any matter until it has been referred to them by the House. There is no committee of the Canadian House, even a standing committee, which has anything but a delegated power. When the House sets up standing committees at the beginning of the session it empowers them at the same time "to examine and inquire into all such matters and things as may be referred to them by the House and to report from time to time their observations and opinions thereon, with power to send for persons, papers and records." However, this latter power, contrary to general belief, is not inherent in any standing committee and is not granted by the rules:[20] it is voted anew at the beginning of each session. The right to call for witnesses and documents is not always given to special committees, although usually it is.[21]

The Work of Committees

The House refers matters to a committee by motion. In the case of a special committee the same motion usually establishes the committee as well. The motion need not name the committee, but it establishes it, gives its numbers and quorum, and (usually) empowers it to call for persons, papers, and records. At this stage a member may move an instruction to the committee should he consider it desirable. The purpose of such an instruction is to give the committee the power to do something which otherwise it would be unable to do. Such instructions are rare as the committees have ample powers to take all but the most extraordinary action.

When a committee has some item of business referred to it, its chairman arranges the first meeting; it is undoubtedly within the power of any member to ask that a committee meet, but the chairman generally takes the initiative. Should there be a number of items to be considered (the Standing Committee on Miscellaneous Private Bills, for instance, may have fifty or a hundred private bills to consider at one time) the clerk of the committee has an agenda printed. The committee meets, and if its work is to extend over a prolonged period of time, authorizes the chairman to set up an unofficial steering committee to assist him in organizing the programme, or he may establish one on his own initiative,

[20]Despite the statement by the Leader of the Opposition in 1956 that "under the rules of this House every standing committee has the right and power to call for the attendance of witnesses and the production of papers and documents." *Debates*, Feb. 29, 1956, p. 1675.

[21]The outstanding exception in recent years was the Special Committee on Estimates. The omission of this power was a matter of deliberate Government policy.

reporting the fact to the full committee at its next meeting. Such a subcommittee represents all parties and is a great help in obtaining advice on the order of business and the length of discussion which will take place. As a general rule, the committee does little real work at its first meeting, merely passing motions to ask the House for leave to reduce i⁺s quorum, to sit while the House is sitting, and to print the minutes of proceedings and evidence. Many committees print verbatim reports of their proceedings. They may do so only with the consent of the House, although permission is never, in practice, refused. These reports are almost invariably printed when evidence is taken on any bill or public matter referred to a committee by the Government. Proceedings on private bills are printed only rarely.

After all these requests have been reported to the House, which passes them, the committee is ready to begin its work. The work of most committees is carried on in an informal and reasonably efficient manner. The clauses of a bill are called in order and amendments are considered as they are made. However, if the committee is to hear evidence on a bill, it hears most of the witnesses before it undertakes this detailed consideration, for the committee members will have read the bill and will be reasonably conversant with its main provisions; besides, they can ask questions later when the bill is considered in detail. Proceedings on a private bill are slightly different; the quasi-judicial nature of the investigation makes it necessary to prove the preamble of the bill first, and then consider the clauses one by one.

By custom the rules of the House are followed in committee where applicable, but by general consent the procedure is kept simple. Formal motions are rarely made unless there is a sharp difference of opinion; and an effort is made to minimize party distinctions. Press and public are admitted except while the committee prepares its report. Since most of the meetings are dull, however, normally no press coverage is given and most of the members attend to the work of the committee and do not speak for publicity. Occasionally some matter which the House has referred to a committee arouses public opinion, generally because of the heat raised in the committee itself. At such times there is a distinct tendency for members to make political speeches at every opportunity and to abandon the search for truth in the quest for political advancement.[22]

[22]Note for example the investigation in 1957 by the Agriculture Committee into alleged over-compensation for diseased sheep. This potentially dull subject was leavened by long and bitter altercations between the Minister of Agriculture and various opposition members. At one point the Minister even offered to fight one of his leading critics who had called him a liar. Standing Committee on Agriculture and Colonization, 1957, *Minutes of Proceedings and Evidence*, p. 266.

THE CHAIRMAN

The chairman has the authority to maintain order; and though his rulings may be appealed to the committee, they cannot be appealed to the House.[23] His position in committee is ambiguous, and its ambiguity arises from his own attempts to participate. He is a purely political appointment, often an older member of the Government party who does not have the qualifications to become a Minister or Parliamentary Secretary.[24] Thus a committee may find its presiding officer arguing for the Government against the members of the committee.[25] The chairman also keeps a close watch over the Government majority on the committee and sends out to the whip's office should his supporters seem weak in numbers. The result is, of course, that the chairman neither receives nor expects any degree of respect from the committee over which he presides, and only the greatest measure of co-operation enables the committee to accomplish its work with any degree of harmony.

WITNESSES

As we have seen, most committees are granted the power to summon witnesses. A member of the committee must first file a statement with the chairman that the evidence is important (S.O. 69 (1)), and the witness is then summoned by order of the chairman. In practice an individual whose evidence is desired is merely invited to attend. A refusal to do so is met by the more formal order to attend. Reasonable expenses will be paid to those from outside Ottawa. Should the evidence of a senator be required, the House as a whole must send a message to the Senate to ask that body to permit one of its members to appear. Permission is normally granted and the senator is given leave to appear "if he thinks fit." Should an officer of the Senate be required, the House sends a similar message, but when permission to appear is granted his attendance is obligatory. A member of the House is invited to appear; he is not summoned.

A stranger who refuses to appear in response to the summons of a committee or who refuses to answer questions in a committee is guilty of a contempt, and the House will take action when the matter is reported to it.[26] There have been several cases in Canada which

[23]*Journals*, July 24, 1956, pp. 920–1.
[24]The exception is the chairman of the Public Accounts Committee: he is now a member of the Opposition. This is a recent change and may not be permanent.
[25]For instance, the chairman of one committee when ruling on a point of order: "I believe that I can speak for the Liberal Party. . . ." Standing Committee on Banking and Commerce, 1956, *Minutes of Proceedings and Evidence*, p. 735.
[26]*Supra*, chap. 3. It is also undoubtedly a breach of privilege for any person to intimidate a witness or prevent him from appearing. There is no example of this happening in Canada.

illustrate this. Twice in 1891 the House was called on to deal with recalcitrant witnesses.[27] The first witness had refused to deliver up his account books to the Public Accounts Committee. He restated his objections to doing so at the Bar of the House, but offered to do so should the House insist. The House insisted and the witness was discharged. Later in the same session the House summoned a witness to the Bar when he refused to appear before a committee. The Speaker issued a warrant for his arrest, but the witness had left Ottawa for an unknown destination. Three years later two more witnesses failed to appear when summoned. A summons to appear at the Bar was also ignored and the two were arrested and brought before the House. They gave a long and complicated explanation for their actions, an abject apology, and a promise of better conduct in future, and were released.[28]

In 1906 a committee attempted to follow this same course. A witness refused to answer questions in committee and a motion was made to summon him to the Bar of the House. The Prime Minister defended the culprit in the House and suggested that committees should avoid prying into private affairs whenever possible.[29] Seven years later, however, the House decided that its investigation into private affairs was warranted and imprisoned a witness who persisted in a refusal to answer.[30]

Committees have the right under statute to take evidence on oath. This was first authorized in an act passed in 1868[31] but the power was limited to committees set up to examine private bills. The committee which was set up to investigate the Pacific Scandal in 1873 recommended that witnesses in that inquiry should also be sworn, and Parliament extended the power to swear witnesses to all committees.[32] That act was disallowed, but following the passage of the Parliament of Canada Act of 1875, Parliament re-enacted the Oaths Act in its previous form.[33] One limit remained on the power given to a committee: before it could administer an oath to a witness, it was forced to report its wishes to the House and was then granted the power to do so. The House, therefore, and not the committee, authorized the administration of the oath. Parliament removed this limitation in 1894 when the Parliamentary Witnesses Oaths Act permitted any committee to administer an oath on its own responsibility.[34] The provisions of this act may be found today in the Senate and House of Commons Act.[35] A large num-

[27]*Debates*, June 16, 1891, cols. 895 ff.; Sept. 1, 1891, cols. 4747–8.
[28]*Ibid.*, June 13, 1894, cols. 4189–92.
[29]*Ibid.*, June 4, 1906, cols. 4451–534.
[30]*Ibid.*, Feb. 18, 1913, col. 3451.
[31]31 Vict., c. 24.
[32]36 Vict., c. 1.   [33]39 Vict., c. 7.
[34]57–58 Vict., c. 16.   [35]*R.S.C.* (1952), c. 249.

ber of witnesses have been examined on oath in committees. The practice today, however, has fallen into disuse, and it is now rare for such action to be taken except when hearing evidence on divorce bills.

Every committee of the House that is given the power to summon witnesses also has the concurrent power to force a reply. Witnesses are as fully covered by parliamentary privilege in committee as they are at the Bar of the House, and no excuse of self-incrimination can be validly advanced. Should the committee require an answer, an answer must be given, and a persistent refusal to comply is reported to the House for action.[36]

COMMITTEE REPORTS

When the committee has concluded its investigation it discusses its report *in camera*. The chairman generally drafts a report and submits it to the consideration of the committee, which may, of course, amend it in any way. When a bill is reported without amendment, the report to the House is a simple statement of the fact and does not need the formal approval of the committee. Minority reports are not recognized in Canadian practice. Reports from subcommittees must be presented to the House by the full committee, and it is in the discretion of the full committee whether such a course is desirable. When a committee has received permission to print its evidence, it is customary to table this evidence in the House with the report.

Reports are presented in both languages to the House by the chairman during routine proceedings. Should any further action be necessary, two days' notice must be given of the motion for concurrence. Most committee reports are not passed by the House but by Committee of the Whole, to which even amendments to bills are immediately sent. Reports which ask for unusual rights or privileges must, however, be passed by the House; these include, as already mentioned, the reduction of the quorum of a committee, the right to sit while the House is sitting, and permission to print evidence. On these occasions the House usually waives its formalities and accepts the reports immediately.

It is possible for the House, on the rare occasions when it does debate a committee report, to move to accept it, reject it, hoist it, or refer it back to the committee with the power to amend it, except of course in the case of special committees, which have to be reconstituted by the House before their reports can be referred back. It is not possible to return a report to a committee with instructions to investigate another

[36]The outstanding case is that of R. C. Miller in 1913 who was imprisoned for refusal to answer questions in committee.

subject; such instructions must be moved as a substantive motion.[37] Nor is it possible for the House to amend a committee report. On the other hand, when a report is referred back to a committee, the committee must present a new report; it cannot merely return the original report to the House.[38]

Assessment

The best that can be said of the Canadian committee system is that when it is given legislation to consider, it does the work reasonably well. Little important legislation is dealt with this way. All private bills must be referred to standing committees (S.O. 105), and many non-contentious Government bills are also referred. Major bills, however, on which there is a sharp difference of opinion, are considered only in Committee of the Whole. The pressure on parliamentary time has not yet become great enough to force a major devolution of work to committees, and the pressure from private members on all sides for full debate in Committee of the Whole has not encouraged the Government to take the step voluntarily.

It is necessary for purposes of evaluation to separate the committees which have investigatory roles into two groups. Those in the first group, which have dealt over the years with a wide range of harmless topics, have probably done their work well. Certainly in many instances they have buried their subject as well as any optimistic Government could hope. Those in the second group, which have been set up to examine politically controversial subjects, have been little less than failures. In any inquiry which is even distantly related to the political situation of the day, most members of a committee go to each meeting in a set frame of mind. As long as the Government has a majority a politically correct verdict will be reached, and few, if any, of the participants will be satisfied that a fair hearing has been held. But even here, the committee may have one redeeming feature. In the course of the investigation the opposition has a chance to demonstrate once again the deficiencies of the Government and if the hearings are sufficiently controversial they are reported in the press. For this reason, perhaps, the opposition is generally found demanding the establishment of committees, and the Government in general against it.

There is no real solution to this problem. It is possible to hope for a

[37]*Debates*, May 19, 1943, pp. 2811–12.
[38]*Ibid.*, June 23, 1899, col. 5745.

change of heart in the members themselves but it is probably too much to expect. The opportunities given to members for this type of investigation are few and the rare occasions on which there is a chance to discover some discreditable facts seem irresistible. The opposition is not alone. The Government members form an equally irresponsible group. Led by the chairman they do everything in their power to minimize their leaders' shortcomings. The only real solution, and one that would kill rather than cure, is to remove such controversial investigations from the House and to use the other facilities at the command of the Government to conduct inquiries.

On some occasions the committees of the House may be used to good effect. There are some matters on which there is substantial agreement or on which there is no political capital to be made. Much valuable work, for instance, has been done by the various veterans' affairs committees. At the end of the Second World War they did an excellent job in drafting veterans' legislation. More recently they have had more limited scope but veterans' organizations submit briefs, departmental officials give evidence, and while little may be done at once, the participants disperse happily and some useful information may be procured. Certainly the members of the committee benefit from an increased knowledge of the problems involved.

There has been considerable agitation over a number of years for the expansion of the committee system. Each member who has a particular field of interest is convinced that there should be a standing committee on the subject. The debates on the resolutions which recommend the appointment of such committees reflect the attitude of the House to the whole committee system. There has been a general belief in the opposition that the establishment of a standing committee on any subject will automatically enable that subject to be studied constantly and will allow the opposition to bring pressure to bear on the Government to amend or introduce legislation in these fields. There is no realization of the fact that such a committee could do nothing until some matter was referred to it. The inactivity of many of the existing committees of the House should be sufficient indication. The committees on Mines, Forests and Waters and on Marine and Fisheries, for instance, hardly met in thirty years until revived in 1958 for the examination of estimates.

The opposition concept of standing committees is perhaps responsible for the absence of reform. Certainly it shows a remarkable lack of any realization of the main function of standing committees, which has been and still is the consideration of legislation referred to them by the House. It is most emphatically not the formulation of policy for Parliament. It is not even the defensive function envisaged by one member who wanted a standing committee "for those who cannot defend themselves."[39]

There are many aspects of Canadian committees which might commend themselves to a committee on revision. The chairmen are undoubtedly far too much Government partisans for their own good or the truly effective working of their committees. They also tend to be elderly and inefficient. At the present time this makes no difference as few contentious issues arise in committee which require either an impartial ruling or skilful handling. If the committees are ever to do more important work and if it should ever become necessary to impose some form of limitation of debate in committee, some change will have to be made in the quality of presiding officers. If younger members were to preside over these committees it might even be possible to use the standing committee chairmanships to provide a source of trained personnel for the three senior posts in the House itself.

Other changes would probably be desirable in the committees themselves. There is as little sense of reality in appointing a committee of sixty members as there in having a Committee of the Whole of 265: it is hopeless to expect a committee of such a size to accomplish any useful work. It is true that the largest committees are not really expected to accomplish anything, but under the circumstances one may fairly ask if they are serving any useful purpose. There is little doubt that small committees of fifteen or twenty members would be big enough to represent all parties and all sections of the country, and would be vastly more effective legislative instruments than are the present cumbersome groups. It could even be hoped that the reduction in size would arouse a sense of responsibility in members which has hitherto been lacking and that the problem of keeping a quorum which has been so prevalent might disappear. A reduction in size would also help those small opposition parties that simply do not have enough members to fill all the places allotted to them on the committees. Members of these parties are constantly faced with the unpleasant alternatives of either not going to a number of their committee meetings, or running from one to the other and being perpetually unprepared for any. On the other hand, there is no doubt that a Prime Minister with a large majority welcomes these big committees as a means of occupying the time of his restive back-benchers.

There is also much to be said for the abolition of specialized commit-

[39]*Ibid.*, Feb. 4, 1957, p. 959.

tees. There is no doubt that some members at least feel that they must be appointed to all the committees which affect their constituencies.[40] They may have no interest in any of the bills that are referred, but their political conscience will not allow them to be omitted from the membership. The specialized committee leads also inevitably to a desire on the part of its members to consider and even create policy: their expertise leads them to believe that only they can truly reflect the wishes of the country on any matter. It is possible that a committee of reasonably intelligent amateurs could do as good or better a job. Should a body of expert opinion ever be needed for an unusual matter, the House can appoint a special committee with all the best it has to offer.

The Government could easily work a major reform without a change in the rules by sending more legislation to standing committees. The present method of leaving most important bills in Committee of the Whole does nothing to encourage a sense of importance or responsibility in the committees. The added reluctance of the Government to accept any alterations in such bills as are sent to committee merely contributes to the same feeling. Two changes are necessary. The Government must be willing to accept, or at least to consider seriously, opposition amendments to bills in committee. The opposition at the same time must show itself willing to abandon its attacks on the principle of bills and concentrate its efforts on the improvement or modification of them through amendments in detail. Together these could make the standing committees of the House vastly more important than they are now.

One thing seems certain. The House must soon resolve to study both the functions and composition of committees. It cannot by itself correct all the defects of the system. To correct them all, some action will be necessary by the Government and by the opposition. Success in the attempt will only be achieved by the goodwill and co-operation of all members. Whatever is done, it is to be hoped that some effort will be made to establish for the committees of the House a useful and effective place in the legislative process.

[40]*Ibid.*, March 18, 1927, p. 1346.

THE CONTROL
OF PUBLIC
EXPENDITURE

12

THERE IS NO PART OF PROCEDURE in the Canadian House of Commons which is so universally acknowledged to be inadequate to modern needs as the control of the House over public expenditure.[1] Ideally, Committee of Supply debates at length and finally approves the estimates of expenditure for the coming year (except items which are governed by statute), Committee of Ways and Means debates the Government's budget proposals and votes the money necessary to cover the expenses, and the Auditor General (an officer of Parliament and therefore not a true civil servant) reports on expenditures to Parliament. But this ideal is modified in practice by the inadequacy of Committee of Supply as a forum for debate on detailed expenditures, and the inability of members of the House to perform their scrutinizing functions properly. The ideal is further limited by the lack of proper facilities for consideration of the Auditor General's report and for examination of the way in which the Government has carried out its programme.

Committee of Supply

Modern supply procedure is similar in its broad outlines to that which existed at Confederation, but the details have changed considerably over the years. For the first seven years of the life of the House various formalities were necessary before supply could be voted. The House resolved itself into committee to consider the portion of the Speech from

[1]For a full account of this subject see N. Ward, *The Public Purse* (Toronto, 1962).

the Throne which related to supply. The committee sat and decided that a supply should be granted to Her Majesty. It reported this resolution to the House which then, by resolution, agreed. As a final step the House agreed to resolve itself on a future day into committee to consider the supply to be granted to Her Majesty. It was this final motion which established the Committee of Supply.

The rule was undoubtedly cumbersome and unnecessarily complicated. There was, therefore, almost universal approval in 1874 when the Minister of Finance moved a resolution to change the practice.[2] The temporary alteration of 1874 was made a standing order in 1876 and has remained virtually unaltered since that time.[3] The Committee of Supply is now established by a simple routine motion early in every session under Standing Order 55: "The House shall appoint the Committees of Supply, and Ways and Means, at the commencement of every session, so soon as an address has been agreed to, in answer to His Excellency's speech." However, the new rule changed little of the important practice surrounding the granting of supply. Every time the Government wished to debate estimates it was forced to move a motion which could be, and was, debated, and at interminable length. These debates were held throughout the session on all matters, relevant and irrelevant, and estimates passed slowly. One might wonder for instance what interest the Canadian House of Commons could have in Irish Home Rule. The House did, however, pass a series of resolutions asking Home Rule for Ireland in amendment to a motion for supply in 1882. More normal perhaps was one debate on a supply motion in 1894 which covered the Lake Erie fisheries, the payment of canal employees, cattle transit, freight rates in the Northwest, the Nova Scotia fisheries, and the Pontiac–Pacific Junction Railway.[4] On some occasions members offered amendments which dealt with their grievances. An important point in this connection is that no notice has ever been required for an amendment to a supply motion; a member who suggested in 1908 that two days' notice should be given was attacked from all sides and the motion was lost.[5]

Obviously the opportunities for blocking supply were practically unlimited and occasionally the Opposition used its rights to the full, so in 1913 the Government introduced (along with the closure) a new rule which made its position much easier. Under this new rule, the House

[2]*Debates*, March 31, 1874, pp. 6–7.
[3]*Ibid.*, March 29, 1876, p. 910.
[4]*Ibid.*, April 20, 1882, pp. 1030–3; July 4–5, 1894, cols. 5234–429.
[5]*Ibid.*, Feb. 12, 1908, cols. 2984–8.

could go into Committee of Supply on Thursday and Friday of any week without motion: the order for supply was read and the Speaker left the Chair at once. The only restriction placed on this new power in the hands of the Government was contained in a clause which prevented consideration on any of these days of any department which had not been called on one of the other three days of the week. The Opposition was thus guaranteed a reasonable number of regular supply motions on which to present grievances and the Government was assured that on two days of the weeks the details of the estimates could be reached without delay.

Various questions of interpretation have arisen over this rule. When it was passed, there was, understandably, some fear that the heading "Civil Government" in the estimates might be used to cover all civil departments and that the Government might thus be able to evade the intent of the rule and call only two "departments" each session. The Prime Minister assured the House that each department would have to be called separately, and in practice, this has nearly always been done.[6] (The heading "Civil Government" no longer exists in the estimates. By consent today, however, certain items in the estimates are considered to have been called when the department under whose Minister they come is opened. Thus for instance the Chief Electoral Officer and Public Printing and Stationery are open for discussion when the estimates of the Secretary of State are called.) A few years later the Government tried to open more than one department on a single supply motion, and the Speaker ruled that the Government was entitled to open any number of departments for which it could get consent[7] (a decision which stood until the revision of 1955 made it unnecessary). On each supply motion, therefore, the Government called a certain number of departments by agreement with the opposition. It was not always easy to obtain consent for as many as the Government wished, but a reasonable number of departments could always be called.[8] Nowadays, a fixed number of departments is called on each of the six annual supply motions.

In the years following the First World War small third parties appeared, and one of the practices relating to the granting of supply— the matter of amendments to the motion—proved inadequate under the new conditions. In 1922, the leader of the Progressive party moved a

[6]Ibid., Jan. 30, 1914, pp. 306–7.
[7]Ibid., March 15, 1921, pp. 957–62.
[8]Ibid., April 11, 1951, pp. 1937–8; April 27, 1951, p. 2497; June 11, 1951, p. 3954; April 26, 1954, p. 4114, etc.

sub-amendment to a motion for the Speaker to leave the Chair for the House to go into Committee of Ways and Means. Some members of the House opposed the motion, and the Speaker made a detailed ruling the next day. In this ruling he reviewed the precedents of sixty-five years, and concluded that, although there was no firm rule on the subject, only one amendment could be moved to such a motion.[9] The Progressives brought matters to a head in the next session and moved for the appointment of a committee to examine the possibility of changing the rules to allow a sub-amendment on a motion that the Speaker leave the Chair for Committee of Supply or of Ways and Means.[10] Both major parties attacked the idea. The proposal was pictured as lengthening the session, confusing debate in the House, and putting too much power in the hands of an unscrupulous opposition. None of the arguments advanced against the proposition bear much conviction with them, but the opposition to the motion was too strong and it was defeated.

The committee of revision of 1925 found an answer to all the problems that had seemed so insuperable in 1923, devoting a section of its report to a discussion of a solution. The committee agreed that an extra amendment could be defended on the grounds that the reason for opposing a motion (put forward in the original amendment) might be acceptable to another group only if somewhat modified. The report did, however, emphasize that only one main amendment could be offered, for if the House negatived the amendment the implication was that it approved of the Speaker's leaving the Chair, whereas if it adopted the amendment the implication was that it did not approve. In either case the matter was settled. The committee therefore recommended that only one amendment should be allowed to a motion for the Speaker to leave the Chair, but that the amendment itself could be amended.[11] In 1927 the revision committee followed the same reasoning and the House adopted a new rule, the present Standing Order 45: "Only one amendment and one sub-amendment may be made to a motion for Mr. Speaker to leave the Chair for the House to go into committee of supply or ways and means."

Between 1927 and 1955 the House largely ignored supply procedure. Suggestions were made which would have limited the length of speeches in committee[12] and would have sent more estimates to smaller com-

[9]*Ibid.*, June 6, 1922, pp. 2519–23. The ruling was equally applicable on motions for the Speaker to leave the Chair for Committee of Supply.
[10]*Journals*, March 19, 1923, p. 212.
[11]*Ibid.*, May 29, 1925, p. 358.   [12]*Supra*, chap. 7, pp. 136–7.

mittees. Nothing, however, was accomplished in these years, although both the Government and opposition were dissatisfied. The Government inevitably tried to introduce its departments with a minimum number of supply motions and the opposition consistently complained that pressure was exerted to force estimates through quickly. This conflict led to the amendments made by the revision committee of 1955, which are still in effect.

Under the new rules (S.O. 56) only six motions are made each session for the Speaker to leave the Chair for the House to go into Committee of Supply. We have already seen the use of these in limiting debate[13] but the new rule has one further advantage—it settles the number of departments which can be opened for debate after the Speaker leaves the Chair on each of these occasions. On the first motion six departments are called; on each of the next four motions, three departments; and on the last motion, all the rest. The new rules passed in 1955 have also extended to three the number of days on which the Speaker can leave the Chair without motion in the House to go into Committee of Supply.

Modern supply procedure has, therefore, become more regimented than it was, although the basic principles have remained the same. Each session a formal motion is passed which actually establishes the Committee of Supply in much the same way that any committee is set up. As early as possible in the session the main estimates for the year are received from the Governor General, are tabled in the House by the Minister of Finance, and are formally referred to the committee. From this time on supply procedure divides itself into two dissimilar parts. The first part consists of the six debatable motions for the Speaker to leave the Chair for the House to go into Committee of Supply. These motions are scattered through the session and give the opposition parties a chance to debate general questions of Government policy and individual grievances. The result of these debates is the formal "opening" of departments for discussion in the committee itself. The second part of supply procedure is more important. On three days each week when the House can go into Committee of Supply without a formal motion, the committee debates the details of the estimates—a completely different proceeding from discussion on motions for supply. For the most part debate on these days is concentrated on small items of administration of interest to individual localities, and this debate provides time for the private member to outline the needs of his constituency. There is no limit to the length of time spent on this part of supply and it

[13]*Supra*, chap. 7, pp. 139–43.

comes to an end only when every member is satisfied that he should not speak further and each individual estimate has passed. When all the items have been passed in this way, they are consolidated into a single Appropriation Act which is normally passed through all three readings in a few minutes on the last day of the session.

There has been general agreement that the regular, fixed-length supply motion has been a vast improvement. But the changes made in 1955 did nothing to improve the consideration of estimates in the committee itself. Long debates are still held on early items, whereas later ones are approved with scant attention. There has been little attempt to fix an outside limit on the number of days spent in Committee of Supply, or to organize the time of the committee more effectively, but an effort is being made to provide a workable alternative in the form of an efficient and satisfactory Committee on Estimates. This attempt will be examined later.

Committee of Ways and Means

Committee of Ways and Means has never aroused as much interest as Committee of Supply. The providing of the money necessary to carry on the business of the country has occasionally been the subject of heated debate, but recently there has been no feeling that the procedure used is inadequate to modern needs.

The old practice of the House was more tedious than it is today. For some years after Confederation it was thought necessary for the House to pass a token item in Committee of Supply (generally a non-contentious one such as the vote for the office of Secretary to the Governor General) before moving to go into Ways and Means. This practice did not cease until 1883, though in 1874 the House had agreed to set up Committee of Ways and Means automatically at the beginning of every session. It was in 1927, as we have seen, that the change in the rules relating to amendments to motions for ways and means took place, along with the similar change relating to supply.

There is only one important occasion on which the House debates a motion for Committee of Ways and Means. It is traditional for the Minister of Finance to review the financial condition of the country at least once a year. On a few occasions in the early years after Confederation he made his budget speech in committee although the practice was never consistent. Now the wording of the rules prevents such a course of action: the Minister makes his budget speech on the motion for the Speaker to leave the Chair, and the debate which follows is limited in length to eight days.[14] At all other times the Speaker leaves the Chair without a motion. This change eliminates much of the uncertainty of the session. The Government can now depend on a lengthy, but fixed, debate on its financial proposals.[15] When it is completed, the resolutions which embody the changes proposed in the Income Tax Act, the Tariff Act, and other fund-raising acts are debated in committee for an indefinite time. When the resolutions are passed, the Government introduces amending bills, which proceed through the usual channels which all bills follow.[16]

Committee on Estimates

Agitation for a Committee on Estimates began in Canada nearly thirty-five years before such a committee was established. The question was first raised in the House in a definitive form in 1921 when a member moved to establish a special committee to examine estimates before they were tabled in the House.[17] The House split on the motion, the Government against it and the Opposition for it. The arguments raised were those which were to be heard many times in the future on similar motions: on the one hand, Committee of Supply was inefficient and could not possibly do its job properly; on the other hand, the Government feared a confusion in constitutional responsibility, and pointed out the technical problems which would have to be met. The motion was withdrawn after debate. The objections in this and following years are surprising, as Great Britain had established a satisfactory Estimates Committee in 1912 without any apparent difficulties.

Four years later another member moved a similar motion. The arguments were much the same as in 1921 with two exceptions. First, the supporters of the motion could now point to the Special Committee on Government Railways and Merchant Marine which had been established to examine and report on the activities of one specific part of the public

---

[14]*Supra*, chap. 7, p. 140.

[15]It is occasionally possible for the Government to present financial proposals without a formal budget debate. In the 1957–8 session the Minister of Finance presented limited amendments to two financial bills in this way; this course of action was not popular with the opposition but he was attacked on moral grounds rather than legal.

[16]For the passage of Government bills see chap. 13.

[17]*Debates*, April 18, 1921, p. 2193. A notice of motion in 1869 which called for a similar committee was removed from the Order Paper before it was raised in the House. *Orders of the Day*, May 17, 1869.

service. This committee did, in fact, examine estimates and there was no reason why the examination of regular departmental estimates could not be the same except on a larger scale. Second, the motion of 1925 suggested that standing committees be used to examine the estimates rather than create a special estimates committee. A committee on revision of the rules was sitting at the time and, by consent, the motion was referred to it.[18] The revision committee did not accept the challenge and in its report recommended that the question be reconsidered by another committee at the next session.[19] This was not done. The revision committee of 1927 considered the reference of estimates to committees "too radical" and made no recommendation.[20]

The Government took the initiative for the first time in 1929, when the Prime Minister moved an instruction to the Committee on Standing Orders to consider the question of revising the rules so that estimates could be referred to a committee.[21] The Committee on Standing Orders recommended that the House be empowered to refer estimates to a standing or special committee without removing them from Committee of Supply: the small committee would be able to consider part of the estimates in detail and the rights of Committee of Supply would not be infringed.[22] In the debate on the report, the chairman of the committee explained exactly what the committee had thought. The proposed small committee was to be used to get information of a factual nature, of interest to a limited number of members, and Committee of Supply was still to be used to debate the contentious items of general interest. The opinion of the House was by no means unanimous in support of the suggestion and the debate was adjourned and never revived.

The House went a stage further the next session. Again a private member moved that estimates be considered in smaller committees, and again the arguments of the previous ten years were advanced. The Prime Minister supported the motion, however, and the House passed it.[23] The matter rested there. The House made no attempt to refer estimates to a committee, except those relating to the railways and merchant marine. There were various further attempts over the next eleven years to revive the subject.[24] In 1933 a member suggested a new committee to consider the question yet again, but his resolution died on the Order

[18]*Debates*, Feb. 25, 1925, pp. 521–39.   [19]*Journals*, May 29, 1925, p. 360.
[20]*Debates*, March 22, 1927, p. 1428.
[21]*Ibid.*, Feb. 15, 1929, pp. 147–9. A private member's motion to the same effect was referred to the same committee.
[22]*Ibid.*, Feb. 21, 1929, p. 307.
[23]*Ibid.*, March 12, 1930, p. 531.
[24]*Ibid.*, Feb. 15, 1933, pp. 2123–47; June 23, 1936, pp. 4124–5.

Paper. Near the end of the 1936 session the C.C.F. questioned the Government on the matter and the Prime Minister advised postponing the question for the time.

'The Second World War revived interest in the question because increasingly large sums of money were being spent every year and little check could be kept. The House complained often of this situation and requests were made for more efficient investigation of estimates. In 1944, for the first time, a committee of the House, after careful consideration, recommended that estimates be not sent to committees. The revision committee reported that such a suggestion struck "at the root of Ministerial responsibility" and restricted criticism of the Government on the floor of the House. It conceded that some estimates could be sent to smaller groups to study detail, but emphasized that such action should be exceptional. The report was at least a triumph for the independence of the committee, for when the Prime Minister discussed it in the House he disagreed strongly with the views expressed in it on this point. He argued that the reference of estimates to committees was not a denial of ministerial responsibility and expressed disappointment that the committee had not seen fit to endorse such references.[25]

The years after the war brought an increased interest in the problem. Government expenditures remained high and no valid reasons could be advanced for preventing a closer scrutiny by the House. One member advanced the novel proposition that estimates should all be considered by a committee first and that they should then be consolidated into one item so that the House could debate all supply together. Shortly thereafter, the Leader of the Opposition took a more conventional stand and merely suggested that all estimates be sent to committees.[26] The committee appointed to revise the rules of the House in 1946 recommended that any of the estimates could be withdrawn from Committee of Supply and referred to a smaller committee. It added several qualifications to this suggestion. Any committee which examined estimates would operate under the same rules as Committee of Supply, but a Minister and his deputy would both be permitted to address the committee. Any member of the House would have the right to appear and take part in the discussion on the estimates themselves and the proceedings of the committee would be printed and distributed under the same rules as Hansard.[27] The House did not debate the report. A member suggested yet again in the next year that estimates be sent to committees,[28] and in the same

[25]*Ibid.*, March 7, 1944, pp. 1255–6.
[26]*Ibid.*, Dec. 18, 1945, p. 3747; March 18, 1946, p. 36.
[27]*Journals*, April 10, 1946, p. 126.   [28]*Debates*, June 25, 1947, pp. 4617–18.

220 / PROCEDURE IN THE CANADIAN HOUSE OF COMMONS

year two more recommendations of a similar nature were made by more influential individuals. The first of these latter was the Auditor General, who stated that committees should be established to "comb" the estimates, in the interests of economy, before they were submitted to the House.[29] The other was the Speaker, who recommended that the House set up a standing committee on estimates.[30] The committee to which this report was referred made no recommendation in its report to the House.

The Government finally took a stand in 1949 which it maintained for six years. The Opposition made its usual case for the appointment of a committee on estimates. The Minister of Finance replied for the Government. For the first time the Government seriously put forward the proposition that to refer estimates to committees would be inconsistent with ministerial responsibility. The Minister of Finance minimized the significance of the customary reference of External Affairs estimates on the ground that foreign policy was largely non-partisan and that the same conditions could not be reproduced in any other department. He further deprecated the idea of exposing civil servants to lengthy examinations before parliamentary committees, both in the interests of the work of the civil service and in view of the danger inherent in questions relating to policy. As a final point he objected to the delegation of authority from the House to a committee. It was the duty of every member to examine the estimates. This responsibility could not be delegated to any smaller group.[31] The question did not die in 1949 in spite of the attitude of the Government. The Auditor General renewed his recommendation for a committee in a memorandum prepared in 1950.[32] The Opposition continued to press for the appointment of a committee.[33] A committee on revision of the rules considered the matter and although unable to agree on any recommendation listed the reference of estimates to committees as a method of saving the time of the House.[34]

The Government finally gave way in 1955. Early in the session the Minister of Finance moved for the establishment of a special committee "to consider such of the estimates as may be referred to it and to report from time to time its findings and recommendations to the House."[35]

[29]Standing Committee on Public Accounts, 1947, *Minutes of Proceedings and Evidence*, pp. 443 ff.
[30]*Journals*, Dec. 5, 1947, pp. 13–17.   [31]*Debates*, Oct. 26, 1949, pp. 1154–72.
[32]Watson Sellar, "Review and Form of Estimates" (mimeo.), March 15, 1950.
[33]*Debates*, June 8, 1951, p. 3853; June 12, 1951, p. 3965; Nov. 17, 1953, p. 99; Nov. 27, 1953, p. 397; June 23, 1954, p. 6525.
[34]*Ibid.*, Dec. 13, 1951, p. 1858.   [35]*Ibid.*, Feb. 8, 1955, p. 937.

The committee to be set up under this motion bore little relation to that which had been visualized over the past thirty-five years. There had been differences of opinion, but in the main what seems to have been visualized was a committee similar to that in Great Britain: a committee able to investigate what it liked and free to interrogate civil servants without the presence of the Minister. What the Minister of Finance offered the House in 1955 was a miniature Committee of Supply: the Government would decide which departments would be referred, the Minister of the department involved would appear with such officials as he chose to bring, and he would answer the questions of the committee as he did in Committee of Supply. The purpose of the committee, in short, was to provide more information for members yet shorten the time taken in Committee of Supply. The Opposition did not meet this motion with any degree of enthusiasm. Members on that side of the House persisted in their demands that a committee similar to that in Great Britain be set up. The fact was that the Government was setting up a committee which, while admittedly similar in name to the British committee, was nevertheless predicated on entirely different assumptions, and the Opposition insisted on equating similarity of name with similarity of purpose and function. The House accepted the motion and the first Special Estimates Committee was established.

In 1956 the Government proposed a similar motion. The Opposition attempted in this session to remodel the committee along lines which it preferred, moving amendments which would have permitted the committee to call for "persons, papers and records" and to examine whatever estimates it chose. Both amendments were negatived and the motion to establish the committee passed.[36] Debate in 1957 followed the same pattern. The Opposition attempted to extend the powers of the committee, and the Government refused to agree. In 1958, however, the new Government had the opportunity to put into effect what it had advocated while in Opposition, and it moved to establish a Standing Committee on Estimates with the same powers of calling for persons and records normally held by other standing committees.[37] At the same time it increased markedly the number of estimates sent to the older standing committees.

Some of the most difficult problems of procedure which were faced by the first Estimates Committee were solved by its change in status from a special to a standing committee. The early committee faced attempts to call witnesses and to request papers, attempts which were

[36]*Ibid.*, Feb. 9, 1956, p. 1041; Feb. 28, 1956, p. 1641; Feb. 29, 1956, p. 1669.
[37]*Ibid.*, May 30, 1958, pp. 679–703.

defeated, but not without heated discussion. Both of these actions are now possible, although the committee has not often availed itself of its new powers, which are in any case of doubtful value as long as there is a Government majority on the committee to defeat any undesirable motions. Moreover from 1955–7 the committee had as one of its members the Minister whose department was under consideration. This practice has now ceased and ministers appear as witnesses only. The question of which departments are to be examined appears still to be in the hands of the Government alone. There has been no apparent tendency to allow the committee itself or the Opposition to determine which departments will be called.

There is no doubt, however, that the whole character of the Estimates Committee has changed. The original purpose was to give the members of the House a greater opportunity to question ministers on details of departmental work in the hope that the later debate in Committee of Supply would be shorter, more general, and better informed. The Government hoped that members would use the committee to obtain locally interesting but otherwise useless facts from the ministers, and that Committee of Supply would be used as a forum for debates on the broad aspects of general policy. There has never been any serious suggestion that the Committee on Estimates would be able to recommend savings. It has always been recognized by even the most ardent advocates of the system that should the committee advise reductions there are always members waiting in the House willing to defend the original estimates. It is significant that even the Opposition has been heard quoting Gladstone's statement that "it is more difficult to save a shilling than to spend a million."

The new Estimates Committee has lost much of its intended purpose. It has now become just another standing committee of the House to which estimates happen to be the thing referred. In its composition, procedure, and reports there is nothing to distinguish it from the other standing committees doing the same job. The committee questions both ministers and civil servants but there seems no hope that its discussions will replace those in Committee of Supply. It has certainly not yet resulted in the saving of any appreciable amount of time in Committee of Supply, for there has been no noticeable lessening of the time which the latter spends on estimates.[38]

[38]One leader of the House has even stated that the House has taken longer in Committee of Supply over the departments which have been considered in the Estimates Committee than when they were debated in supply only. W. E. Harris, "A More Business-like Parliament," *Queen's Quarterly*, Winter 1957, pp. 540–7.

However, any judgment on the Estimates Committee must await the further development of its procedure. In the past, criticisms have been harsh and largely unmerited. Certainly much information was obtained even before it became a standing committee.[39] But even this achievement was decried by some: one leading member of the Opposition called the committee a "sham and a delusion," and his leader asserted that the committee offered "little in the way of real information."[40] These statements perhaps indicate little more than the frustration of an Opposition which was denied the opportunity to debate what it liked in the way it desired. The additional charge that "all that is to be presented to the committee is the evidence which the Government is prepared to have presented to it" was a startling admission of defeat for any competent Opposition party.[41] Since the establishment of a standing committee these complaints have disappeared although there is still a noticeable lack of enthusiasm over the work of the committee.

Sessional Committee on Railways, Air Lines and Shipping

Several other committees have been used to study estimates before they are considered in supply. The oldest of these committees is the Sessional Committee on Railways, Air Lines and Shipping Owned and Controlled by the Government.[42] The government of Canada has been in the railway business virtually since Confederation. The Intercolonial and Prince Edward Island railways had been under government control for nearly fifty years when the acquisition of transcontinental lines made the government the largest railway operator in Canada and brought it into active competition with the privately owned Canadian Pacific Railway. At that point the government decided to operate the government railways through a normal corporate structure and not as a department of government, so that the railways could be kept free from political patronage, influence, and interference. The arrangement was only moderately satisfactory. Members asked questions in the House about the daily running of the railway, and accusations of patronage in the

[39]The committee proceedings ran to 928 pages in 1955; 919 pages in 1956; 132 pages on one department in 1957; 599 pages in 1958; 519 pages in 1959; and 524 pages in 1960.

[40]Debates, Feb. 26, 1957, p. 1657; Feb. 28, 1956, p. 1648.

[41]Ibid., Feb. 28, 1956, p. 1639.

[42]Up to 1958 this committee was known as the Sessional Committee on Railways and Shipping, Owned, Operated and Controlled by the Government. It is to be distinguished from the Standing Committee on Railways, Canals and Telegraph Lines which is set up under the rules to consider private bills.

awarding of contracts for materials for the lines were always current. More serious questions arose over the production of information which could adversely affect the competitive position of the government railway.

These problems were presented to a special committee of the House in 1921. The annual report of the government railways and the report of the Minister of Marine to Parliament on the government merchant marine were referred to the committee for study, and the House asked it to answer five questions: What information about operations should be given to the House in the public interest? When, and by what method, should this information be given? What system of auditing should be used and how much detail should be shown in the annual report? What improvements could be made in the management? Should the committee itself be continued, and for what purpose? The committee conducted an extensive investigation into all phases of railway and shipping operations. It examined the accounting system of the railway and received reports in which the various departments of the railway expressed their opinions on the publication of details of operations. Altogether, it took nearly five hundred pages of evidence. Unfortunately, however, it neglected to answer the questions which it had been asked; it merely reported to the House that it had not had the time necessary to make a proper report on the matters referred to it.

The committee then disappeared for three years. In 1924 it was revived under the same general terms of reference as it still has. The House has not asked specific questions again. Today, the estimates and reports of the Canadian National Railways and Trans-Canada Air Lines together with the estimates required to cover the deficits incurred in various interprovincial ferry services are all referred to the committee, and the officers of the companies appear before it and give evidence. The committee allows much greater latitude in questions than the House does, and members inquire into local services and corporate policy as well as the financial affairs of the corporations. There are, of course, refusals to answer questions on matters which the management consider affect their competitive position. The committee has in the past appointed unofficial subcommittees to examine specific points which could not easily be settled in the full committee.[43] It has also taken evidence *in camera* on subjects which the railway felt should not be divulged.[44]

[43]See Select Standing Committee on Railways and Shipping, 1932, *Minutes of Proceedings and Evidence*, pp. 34–40.
[44]See Select Standing Committee on Railways and Shipping, 1931, *Minutes of Proceedings and Evidence*, p. 109. A subcommittee was appointed to look into the question of salaries paid to the officials of the Canadian National Railways. The facts provided are not printed in the proceedings of the committee.

Over the years the Committee on Railways and Shipping has performed a useful function. For one thing, the officials of the railway no less than the members of the House seem to appreciate the opportunity for an exchange of ideas. Moreover, the existence of the committee undoubtedly lessens the pressure for information in the House itself; and the fact that a member of the committee can question the officials who are directly responsible for the operation of the companies removes many problems from the Minister of Transport. But the exact powers of the committee have never been defined. In some ways its meetings represent the stockholders' meetings of a normal corporation, but they do not in fact perform the same function and are not likely ever to do so.[45] The committee has never failed to approve the plans for expenditure or policy of the C.N.R. and T.C.A. and could hardly do otherwise, since the plans have been approved in advance by the Government and since the Government always has a majority on the committee.[46] It is unlikely, therefore, that the committee will ever assume too great a controlling role in the operation of the railway. Its function remains largely an investigatory one and has been carried out with marked success over the years.[47]

Other Standing Committees

Since 1946 the House has used the Committee on External Affairs, and, more recently, other standing committees, to examine estimates.[48]

[45]The government in law is the shareholders' representative. One may thus take cautiously a recent statement of the President of the C.N.R. that if the committee did not approve his rolling stock purchases he would have some freight cars for sale (Sessional Committee on Railways and Shipping, 1956, *Minutes of Proceedings and Evidence*, p. 294).

[46]See, e.g., the question of a hotel contract in Montreal, in Sessional Committee on Railways and Shipping, 1955, *Minutes of Proceedings and Evidence*, p. 162.

[47]The President of the C.N.R. has recently expressed some doubts about the usefulness of this committee. He stated emphatically that it was spending too much time on questions of detail and should shift its investigation to policy matters (Sessional Committee on Railways, Air Lines and Shipping, 1959, *Minutes of Proceedings and Evidence*, p. 211). It will be interesting to see the result of this suggestion on future committees.

[48]In 1958 the House referred appropriate estimates to the Standing Committees on Railways, Canals and Telegraph Lines, Industrial Relations, Mines, Forests and Waters, Marine and Fisheries, and Veterans Affairs. In 1959 only Marine and Fisheries, Veterans Affairs, and Mines, Forests and Waters were used; in 1960 Mines, Forests and Waters and Veterans Affairs; and in 1961 Veterans Affairs.

These committees have all the powers to call for persons and papers of any standing committee. They examine the Minister and such officials as seem necessary, and finally report to the House their approval of the estimates. It is difficult to assess the value of this new practice. As on all occasions of this sort a large amount of information is collected from the departments examined and members have an opportunity to question officials as well as ministers. But the departments which have been examined so far have been largely non-contentious, and the activity of the standing committees has been more an attempt to keep a huge majority busy than an attempt to extract information for the House. The real test of the system will only come when there is a sharp difference of opinion over some item or department and the opposition is willing to make its position felt in committee and in the House.

Committee on Public Accounts

In the Committee on Public Accounts the Canadian House of Commons has had the unusual experience of having a committee which has become more inactive. Canada has had a Committee on Public Accounts since Confederation, and although the committee was most active in its early years, it has until very recently been largely dormant. The early committee had the public accounts referred to it regularly. It heard witnesses, examined a few items carefully, and reported frequently to the House on specific items.[49] The committee undoubtedly performed a useful function, but the over-all effect was slight. The Government tended to ignore the reports of the committee and the Opposition too often used the committee for its own partisan advantage.

Since 1930 the public accounts have been referred to the committee only intermittently. All parties seem to have lost interest in the principle and faith in the proceedings of the committee. There is certainly reason for this attitude. A committee which is appointed to investigate Government expenditures after they have been made is bound to labour under a disadvantage. Most of the irregularities have already been discovered and made public by the Auditor General and little can be gained from a public confession of error by the departments themselves. The fact also that the committee is dominated by the Government and will presumably let little be known to its discredit lends an air of fatalism to the whole proceeding.

In the 1958 session the Government revived the Committee on

[49]In 1891 for instance it reported thirty-four times and in 1907–8 forty times.

Public Accounts, which with Government approval, elected a member from the Opposition to the chair. This appointment, the first in the history of the Public Accounts Committee, is of doubtful significance. The power of a chairman is limited under any conditions and disappears entirely when he is faced with a committee dominated by a hostile majority. At any rate, the results were not encouraging on this occasion. The Government had changed within the preceding year, so the accounts were not those of the party in power and the majority thus had a free hand to carry on the investigation it liked. The proceedings of the committee were neither informative nor dignified. Witnesses were bullied and some members were obviously more interested in discrediting the past Government than in discovering facts. The committee has also met in each session since with somewhat better results.

The functions of the Public Accounts Committee have occasionally been taken over to a limited extent by special committees. During the Second World War a Committee on War Expenditures was appointed to examine war spending, with a view to suggesting economies. It divided itself into subcommittees and reported at length to the House. Security restrictions did not allow all the proceedings of the committee to be published but many of its meetings were public. The committee did not meet all the demands of the Opposition for information but it was generally agreed that the organization of the committee itself was satisfactory and that it did its work with commendable efficiency.

A similar committee was set up in peacetime (1951) to examine the expenditures of the Department of National Defence, but it was doomed to failure from the outset. For years the Opposition had been asking for a committee to examine national defence policy and expenditures and only reluctantly accepted this committee as a substitute. The committee however, was limited in its terms of reference and did little, if anything, to satisfy the Opposition demands for a closer examination of expenditures.

Conclusions

In conclusion it can be said that the Canadian House has not yet evolved an efficient or satisfactory system of controlling Government expenditure at any stage. Part of the problem is undoubtedly the natural disinclination of any Government to expose itself to unnecessary criticism; another part is distrust of the motives of the opposition. Canada has tended to run to long uninterrupted periods of one-party power. An inevitable result is that by the time these periods are well advanced the opposition has abandoned any hopes it may have had of helping to cut down expenditures in the interest of economy and is making strenuous efforts to discover damaging evidence of waste and extravagance to be used to defeat the Government at the next election. It is only natural that no Government wishes to encourage this form of investigation and as its tenure of office lengthens it becomes more intolerant of such interference.

The feature of the British system which has forced a change in the traditional methods has been the limit placed on discussions in Committee of Supply. Such a change may yet be necessary in Canada. There is evidence to indicate that the Government in the past has considered a rule which would limit the number of days allowed in Committee of Supply. Such a limitation might well be more advantageous to the opposition than to the Government, for, should a limit of this type be accepted by the House, no legitimate objection could be raised to strengthening the other instruments of control.

Further changes could well be made. The estimates could be made less numerous and more explanatory. The present trend toward using standing committees for non-contentious estimates could be extended, and a regular rotation of departments arranged so that the whole service could be examined every two or three years. The Public Accounts Committee could certainly be used to better effect if an honest effort were made on both sides to review the Auditor General's report and the public accounts with a view to providing a check on waste.

The great change that is needed throughout is the growth of a spirit of co-operation. The Government will have to accept a greater degree of opposition control over the investigations of the committees and a more efficient examination of its accounts. The opposition will have to abandon in committee its exclusive search for election material and show a greater realization of the objectives of an Estimates Committee or Public Accounts Committee. Behind this change on both sides of the House is the need for a real acceptance of the principle that the granting of supply is the most important function of the House and one for which all parties should hold themselves responsible.

GOVERNMENT BILLS AND PUBLIC BILLS

13

THE MOST SIGNIFICANT DIFFERENCE between Government bills and public bills is that although virtually all of the former which are introduced in a session are passed, few, if any, of the latter are. Their content and aim is similar, although constitutional practice limits the scope of the initiative of the private member. The procedure used in the consideration of these two types of bill is the same, and is similar to the procedure used in Great Britain for over four hundred years. Both types are subjected to three readings and consideration in committee, and each stage is restricted to a specific examination of some one aspect. First reading is a mere formality. On second reading the House approves the principle of the bills. In committee it examines the details clause by clause. On third reading the House gives further consideration to the bills in their final form. Each step still fulfils its traditional function today, and however laborious the process may seem, the House of Commons has found it adequate to its needs.

The time allotted in the agenda of the House for Government and public bills varies widely of course. We have already examined the gradual development of Government supremacy over the time of the House and the subordination of private members' business.[1] Today, the Government has virtually all the days in the session under its control. Public bills are reached for certain on only two days in a session, and occasionally after private bills on Tuesday and Friday.[2] In practice this

[1]*Supra*, chap. 5.

[2]The 1960 and 1961 committees on revision of the rules recommended a sessional change in Standing Order 15 to give public bills precedence over private bills on Fridays. This change, tried in the 1961 and 1962 sessions, has now become permanent. Even this change has not had an appreciable effect on the number of public bills passed. For private bills see *infra*, chap. 14.

means that few public bills have any chance of passing the House—only the most simple ones, on which there is no debate,[3] can pass. Most public bills are talked out by the House.

The rules of the House have always contained certain regulations concerning the passage of bills. Some of these indeed are so obvious that it is strange that they have been written down. In the light of the vast mass of customary procedure which the House of Commons has inherited, it seems superfluous for it to specify that every bill shall receive three readings on different occasions. It is equally extraordinary that the House should consider it necessary to exclude the introduction of bills in "blank or imperfect shape."[4]

Introductory Procedure

The standing orders which relate to Government and public bills have been virtually unchanged over the years. Any member must ask leave of the House to introduce a bill. At this time he mentions its title, and must explain its provisions if he intends to do so at all, for if he finds that his motion for leave to introduce a bill is opposed he cannot, except by consent, make a later explanation.[5] Until 1913 the motion for leave to introduce a bill was debatable and occasionally the House considered a bill at length at that time.[6] Nowadays, the House does not normally refuse its permission to a member who may wish to present a bill, although examples of refusal may be found.[7] When the House does grant permission, the motion for first reading is always put without amendment or debate.[8] The House may divide on this motion and defeat it although such action is as rare as a refusal to permit the introduction of a bill.[9] First reading passed, the bill is automatically ordered for second reading "at the next sitting of the House." This wording does not mean that the House will debate the bill on the next sitting day; it merely indicates that when the bill takes its place on the Order Paper for second reading it will be called in its proper order

[3]Two public bills which have passed recently merely changed the name of the sponsors' constituencies.
[4]1867 Rule 43, now S.O. 75, and 1867 Rule 40, now S.O. 72.
[5]*Debates*, Feb. 22, 1932, pp. 380–3.
[6]*Ibid.*, April 28, 1882, pp. 1202 ff.
[7]*Ibid.*, May 2, 1879, p. 1696.
[8]1867 Rule 42, now S.O. 73.
[9]*Debates*, Feb. 26, 1934, pp. 926–8. On that occasion the sponsor, understandably enough, protested that the House did not even know what was in the bill it had just defeated.

when "Public Bills" or "Government Orders" are the order of the day. As has already been explained in chapter 9, public bills are called in a rigid order under the rules, whereas Government orders may be called in any order that the Government sees fit.

Money Bills

This introductory procedure is complicated if the bill is to be a money bill. In 1867 the rules contained special provisions about bills relating to trade and about money bills: both were to be preceded by a resolution which was debated in Committee of the Whole, and both followed the same procedure. In 1927, the House repealed the rule which related to trade bills on the grounds that it was useless and tended to encourage repetition of debate,[10] but the initial committee stage for money bills has been retained to this day (S.O. 61). A money bill is thus preceded by a resolution which is drafted in vague terms. It reads that "it is expedient to introduce a measure" to accomplish certain stated ends. Only the barest outline of the objectives of the measure are stated and the committee debates only the expediency of the measure proposed.

Further formalities complicate the introduction of a money bill. The British North America Act (s. 54) clearly states that the House may not pass any bill "for the appropriation of any part of the public revenue, or of any tax or impost, to any purpose" until the Governor General has indicated his recommendation. Until the revision of 1955 the Minister in charge of the bill announced the recommendation of His Excellency at the earliest possible stage, when he moved that the House go into Committee of the Whole to consider the resolution on which the bill would be based. Since 1955, the same general formalities have been observed of obtaining the written recommendation from Government House, but the information that His Excellency recommends the resolution to the House is now printed in the Orders of the Day. The Minister makes no announcement to the House. A bill which affects the rights, property, or prerogatives of the Crown must also be accompanied at some stage in its progress by the consent of the Crown. This may be announced at any stage of a bill's passage through the House, although normally before second reading. The Minister in charge merely states in the House that the Governor General has been made acquainted with the purpose of the bill and has given his consent for the House to do with it as the House sees fit. A public bill introduced by a private mem-

10*Journals*, March 22, 1927, p. 337.

ber which affects the prerogatives of the Crown must be withdrawn if the Crown withholds consent.

Before a resolution for a money bill can be considered in Committee of the Whole the Minister in charge must give two days' notice in the *Votes and Proceedings* of its introduction. At the appropriate time the resolution appears on the Order Paper under the heading "Government Notices of Motions." For sixty years these notices of motions appeared in the daily routine of business and could be debated. The revision of 1927 made them non-debatable and in 1955 the House agreed to put them under routine proceedings so that they could be called every day. The House, of course, may still divide on the motion.

When the House approves the notice of motion it appears under "Government Orders" on the Order Paper and may be called for debate in Committee of the Whole on any Government day in the future. Up to 1952 the motion for the Speaker to leave the Chair for consideration of a money resolution was debatable and the House occasionally took advantage of its opportunities. There seems little doubt that when the Government passed Rule 17A in 1913 it intended that this motion should not be debatable, but the rule was poorly drafted and the motion remained undisturbed. Mr. Speaker Macdonald began to change the practice in 1952 when he ruled that debate at this stage was in order only if directed to the negative of the question.[11] The next year he reversed his ruling and established the principle that no debate could be in order at this stage: the question henceforward was to be decided, by a vote if necessary, at once.[12] This practice has now been accepted as fixed, and in 1955 the House passed Standing Order 53 to conform.

The House may spend much or little time in Committee of the Whole on a resolution, but whatever time it spends is wasted. The House as a whole knows nothing of the bill. It has before it only the brief sweeping summary of the object of the bill prepared by the Minister. The Minister himself cannot, under the rules, divulge the terms of the bill to the House, and the House must thus debate the subject in the most general way. The most common result is that much of the debate (which follows the general rules of committee debate) is aimless, and anticipatory of debate on second reading.

When the House is satisfied that it has exhausted the possibilities

[11]*Ibid.*, June 18, 1952, pp. 534–5. Mr. Speaker Glen had made a similar ruling in 1942 but the House did not accept the new practice. *Debates*, Feb. 23, 1942, p. 800.

[12]*Journals*, March 26, 1953, pp. 419–21.

of the resolution, it passes it, possibly after a division. The Chairman reports the resolution to the House and the Minister in charge at once moves for the House to concur in it. When this motion is passed it is assumed that the House has ordered the Minister to introduce a bill, he complies, and first reading follows at once. The bill is also ordered for second reading later. The House may divide on these later stages although it is unusual for it to do so.

Second Reading

At this point—second reading—the procedure on money bills become identical with that on other Government bills and on public bills. Second reading involves a debate on the principles of the bill; the clauses cannot be debated or even referred to in passing. Amendments are possible, but must be couched in general terms. A complete negative is impossible although much the same result may be achieved with a resolution which differs from the principle of the bill in some details. It is much more common, however, to move a simple hoist or to refer the subject-matter of the bill to a committee before giving approval to its principle on second reading.

The debate on second reading is the most interesting and informative of any stage. Every member has a copy of the bill, which has been printed in both English and French, and the opposition has ample ammunition for its attack. The Government makes an effort to present its case in a persuasive way. The arguments on both sides are fresh, at least in the early stages of debate, and the House is willing to listen. This debate, therefore, often takes days and exhausts the resources of both sides. When the House is ready, it votes on the amendments proposed, approves second reading, and refers the bill either to a standing or special committee or to Committee of the Whole.

Committee Stage

Few Government bills are referred to standing or special committees. Technical bills of interest to a limited number of members and occasionally non-contentious bills are referred to small committees,[13] but the

---

[13]Revisions of the Bank Act and bills for equal pay for equal work, unemployment insurance for fishermen, and control of the salmon fisheries have all been sent to small committees recently.

House as a whole carefully guards its rights of debate in Committee of the Whole, so when bills are sent to small committees they must be reported back to the House and are then sent to Committee of the Whole. At these times, all members may speak in Committee of the Whole but the Government exerts such pressure as it can to keep the debate brief.

Before the Speaker leaves the Chair for the House to resolve itself into Committee of the Whole on a bill, it is proper for a member to move an instruction to the committee. The purpose of such an instruction is to confer on the committee powers which it would not otherwise have, but since it already has the power to make all the amendments which are normally desirable, few instructions are in order. The most common instruction is for the committee to divide a bill which has been sent to it, or to consolidate two bills. It is not in order to debate an instruction (S.O. 32). The motion for the Speaker to leave the Chair which follows an instruction is not debatable either.

In Committee of the Whole the preamble, if any, and the title of the bill are postponed and the various clauses of the bill are called in their numerical order (S.O. 78). By tradition, the committee holds a general debate, similar to that on second reading, when clause one (usually the short title of the bill) is called. The rules expressly forbid such a practice but it is now well entrenched. When the first clause has carried, debate becomes more relevant and speeches become shorter. Amendments are offered and are occasionally accepted by the Government. It has never been necessary to give notice of these amendments.

Committee stage may conclude in one of three ways. First, a member may move the dilatory motion that the committee rise or that the Chairman leave the Chair; this motion is always in order and, if carried, removes the bill from the Order Paper. Second, if the committee wishes to postpone consideration of the bill until some future time, a motion may be made that the committee rise, report progress, and ask leave to sit again; this motion is normally made if the committee is still sitting when the regular adjournment hour arrives. Third, when Committee of the Whole concludes its study of a bill, the Chairman reports the bill to the House, noting in his report whether or not any amendments have been made. Under the old written rules an amended bill was opened again for debate and amendment at this stage, but in practice a motion for concurrence in the amendments was made and decided at once. The revision of 1955 brought the written rules into line with the practice (S.O. 78 (2)).

Third Reading

A bill reported from Committee of the Whole without amendments may be ordered for third reading immediately (S.O. 78 (2)); but a bill reported with amendments cannot be so ordered except by consent of the House, though this is commonly given. No bill, whether amended or not, can, however, be given both second and third reading on the same day (S.O. 75). The motion for third reading is debatable and members may move amendments. At one time specific amendments were common on third reading, but members now customarily move that the bill be referred back to Committee of the Whole with instructions to amend it in certain specified ways. It is also possible to move a hoist at this stage.

A bill used to go through one more stage before being passed: after third reading the sponsor moved a final motion that the bill "do now pass and the title be as on the Order Paper." However, since amendments made during the passage of the bill rarely made a change in the title desirable, in 1958 the Speaker asked for, and received, permission to eliminate this final motion which had no basis in the rules of the House. This motion has now been combined in an abbreviated form with the motion for third reading, and now reads "that the bill be now read a third time and do pass."[14]

Senate Amendments

The bill, approved by the Commons and reprinted if amendment has made it necessary, is sent to the Senate where it undergoes another three readings. If it passes without amendment, the Senate sends a message to the Commons to inform them of the fact, and if amendments are made the attention of the House is drawn to them when the bill is returned. These Senate amendments must, of course, be considered by the House. Up to 1955 Senate amendments to Government and public bills were allotted separate places on the Order Paper: the former under "Government Orders" to be called when the Government wished, and the latter only on Monday and after private bills. The result was that by the end of the session no Senate amendments to public bills could be considered, as by that time Monday had always become a Government day. In 1955 an entry was made in the rules which

[14]*Debates*, May 14, 1958, p. 84.

gave Senate amendments to public bills a reasonable precedence any time public bills were considered, so now they can be reached in private and public bill hour any Tuesday or Friday in the session.[15] The amendment did not change the procedure with respect to Government bills, and it was not a significant one, for few public bills ever progress far enough to come under the provisions of the new rule.

The Commons sends a message to the Senate, whether it approves by motion the amendments the Senate has made, or whether, as it may, it rejects them. In the latter case, should both sides remain firm the bill may die at prorogation. As a last resort, either House may request a conference to come to an agreement on suitable amendments. The idea of a conference was first written into the rules in 1867: Rule 99 stated that if the House requested a conference it must prepare and agree on its reasons and present them to the Senate. The conference was a conference in name only: whichever House requested the conference drew up a statement of its reasons and both houses appointed "managers" who met at an agreed time; one of the managers from the House which requested the conference read the communication from his House and it was accepted by the other House; both groups then reported to their respective houses. The value of such a conference can well be imagined. In an attempt to simplify this cumbersome procedure, both houses passed resolutions in 1905[16] which were added to the rule book in the revision of 1906. The rule, which still exists, allows the managers to meet in a free conference to work out a compromise. If the two houses cannot agree after this meeting, the bill dies, but if the compromise amendments prove suitable, the houses exchange messages to inform one another of the success of the conference. After this exchange the bill awaits royal assent.

The Question of Efficiency

The principles on which Government and public bills are considered in the House of Commons have never been seriously questioned in Canada. Three readings and committee stage give ample opportunity for full debate on every bill; even when the closure rule is in use the right to full debate is not seriously challenged. Occasionally the House

[15]They have precedence after public bills which are to be given third reading; reports on public bills from Committee of the Whole or a standing committee; and public bills which are to be considered in Committee of the Whole; and before public bills which are scheduled for second reading.

[16]*Debates*, July 12, 1905, col. 9280.

even manages to hasten the passage of bills; its treatment of supply bills often provides a case in point. The House spends weeks in supply and discusses the estimates at length. On the last day of the session the Government introduces a resolution to authorize the grant of money voted, and the members of the House hold this resolution in committee barely long enough for it to be read. It is reported, and three readings follow, by consent, at once. The total time for all stages is no more than three or four minutes. Non-contentious bills may be processed nearly as fast: members make a few speeches on second reading and ask a few questions in Committee of the Whole; third reading follows at once without debate. On one occasion at least the House has been so willing to pass a bill that the Government did not have time to move amendments in committee. The House was then forced to revert to committee to enable the Government to amend its own bill.[17]

The House has, of course, made some changes in this branch of its procedure. The passage of bills does not operate as a completely independent unit, but as an integral part of the whole, and the rules which govern debatable motions, amendments, and relevancy, for instance, all contribute to the efficiency of this part of the work of the House. These rules are, in fact, the moderating factors which enable the House to employ a system which has developed little over hundreds of years. The reforms of procedure which will be necessary in the future to enable the House to complete more work and do this work more effectively will be reforms of details rather than of the broad principles common to all British parliamentary systems.

[17]*Ibid.*, April 10, 1957, p. 3394.

PETITIONS AND PRIVATE BILLS

14

THE STATEMENT of Redlich in 1908 that "the venerable institution of petition, the oldest of all Parliamentary forms, the fertile seed of all proceedings of the House of Commons, has but little life at the present day" is as true in Canada as it is in the United Kingdom.[1] The right to petition Parliament for the redress of grievances beyond the power of the courts to set right has been based in Canada on tradition and the inheritance of our parliamentary forms from Westminster. The right to petition in Canada has always been regarded as a quaint survival to be used on increasingly rare occasions, and not primarily as a fundamental right to be jealously guarded.

Petitions may be divided into two categories. Less important in terms of procedure are public petitions, that is, petitions meant to benefit the public, in which the House is asked to take action to right an alleged public wrong or to alter the general law of the country. Less picturesque, perhaps, but more important procedurally, are the petitions on which all private bills must be based and which must be presented to and accepted by the House before the private bills themselves are presented. These petitions, or more particularly the private bills which issue from them, are meant to benefit a person or a particular group of persons, not the public in general; today, for instance, private bills consist mostly of divorce bills and bills for the incorporation of companies. The procedure followed by petitions of this second kind is similar to, though naturally more important and intricate than the procedure followed by public petitions, which will be discussed first.

[1]J. Redlich, *The Procedure of the House of Commons* (3 vols., London, 1908), II, p. 239.

Public Petitions

WRITTEN RULES OF PRESENTATION

The rules which control the presentation of petitions have changed much since Confederation, when the House adopted four rules to govern petitions.[2] The first of these made both the presentation and reception of petitions a part of the daily routine proceedings of the House. The others controlled petitions more directly. The second stated that a petition was to be presented by a member in his place in the House and he was to assume responsibility that it did not contain "impertinent or improper matter." According to the third rule, a member who presented a petition had to endorse it and could make only a short statement of its contents; the form in which the petition was to be presented was also regulated. The last rule referred to later proceedings on petitions. When a petition was judged to be in order, it was to be brought to the Table and no debate was to be allowed. Under certain limitations, if an immediate remedy was necessary, a discussion could take place.

These rules remained unchanged until 1910, when the House approved a new method of presenting petitions.[3] The old method was retained for those who wished to draw attention to the content of their petitions. At the same time the presentation of petitions was removed from routine proceedings, although under another rule it was still possible to present a petition at that time. Another change was that a member no longer had to present his petition from his place in the House, but could file it with the Clerk at any time during the day, and if he filed it before 4 P.M. it was to be recorded as presented on that day. The revision committee of 1925 recommended that the time for the reception of petitions be extended to cover the whole of the afternoon sitting. The House did not pass that report, but in 1927 it abolished the time limit entirely. The rule today stands as it was left in 1927; petitions may be filed with the Clerk at any time during the sitting and are recorded the same day in the *Votes and Proceedings*.

RULINGS OF SPEAKERS

The printed rules, however, do not give a clear picture of the situation. While the few rules were slowly being altered by the House to meet changing conditions, the Speakers of the House were applying British precedents to the petitions presented. The rulings of Speakers over the

[2]1867 Rules 19, 85, 86, 87.
[3]1910 Rules 25, and 75 (1) and (3).

years thus form a comprehensive case law which must be examined to discover the significance of petitions today.

Any person resident in Canada may petition the House. It is well understood that non-resident aliens do not have the right to petition Parliament, but this rule is not enforced if the petition is for a private bill. At one time the House refused to consider any such petitions, but the directors of an American insurance company which did business in Canada successfully presented a petition to the House in 1878 for an amendment to the Insurance Act.[4] Five years later a Speaker ruled that if the subject-matter of an alien's petition came within the jurisdiction of the House, it could be considered.[5] Other petitions from Americans, however, which dealt only with public policy, have been rejected.[6]

The form of petitions always comes under close scrutiny. The petition must be addressed to the "honourable the House of Commons in Parliament assembled"; it may not be addressed to the Prime Minister and the Government[7] or to any other group or person. It must also conclude with a prayer which summarizes the action desired by the petitioner. A remonstrance or a memorial should not be presented, although should such a document be respectfully worded and conclude with a prayer, the House may accept it. No appendices of any description may be attached.[8] Petitions may be written in either English or French. One person may petition the House and always does when applying for a divorce bill. When three or more individuals petition, at least three signatures must appear on the sheet which contains the prayer.[9] The signatures must be written, not typewritten or printed.[10] Thus no petition can be transmitted by telegraph.[11] A petition from a corporation should have a corporate seal attached.

Petitions, however presented, must be sponsored by a member of the House, who is expected to ascertain that they are in order before presentation. A member cannot be compelled to present a petition although there are examples of members who have presented petitions with which they disagreed.[12] If a member elects to present a petition in the House he is not entitled to read it. He must content himself with,

4Debates, March 11, 1878, p. 950.   5Ibid., March 8, 1883, pp. 138–9.
6Ibid., Feb. 19, 1877, pp. 93–4; Journals, March 30, 1880, p. 165.
7Debates, May 18, 1923, p. 2885.   8Journals, Feb. 19, 1879, p. 18, etc.
9Ibid., April 16, 1874, p. 67; March 30, 1882, p. 231; Jan. 31, 1913, p. 210, etc.
10Ibid., May 26, 1938, p. 373.
11Debates, March 10, 1870, p. 46; May 1, 1872, col. 256.
12Ibid., June 9, 1947, p. 3912; Feb. 9, 1949, p. 371.

at most, a brief statement of the authors, the number of signatures, and the allegations it contains. He may read the prayer, however.

RECEPTION IN THE HOUSE

When a public petition is presented it is referred automatically to an officer of the House, the Clerk of Petitions (in practice today not a separate officer, but merely one of the clerks of committees who has been assigned to the post), who reports to the House whether or not it contains any irregularities. Should it be in proper form, it is deemed to have been received when the Clerk of Petitions tables his report (S.O. 70). At this time the petition may be read to the House by one of the clerks at the Table,[13] but only if the House itself approves. There has been some confusion over the position of the Clerk of Petitions. At one time, when he reported irregularities in a petition his report also recommended that it should not be received,[14] and the Speaker did not make a formal ruling. The custom today is that the Clerk of Petitions merely reports to the House any breach in the rules in a petition and the Speaker makes a formal ruling that the petition is inadmissible.[15]

LIMITATIONS ON SUBJECT-MATTER

A petition must, of course, relate to a matter over which Parliament has control. In a federal country this stipulation limits at once the range of subjects which may be raised. The House will not receive a petition relating to a matter which has been delegated to another body. Ever since 1874 when it gave the courts its privilege of judging controverted elections, the Commons has refused to receive petitions which related to such electoral problems.[16] On a more recent occasion a matter which had, by statute, been allocated to a public corporation was judged to be beyond the authority of the House and a petition which requested interference by the House was rejected.[17]

As a corollary, a petition may not ask for the expenditure of money. Most of the petitions which have been rejected over the years have been condemned for this reason alone—petitions asking the House to build a harbour of refuge and to assist in the construction of railways and canals, and in public projects. A petition which merely asks for "appropriate measures" to be taken or for "such measures as the House may think expedient" is accepted as it does not entail any specific

[13]*Journals*, Feb. 22, 1938, p. 97; *Debates*, Feb. 10, 1942, pp. 443–4.
[14]*Journals*, July 1, 1938, p. 571; Aug. 24, 1946, p. 767, etc.
[15]*Ibid.*, April 12, 1956, p. 389, etc.
[16]*Debates*, April 20, 1874, p. 39; *Journals*, May 6, 1926, pp. 292–5, etc.
[17]*Debates*, Feb. 16, 1956, p. 1231.

expenditure. Acceptance in this case is equivalent to acceptance of a private member's motion which calls for the Government "to give consideration" to action which might entail expenditure. The Government is left free to decide what action, if any, is desirable, and to recommend such expenditures as are necessary.

Petitions which ask for the imposition or relaxation of customs duties are in a somewhat different position. Up to 1876 these petitions were rejected as it was judged that to grant them would impose a charge on the people.[18] The House altered its practice in 1876 and since then petitions on these matters have been received.[19] Requests for a bounty to be paid to an industry are received only if they are presented by persons not directly interested.[20]

These rulings have accumulated in the House over the years and are now as firmly entrenched as the standing orders. These rulings and the procedure surrounding the reception of petitions have acted, in recent years in particular, to discourage petitioning. At many times the House has shown itself willing to waive its rules, however strict, to allow the introduction or the passage of a measure it desires, but it has consistently refused to do the same with petitions. Not only is the possible subject-matter limited today, but the forms are strictly observed. The examination by the Clerk of Petitions ensures that many petitions will never be received by the House. Even if they are drafted properly and deal with a proper subject, the petitions cause little stir in the House: the Speaker informs the House that they may be received and they disappear from sight without comment. At best a member may present a petition in person and read the prayer; his fellow members nod agreeably and the petition disappears; there is no debate. The result of these restrictions and this procedure is that petitions are of little use today. Petitions for private bills are still common, but the old tradition by which an individual could pray for redress of wrongs and expect an alleviation of difficulties has fallen into disuse. It is unlikely ever to be revived.

Private Bills

Private bills differ from public bills (which were discussed in the previous chapter) both in content and in method of passage. By definition they are bills which are passed for the benefit of a person or a

---

[18]*Journals*, March 11, 1875, p. 205; Feb. 23, 1876, p. 76, etc.
[19]*Ibid.*, March 6, 1876, p. 107; March 13, 1876, pp. 130–1, etc.
[20]*Ibid.*, Feb. 16, 1877, p. 37.

group of persons. It is this aspect which gives private bills their peculiar nature, as Parliament when it passes them acts largely as a court of law. The persons affected petition Parliament to grant some extraordinary favour and allege as they do so some set of facts. The House examines the facts presented and decides whether or not the bill should be passed. Should evidence be necessary, witnesses are heard in the standing committees to which all private bills are referred.

DIVORCE BILLS

Divorce bills illustrate the procedure most strikingly in the Canadian House. The innocent party to a divorce in either Newfoundland or Quebec may petition Parliament for a private bill to dissolve the marriage. The petition alleges a matrimonial offence and prays for "relief." Since 1934, because of a difference in fees (as will be explained later) these petitions are first heard in the Senate before its Committee on Divorce. If the offence is established the bill is passed and sent to the Commons. Most divorce bills are uncontested, and pass the House without question. Should any doubt arise in the mind of any member of the House, or should the participants in the case wish to be heard, the Standing Committee on Miscellaneous Private Bills has the authority to rehear the case. Petitioner and respondent may be represented by counsel, witnesses may be heard, and in nearly all respects the committee functions as a court of law in establishing or disproving the facts alleged. The House deals with the bill on the basis of the report from the committee.

NOTICE OF PETITION

Before a private bill can be introduced in the House certain formalities must be followed. The most important of these is the requirement that notice be given in the *Canada Gazette* and in other newspapers in any areas affected of the intention of the sponsors to petition for a bill (S.O. 96). The purpose of the rule is to make certain that all those interested in a bill which is to be presented will have ample opportunity to oppose it. The House introduced this safeguard in 1867 in a simple form (Rule 51). Notice was to be given in the official *Gazette* and in one local newspaper—in Quebec notice was required in both English and French and in one English and one French newspaper. The House has changed the rule many times since, but in largely inconsequential ways.[21] In 1874 English and French notices were required in Manitoba

[21]*Ibid.*, May 22, 1874, p. 307; *Debates*, Oct. 10, 1903, col. 13549, and July 10, 1906, col. 7605; *Journals*, March 22, 1927, pp. 349–53.

as well as in Quebec. The House expanded the rule in 1903 to correspond to a similar rule in the Senate and added the present sections which deal with notice for specific types of bills. The revision of 1906 added a section which established the proper method of communicating the notice to any provincial or municipal authorities concerned. A substantial number of minor changes were made in 1927.

FEES

A petitioner for a private bill, in addition to providing proof of proper notice, must pay a substantial fee. The rule in 1867 (Rule 58) was simple: the petitioner paid the cost of printing and a general fee of $100. As the rule properly observed: "The expenses and costs attending on Private Bills giving an exclusive privilege, or for any object of profit, or private, corporate, or individual advantage; or for amending, or extending or enlarging any former Acts, in such manner as to confer additional powers, ought not to fall on the public." These fees have been steadily increased.[22] In the year 1874 the House accepted a recommendation from a standing committee and increased the general fee to $200. The revision of 1906 added a new set of additional fees—for late deposit of a bill with the Clerk of the House, for late presentation in the House, and for the suspension of any rules to assist the passage of a bill—and it also set a sliding scale of fees for bills of incorporation dependent on the proposed capitalization of a company. The House doubled these last-named fees in 1927. The most significant amendment was that made in 1934. The Prime Minister at that time announced that it was the intention of the Government to encourage the introduction of private bills in the Senate. The House, therefore, agreed to raise its general fee for private bills to $500. Since the level of Senate fees has remained low, and since the general fee is payable only in the Chamber in which the bill originates, this measure has succeeded in transferring the introduction of virtually all private bills to the Senate.

PRESENTATION OF PETITIONS

An individual who wishes a private bill, even if it is to originate in the Senate, must petition the Commons; at one time it was necessary to petition the Commons, the Senate, and the Governor in Council, but this third petition was abandoned in January 1955. The petitions on which private bills are based follow the same patterns as public petitions. They are all sponsored by a member, are couched in the same elaborately

[22]*Journals*, May 22, 1874, p. 306; *Debates*, July 10, 1906, col. 7605; *Journals*, March 22, 1927, pp. 346–7; *Debates*, June 30, 1934, pp. 4509–10.

respectful terms, and must conform to the same general set of rules. The House insists on one further restriction: petitions for private bills must be presented within a certain period of time from the beginning of the session: in 1867 within three weeks, in 1876 ten days, and in 1893 three weeks, but throughout this period, almost yearly, the House passed sessional orders which extended the time. Finally in 1906 the House extended the limit to the present six weeks.[23] The rule (S.O. 93) may be suspended, but only after a favourable report from the Committee on Standing Orders. This is done each session for a few petitions, but the old slovenly habits have largely been eliminated.

Each petition for a private bill to incorporate a railway company or canal company should be accompanied by a map which shows the route which the new work will take (S.O. 98). The House adopted the rule in 1903 following the report of a joint committee of both Houses on private bill procedure.[24] Changes were made in 1927 which did little to alter the rule.

EXAMINATION OF PETITIONS

The examination of petitions has developed slightly since Confederation. In 1867 (Rule 53) all petitions for private bills were referred at once to the Committee on Standing Orders, which established whether the rules had been followed and reported to the House. The revision of 1906 introduced the Examiner of Petitions for Private Bills who took all petitions for private bills under consideration. Those which conformed to the rules were so reported to the House and proceeded through their various stages of debate, and those which contravened the rules were referred automatically to the Committee on Standing Orders for its recommendation. In 1927 the House made minor amendments: the Chief Clerk of Private Bills was made *ex-officio* Examiner of Petitions for Private Bills, and in cases of doubt about compliance with the rules, the Committee on Standing Orders was to consider the petition and report to the House. Nowadays, when petitions for private bills are received they are all examined by an official of the House, the Examiner of Petitions for Private Bills (who is also the Chief of the Committees and Private Legislation Branch) to ensure that all the necessary formalities have been fulfilled. In particular the Examiner satisfies himself and reports to the House that the proper notice has been given according to the rules of the House. If there is any doubt on this point, the

[23]1867 Rule 49; *Debates*, March 29, 1876, p. 909; *Journals*, March 25, 1893, p. 201; *Debates*, July 10, 1906, col. 7603.
[24]*Debates*, Oct. 10, 1903, col. 13549.

Standing Committee on Standing Orders automatically will consider whether or not the petition should be received (S.O. 100).

THE FORM OF PRIVATE BILLS

The standing orders control not only the form of the petitions on which private bills are based, but also the form of the bills themselves. In the early years of the House private bills were often drafted in a haphazard way and members and committees complained about the general confusion which surrounded their introduction. In response to these complaints the House in 1883 adopted the recommendation of the Standing Committee on Railways, Canals and Telegraph Lines and made a rule that any private act of incorporation should include specific clauses from the general act relating to such bills.[25] Departures from the general form were to be specially noted, and any bill which deviated from this rule would be returned to its promoters.

In 1887, after further study of the matter by a special committee, a model bill was drawn up to which all bills for incorporation had to conform.[26] Unusual provisions in proposed bills were to be marked and were to be "clearly specified" in the notice of application. In the revision of 1887 the House also added two rules, one of which remains among the standing orders. This rule (S.O. 99) requires the production of a map or plan with every bill to incorporate a railway or canal company.[27] The map must also show other similar works in the neighbourhood, because, as the House noted in 1887, bills had frequently been presented to construct railway lines on land which was already occupied by existing lines. The other rule introduced in 1887 required a statement of the capital proposed to be raised and the method to be used in raising it. The purpose was to discourage the incorporation of fictitious companies which would obtain a charter and then sell it to others who were willing and able to do the work. By 1927 the problem had apparently disappeared. Promoters no longer produced the information required and the House assumed that the committee which examined the bills could obtain the information if it needed it.[28] The rule was therefore removed. The House changed little else in 1927 except to add a clause which provided for an Examiner of Private Bills. This

[25]*Debates*, April 20, 1883, pp. 741–3.
[26]*Ibid.*, June 18, 1887, pp. 1115–16.
[27]This map presumably could be the same one presented with the petition under S.O. 98, although S.O. 99 demands more information to be included on the map presented to the committee. In practice no maps are now filed at any stage.
[28]*Journals*, March 22, 1927, p. 355.

officer is entrusted with the duty of seeing that proposed bills conform to the rules (S.O. 97).

INTRODUCTION OF PRIVATE BILLS IN THE HOUSE

For nearly forty years after Confederation, private bills, although based on petitions, were introduced in the same manner as other bills. When a petition had been reported by the Committee on Standing Orders, the sponsor moved for leave to introduce his bill. The motion was made immediately before the order for private bills was read on Monday, Wednesday, or Friday. It was necessary that the bill be printed in both French and English by the government contractors, and presented within the first four weeks of the session, although this period was usually extended if the time for the reception of petitions had been extended.

FIRST READING

The revision of 1906 eliminated the old motion for leave to introduce a bill and the formal motion for first reading, and in 1955 the House extended automatic first reading to include private bills from the Senate. Today, therefore, the first reading of a private bill is a simple matter. Once the petition for a private bill has been favourably reported on, either by the Examiner of Petitions for Private Bills or the Committee on Standing Orders, the Clerk of the House lays the bill on the Table and it is recorded in the *Votes and Proceedings* as having been read a first time (S.O. 103 (1)). In the case of private bills which originate in the Senate, the Senate informs the House of the passage of a particular bill; the Speaker then reads the message to the House, the fact is recorded in the *Votes and Proceedings*, and again first reading is assumed (S.O. 103 (2)).

For six years after Confederation the House referred all private bills to standing committees after first reading. This arrangement proved to be unworkable. Under the rules, all bills had to be printed before presentation to the House, but committees often found that, in the rush of business, private bills were being presented, referred, and posted for consideration before being printed. In 1873 the House therefore agreed that private bills should be referred to committee only after second reading.[29]

SECOND READING

Second reading generally follows soon after a bill's *pro forma* first reading. Unlike public bills, private bills are reached and debated

[29]*Ibid.*, May 15, 1873, pp. 350–2.

regularly. They have precedence on three private members' Mondays and for two hours each week throughout the session.[30] When the Clerk reads the order for private bills, the member whose bill has precedence moves the usual motion for second reading. Bourinot records that at this time counsel may be heard at the Bar of the House both for and against the bill;[31] however, such a procedure has never in fact been attempted, and it is doubtful whether it would be countenanced by the House today. Second reading is rarely opposed, for a private bill is based on allegations of fact which can be proven only in committee. Second reading, therefore, is conditional on the proof in committee of the preamble of the bill: it is not full and unqualified approval of the principle of the bill. The usual amendments are in order at this stage, although opponents of bills generally content themselves with moving a hoist. One amendment which has been used occasionally is that which postpones second reading and sends the subject-matter of the bill to committee. This amendment, though in order, is meaningless on a private bill for the reason already mentioned—that the subject-matter of a private bill is automatically sent to committee after second reading.

REFERRED TO STANDING COMMITTEE

Under Standing Order 105 private bills are sent to specific committees. A few go to the Standing Committee on Banking and Commerce, a few more to the Standing Committee on Railways, Canals and Telegraph Lines, and all the rest, including divorce bills, to the Standing Committee on Miscellaneous Private Bills. In these committees the bills are submitted to a searching examination. Witnesses may be summoned and petitioners heard for and against. The first business of the committee is to prove the preamble of the bill which sets forth the allegations on which the remainder of the bill is based. Should a committee decide and report that the preamble of a bill is not proven the bill cannot go further without a special order of the House (S.O. 110).

Other rules also apply to standing committees when they are considering private bills. In 1867 (Rule 60) ten days' notice was required of a committee meeting on a private bill originating in the House, and two days' notice on a bill from the Senate. No motion for the modification of this rule would be considered unless the question had been referred to the standing committee concerned or unless two other committees had so reported. A further section required the Clerk of

---

[30]*Supra*, chap. 5.
[31]Sir John G. Bourinot, *Parliamentary Procedure and Practice in the Dominion of Canada* (1st ed., Toronto, 1884), p. 640.

Private Bills to give ten days' notice in the *Votes and Proceedings* of the bills to be considered by committees, and to give one day's notice of committee meetings on private bills. The House altered the rule slightly in 1873 when it reduced the length of notice to one week and (for Senate bills) one day and removed the requirement for the publication of the notice of committee meetings (S.O. 106).

The remainder of the rules which relate to private bills in committee are of little interest. The chairman is given both an original and a casting vote (S.O. 107). Both the chairman and the clerk of a committee must initial the various sections of the bill when they are passed and sign the bill (S.O. 111). These rules have been changed over the years only in unimportant details.

When a committee has completed its examination of a private bill it must report it back to the House (S.O. 109). It has wide discretion in its reports. It may merely report the bill with or without amendment. It may report the preamble not proven. It is also empowered, and even enjoined, to examine its bills and satisfy itself that the rules relating to notice have been sufficiently met (S.O. 108). As has already been mentioned, if a committee reports that the rules have not been complied with, the bill may not proceed further until a new report is made on it by the Examiner of Petitions for Private Bills or by the Committee on Standing Orders. Should a committee amend a bill extensively, the committee or the Clerk of the House may order the bill reprinted before further consideration is given to it. The cost of such printing is borne by the promoter.

COMMITTEE OF THE WHOLE

Until the revision of 1906 private bills followed normal bill procedure in Committee of the Whole. Each bill was separately referred to Committee of the Whole, was considered there, and was reported back to the House. On most occasions this procedure led to an abnormal waste of time. Few bills could be passed in the short period allotted each week, as the formalities of changing the House into Committee of the Whole and back again were tedious and time-consuming. The House therefore adopted a new rule in 1906 which allowed it to refer to Committee of the Whole in one motion all private bills reported to the House by standing committees. Committee of the Whole then considered as many bills as possible in the time available and reported those completed to the House. At the expiry of the private bill hour the bill under consideration retained its place at the top of the Order Paper.

This rule has proved satisfactory and the House has made only one change: in 1955 it amended one section of the rule so that, although the bills which had not been debated in Committee of the Whole in the time allotted for them retained their places when the committee reported to the House, any bill still under discussion dropped to the end of the list of private bills (S.O. 20 (2)).

THIRD READING

A private bill reported from Committee of the Whole is generally given third reading at once. The House may debate a contentious bill, and on third reading the usual amendments are sometimes moved. Standing Order 112 states, however, that before moving any "important" amendment, a member must give a full day's notice, but it does not attempt to define "important." And Standing Order 114 stipulates that any serious amendment made by the Senate in a private bill must be referred to the standing committee which considered the bill before it can be passed; but this order is of little significance today, for few private bills originate in the House of Commons and the Senate is, of course, unlikely to amend its own bills.

Efficiency of Procedure

Private bill procedure today is of little concern to any member. The vast majority of private bills in any session are divorce bills and excite no interest: various individuals and parties provide some opposition, but their opposition is based on a belief that the subject is not a proper one for Parliament. The solution to this problem lies in the elimination of divorce bills, not in improvement of the rules.

An amendment which would guarantee a vote on every private bill presented to the House would, however, be valuable. On several occasions a small minority of the House has managed to prevent the passage of private bills by the simple expedient of talking out every private bill hour. In 1928 two innocent bills were sacrificed by members who opposed the establishment of a divorce court in Ontario. The two bills were never even reached on the Order Paper. Similarly, in 1957 one bill was blocked in much the same way: every other private bill was passed but the one. A small group in the House was determined that it should not go through, and against this opposition all the rules were useless. There seems little reason why this system should be continued, and in this connection the outcome of the 1928 episode is interesting. It was a recommendation in 1929 by the Standing Committee on Standing Orders that when a private bill had been reported from standing committee and had been considered in Committee of the Whole at two sittings, it should, if not otherwise disposed of, be put down at once for third reading. The motion for third reading would then be put without debate at the next opportunity.[32] If this recommendation had been accepted, a repetition of the 1928 incident would have been made impossible.

There is, of course, no effective procedural answer to the mass obstruction of divorce bills carried on recently by the C.C.F. Their device is simple: debate every one of the hundreds of divorce bills in Committee of the Whole. As each member of the party can speak as often as he likes, and as private bill time is limited, the procedure is unbeatable, unless the session is extended and the bills become the only business of the House until the party becomes exhausted.

For the remainder of the private bills—the bills of incorporation and similar subjects—the rules are adequate to the needs of the House. Few companies need this cumbersome form of incorporation and the time and facilities of the House are sufficient to meet the strain.

[32]*Journals,* Feb. 21, 1929, p. 78.

CONCLUSION

15

THE HOUSE OF COMMONS has not yet been faced with a situation which demands a drastic alteration in its procedure. This is perhaps as well, for there is little satisfaction any member can take from the procedures used today in Ottawa. The rules of the House are sufficiently antiquated that they are still excellently suited to preserve the rights of all members at the expense of efficiency. It is sheer good fortune that no excessive strain has ever been put on the Canadian House. The possibility that this may happen in the future cannot be overlooked.

Any changes made in procedure in the future will probably have one of two separate ideas behind them. There will be a desire on the part of some merely to shorten the session, and there will be a desire on the part of others to make the House of Commons a more efficient body. Neither of these ideas is in itself really adequate. The mere shortening of the session may appear attractive to members who feel now that they are underpaid and are given insufficient time to maintain a business in their home constituencies. This feeling is, obviously, not a sufficient justification for altering the procedure of the House, although it may be a convincing argument for increasing the pay of members. The only really acceptable version of this argument is the one which contends that the session should be shortened now, so that in future, when the House has more work to do, the session can be again extended.

A desire for efficiency is, on the surface, commendable. But again, we must be careful that in a blind search for efficiency we do not lose the essence of the parliamentary system. Clearly, a rigidly controlled Parliament and a muzzled Opposition would, in one sense, form the most efficient legislature possible to devise. But the important fact is that Parliament, by its encouragement of an Opposition, is deliberately using means which are apparently inefficient in order to achieve efficiency in its ultimate aims. We encourage slow procedures, such as three readings of bills, because we feel that better legislation results if full publicity is given to the activities of the Government. No matter how efficient we wish to make Parliament, we must not lose sight of these democratic necessities.

The cure for Parliament's problems is, then, not a simple one. It must, in all likelihood, combine both of these elements while keeping in mind the structure and principles of the system. There seems little doubt that the trends of the last fifty years must be continued and that the Government must be given greater control of the House. At the same time it is highly desirable that some of the rules which restrict the private member should be relaxed to give him greater freedom in the use of the time which is supposed to be his. It is not the basic features of procedure which will have to be changed, rather it is the details.

Several improvements could be made to increase the work done by the House as a whole in the same amount of time. The Government in particular should make an effort to have its work properly organized before the session begins. When the Speech from the Throne is written all the major items of Government business have been settled. There is no possible excuse for delaying the introduction of this legislation, and yet, year after year, the Government introduces major items of business in the last month of a six- or eight-month session. Under these conditions the House may have to sit even longer—an unpopular choice—or rush the bills through. Doubtless there is no escaping these alternatives on occasion, when unusual situations require immediate solutions, but there is a strong suspicion that the Government does not dislike the idea of leaving the House on the horns of this dilemma.

Two other changes could be made which would affect members themselves more closely. The realization that they have a full-time job in Ottawa is long overdue. The real problem of parliamentary time today is the reluctance of the members to do a year's work for a year's pay. This reluctance appears in two forms. Some members, particularly those from the east and the west coasts who cannot get home on weekends, become restless after six or eight months in Ottawa and are quite willing to restrict debate on supply or on legislation in the interests of returning home. The Government knows this restlessness well and the knowledge assists materially in getting awkward legislation through the

House with a minimum of debate. It is true that time must be allowed for members to return to their constituencies, but periodic recesses could be allowed and a long summer recess could be planned.

More important, the primacy of their parliamentary employment must be brought home to those members from Ontario and Quebec who persist in spending long weekends at home. If Parliament is to make the best use of its time this notorious "Tuesday to Thursday" group must be eliminated. No change would be needed in the rules of the House. Under a standing order passed in 1867 every member is bound to appear at every sitting of the House and at all committee meetings. This rule has not been enforced for eighty years, but is still in the standing orders and could be applied should the House wish.

A final change which would save a large amount of time for the House would be the elimination of the lunch and dinner breaks. In a normal week the House rises once for lunch and three times for dinner, a loss of seven and a half hours. As the longest normal working day of the House is only five and a half hours, the total loss in each week is thus nearly one and a half sitting days. This loss is, of course, accentuated when the House sits longer hours and for six days a week near the end of the session. The elimination of meal breaks would not be popular among members, least of all, presumably, among those members who would then be scheduled to speak. It is a problem which was overcome in the United Kingdom many years ago, and which could be equally well met in Canada.

Several changes could also be made in the rules which would directly or indirectly benefit the private member. The notice of motion is the easiest way in which a private member can put forward his ideas to the House, but far too few opportunities are given for debate on these motions in the House. Three amendments could be made which would increase their effectiveness. First, before every day on which notices of motions are to be called, a ballot could be held for precedence in debate.[1] There is at present an element of farce in submitting forty or fifty notices of motions knowing that only the first half-dozen have any chance of being discussed. There is no particular advantage in giving precedence to the notices of motions which are submitted first (or, as now, to those submitted by the opening day of the session), and a ballot would give all such notices an equal chance on all days. Second, the time spent on any one notice of motion should be severely limited.

[1]The House has moved part way in this direction, but the practice does not extend far enough, and depends only on the Speaker's instruction rather than on a written rule.

Many notices are of limited interest and their subjects could be adequately covered in a period of, say, two hours. The result would be the discussion of three notices of motions each day instead of one as at present. Third, the length of speeches on notices of motions could be cut to twenty minutes for the mover and ten minutes for each of the other speakers. Combined with a two-hour limit on the debate, this reduction would mean that at least eleven speakers would be able to express their views on the subject raised, a number which, while not exhausting the resources of the House, would be adequate for most matters.

A final improvement might be made in the system of motions. There is no doubt today that the Government makes certain that virtually no private member's motion is passed. No matter how encouraging the Government sounds, and many times ministers may be found supporting such motions, there is always just one more Government backbencher ready with a speech at adjournment time so that the House does not have an opportunity to vote. The problem could be solved by adding to the rule a clause which provided a mandatory vote on these motions at the end of the limited time allowed for debate. Nothing would result from this vote of course, as the motions are so phrased as to be harmless except as an expression of opinion, but a vote would at least allow the sponsor an opportunity to gauge the support in the House for his ideas.

The other instrument at the disposal of the private member for making his legislative wishes known—the public bill—should also be improved. Here the change must come from the members themselves; it is not really dependent on a change in the rules of the House. There is no doubt that in the past the Government has been encouraged to make changes in the law as a result of public pressure in support of these bills, for though the bills may not have been passed, the Government itself finally took action. It is doubtful if this haphazard system of pressure is the best use of public bills, however. At any rate, the private members in Great Britain have used this same instrument in a different way. In the British House it is understood that in each session a few public bills will be debated, and probably passed. A ballot is held[2] and those who win have at least an opportunity of direct legislative action. On the other hand, the members who have this opportunity often (although not always) concentrate on achieving relatively small im-

[2]Now a feature of the Canadian House as well. Like the ballot on motions, it is held on the opening day, before the bills are introduced in the House, but exists only on the basis of a Speaker's instruction, and not on the rules.

provements in the general law. There is not the dispersal of effort on wide questions of policy on which there may be strong party divisions that we find in Canada. The result is that many aspects of the law in Britain have been improved by the private members of the House, whereas in Canada it is only an occasional member who can point to any success of his own beyond changing the name of his own constituency.

It would, perhaps, also be possible to relax the custom which surrounds the use of the adjournment of the House to discuss a matter of urgent public importance. This rule has developed in an unexpected way over the years, and has become a negligible factor in our procedure. This trend could be reversed merely by the Speaker's allowing more motions of this kind to go forward. Certainly on occasion the Opposition has tried to move the adjournment when it was unjustified, and when, for instance, a supply motion had been called for the near future. But on many occasions the adjournment has been refused on the grounds that the matter which the mover wanted discussed could be raised on estimates in supply or at some similar time. These opportunities are not always suitable and the House should be allowed a better method of concentrating debate on one particular subject. One further point should, perhaps, be made. The adjournment motion is essentially the weapon of a single member or a group of members. It should rarely be used by the leaders of the opposition, who have ample opportunity to decide what amendments are to be moved to supply motions or to make arrangements with the Government to debate specific issues. The back-bencher has none of these advantages, and the adjournment motion should be his substitute.

Two other changes could be made in the rule relating to these adjournment motions. The first was suggested by Mr. Speaker Fauteux and deserves more attention than it has so far had. It was that the debate on an adjournment motion should be postponed until the evening of the same day, when it could be debated for a suitable length of time without unduly disturbing the work of the House. A second change—a strict time limit on speeches—would enable more members to participate in the debate. If a subject is of "urgent public importance," a large number of members will want to speak on it, and most of them could say all that is necessary in ten or fifteen minutes.

Changes in the committee system of the House would also be of use to the private members. If specialized committees were eliminated, there would be no pressure on a member to belong to a large number of committees of interest to his constituents: he would then probably belong to only two or three and be able to give a proper amount of time to their work; and if the House went a further step and reduced the size of the committees, he would not need to belong to more than one. The combination of these two changes might have some unusual results. A member from a wheat-farming riding might be forced to spend part of his time examining a bill relating to the east-coast fisheries, and such an examination by a disinterested member might produce better results than a similar examination by an expert member with a well-developed set of prejudices. In any event, all the committees could be widely representative of all sections of the country.

Certainly, the House would be well advised to alter its method of electing committee chairmen. The post should be one of prestige, and should be looked on as a step towards something better. The chairmen should be picked from among the most able of the supporters of the Government, and, as the position does not require any excessive separation from active politics, should be able to look forward to political promotion, the best of them being kept as chairmen until one of the senior posts in the House itself became vacant.

One improvement in the committee system which could be made without any change in the rules would be the reference of virtually all Government legislation to standing committees. A few bills could be excluded—those consequent on the budget, and the appropriation bills —but if the remainder were sent to committee the pressure on the House would be lessened and the committees would gain a prestige which they lack today. If the specialized committees were eliminated and the committees themselves made smaller, there would certainly be enough members on them to do the job thoroughly.

Three exceptions could be made to this general change in committees. The Committee on Miscellaneous Private Bills could be maintained as a specialist committee to which all private bills were referred. The other two exceptions could be the Committee on Estimates and the Public Accounts Committee. These two have limited and well-defined functions to perform and should be maintained. Some features of these two committees could be altered. They could be increased in size slightly, and be authorized and encouraged to divide themselves into subcommittees. They could also be given a small staff to assist them in their investigations. In particular, the estimates as a whole could be referred to the Committee on Estimates with the power to examine any department or items it chose. A report could be submitted near the end of the session on the work the committees had been doing.

It is true that in the case of the Estimates Committee this report would probably reach the House after the items examined had been passed, but no one seriously expects the Estimates Committee to recommend savings. Its true value, and that of the Public Accounts Committee, is publicity and the collection of information. No Minister and no department welcomes adverse publicity and the ultimate result will probably be as favourable as if the House debated every report.

With these changes in favour of the private member, the Government must also have a few changes made which will enable it to do its work more efficiently. The most valuable change under present conditions would be a further limit on the length of speeches. A limit on speeches works two ways. It does shorten the speeches of a few, but it also has the opposite effect on some members to extend their speeches to the allowed limit. There is no doubt that the British House, with no official time limit, but with a strong tradition of brevity, has been more successful in limiting the length of speeches than has the Canadian House with a formal limit. Since it lacks such a tradition, the Canadian House could well re-examine the forty-minute rule: surely many would agree that thirty minutes in the House is adequate and twenty minutes on any item in Committee of the Whole. A further limit of ten minutes on any one item in Committee of Supply could be added, not of course to include the time taken for brief specific questions.

Along with a time limit on speeches in supply could go one or two more changes. The House should find it possible to agree on a generous over-all time limit for Committee of Supply. It need not yet be as strict as the limit imposed in the United Kingdom, but perhaps thirty-five days would be sufficient. Within this limit debate should be in the hands of the opposition parties, with the acknowledged right to raise such departments as they like. Undoubtedly there would be some initial friction between the opposition parties over the choice of departments. But this problem has been settled on other occasions, the most notable being the speaking roster in debate. In that case the Speaker chooses members from the opposition parties in a well-recognized and accepted rotation depending on the size of the parties on that side of the House. A similar agreement could surely be arrived at by the opposition whips for the debating of items in supply. If, indeed, the Committee on Estimates (and the other standing committees that examine estimates) prove to be a success, there seems little reason why the standing committees could not be left to discuss details of estimates and gather the minutiae so dear to the heart of a member, and why the House itself could not consolidate all of the estimates for each department under one heading and hold a general debate on departmental policy on that one item. Should the House not like this proposal, it might agree to limit the debate on the first item of the estimates to one day, so that the details could be reached in good time.

Two reforms could also be made in the procedure relating to the passage of bills to make the work of the House more efficient. The royal recommendation of a money bill is required under the constitution, but the preliminary resolution stage exists only in the rules of the House, and could be eliminated. The debate on the resolution is ill informed and, when it is not, is repeated in later debates. The argument that it is a protection of the House against executive or royal power is merely a historical relic, and the further argument that discussion is concentrated at this stage on the financial provisions of the bill is simply not true in Canada. The abolition of the resolution stage would merely eliminate days of repetitious debate.

If the resolution stage is not abandoned, at least the rules on relevancy and repetition should be rigidly enforced. They should also be applied at later stages to eliminate the repetition on second reading and on clause one in Committee of the Whole. The need here is not so much for new rules as for a proper application of the rules which exist today.

The Government and the House should also devise some protection against the flood of improper questions which deluge them. The most effective means would be the virtual abolition of the daily questions on the orders of the day. The right to ask such questions could be reserved, as the rules now allow, for questions of urgent national importance. A member wishing to ask such a question should be required to submit his question to the Speaker in advance and to give notice to the Minister of the department concerned. In place of the present daily oral questions, the time for starred questions could be extended to five days a week. No great notice would need to be given; but the questions would have to be submitted the evening before for printing on the Order Paper. They would have to be in a proper form and deal with a proper subject before they could be printed, and would, of course, be followed at once by supplementary questions. The principle of giving written answers to other questions would be preserved as it is at present.

Finally the Government must be given an efficient rule by means of which it can end debate on any motion within a reasonable time. The pipeline debate illustrated how inefficient the present closure rule is, and how unfair it can be to an Opposition. A new rule should be put in its place which will protect both sides of the House, a rule which is clearly worded so that the House will be certain what subsidiary motions, if any, are covered by a closure motion. It should provide specifically that all the clauses of a bill must be called at least, before the closure is applied on them. The House may feel that two days is not sufficient time to debate a motion under closure, and that more specific limits should be set for each stage of a bill and for substantive motions. Perhaps the House would prefer in the future to leave the final decision in the hands of the Speaker as it is in the United Kingdom. Whatever is done the rule cannot be abolished. It must be revised and improved.

Any new rules which strike deep at the rights of members must also be dependent for their success, indirectly if not directly, on the respect in which the Chair is held in the House. As restrictions on the rights of the House increase, the tact and impartiality of the Chair will become increasingly important. A change in the status of the Chair is probably the most important single step which could be taken at the present time. The changes in themselves might be relatively small, such as abolishing appeals or making the post of Speaker permanent, but they would in turn make possible more sweeping alterations in the rules themselves as they became necessary.

It may be desirable in the future to pass some stringent rules to limit debate. It may be necessary to put more power into the hands of the Speaker to enable him to enforce the rules on repetition, relevancy, and the reading of speeches. All such developments must, in the last analysis, depend on respect for the Chair. It is impossible to establish a tradition as easily as to pass a standing order. The Chair is one of the elements in Parliament which depends almost entirely on tradition for its success, and this must be built up slowly over the years.

Finally, as important as any factor in the whole development of parliamentary procedure is the parallel development of the attitudes and actions of members of the House. No set of rules, regardless of their skilful drafting and impartial application, can succeed if the feeling of the House or of any significant body of members is against it. The reluctance of members to remain constantly in Ottawa until their work is done has already been mentioned. But further changes in attitude will be needed. Relevancy, for instance, can be maintained only with a maximum of co-operation from all sides. The custom which requires speeches to be made extemporaneously rests on this basis also and can be enforced only with the goodwill of the members as a whole. The committee system can be changed, but the change will mean nothing if members persist in their refusal to attend meetings and if those who do attend go with preconceived ideas in their minds.

The development of the rules in the House of Commons of Canada has now entered a most interesting stage. After ninety-five years the House has evolved a set of rules, distinctively Canadian, but which is today barely adequate to its needs. The next phase of development will undoubtedly be one in which the rights of members to obstruct by means of virtually unlimited debate will be curtailed and the power of the Government to control the time of the House will be increased. The traditions of the Canadian House are against such a development, and it will not be easy. It is impossible to believe that members of Parliament are entirely insensible of the need for change. Leaving aside the perennial small group of eccentrics who will not accept any alterations in the rules no matter how innocuous, it should not be impossible to find enough members with the good of Parliament at heart to make a serious effort to improve procedure. This should not be a matter of Government *versus* Opposition. Change should not be considered as taking away "rights" or merely giving "power" to the Government. It should be a challenge to all members on all sides to find new ways of making Parliament do its work better.

The future, therefore, is uncertain. There is no doubt that today new rules are needed in the Canadian House. Parliament is still lost in a morass of detail and spends too little time on the really important issues of a session. This is a tendency which has been growing over ninety-five years and so far the necessary changes have been slow in coming. Considering the past it is possible to hope that the good sense and moderation of the House will be able to meet the challenge and that changes however small and slow will be made in time to meet the strains of the future. What is more important, however, is that the House should look now to the foundations of its future rules so that when new rules are passed it will be possible to make them truly effective.

ABSENTEEISM. *See* Attendance in House
Act of Union, 12
Addington, H., 55
Address to the Governor General for papers. *See* Papers presented to the House
Address in Reply to the Speech from the Throne, 95, 97–8, 102, 105, 110; length of debate, 14, 27, 28, 119, 138–40; length of speeches on, 28, 137n; amendments to, 109, 110, 139–40, 178, 180; closure used, 120n, 125, 126–7; time of divisions, 140
Adjournment, 166, 172–6
    not debatable, 168, 172–3, 176
    debatable, 172; by agreement, 173
    under Standing Order 26, 23, 173–6, 256; limitations, 79, 173, 174–5; suggested reforms, 175, 256
    See also: Motions, debatable; Motions, dilatory; Sittings of the House, hour of adjournment
Allocation of time. *See*: Address in Reply to the Speech from the Throne; Committee of Supply; Committee of Ways and Means; Limitation of debate
Amendments, 176–80, 237; previous question and, 120, 120n; in writing, 167; seconded, 167; numbers of, 176–7; content, 177, 178, 233; relevance, 177, 180; repetition, 178; money, 178–80; negative, 178, 233. *See also*: Hoists; Standing orders, amendments to
Anglin, T. W., 59, 60, 61, 62, 65, 66, 80
Anticipation, 109, 178, 180
Applewhaite, E. T., 74
Appropriation Act, 216, 257
Attendance in House, 89–90, 188–9,

254, 260–1; compulsory, 8, 89–90, 254; record of, 89
Auditor General, 211, 220, 226, 228

BAIN, T., 62
Balfour, Lord, 118
Bank Act, 233n
Bank of Canada, 156, 179
Bar of the House, 11, 31, 39, 40, 46, 49, 52, 89n, 205, 206, 248; examination of witnesses at, 30, 32, 45, 50–2
Beaubien, A. L., 186
Beauchesne, A., 153, 170
Beaudoin, L. R., 58, 63n, 64, 66, 68–9, 70, 71, 74, 84, 85, 104n, 165, 186n
Belcourt, N. A., 62n
Bennett, R. B., 37–8, 59, 129
Bilingualism, influence on procedure, 12, 61–3, 166, 167, 187, 187n, 233–4, 247
Bills
    Government: sent to standing committees, 14, 233, 257; defined, 19n; in Committee of the Whole, 229; first reading, 229, 230–1; second reading, 229, 233; third reading, 229, 235; introduction, 230–1; sent to special committees, 233; committee stage, 233–4; Senate amendments, 235–6; affecting prerogatives of Crown, 231
    money, 7; introduction, 27, 108, 231–3, 259; first reading, 233; second reading, 233
    private: revision of rules relating to, 18, 19, 26; defined, 19n, 242–3; fees, 22, 243, 244; divorce, 39, 98, 206, 238, 240, 243, 248, 250, 251; in standing committee, 203; sent to standing committee, 207, 247, 248–9, 257; introduction, 243,

12, 253. *See also* Address in
Reply to the Speech from the
Throne
Speeches: length of, in House, 5, 22,
24, 25, 27, 28, 119, 133–7, 144,
258; extemporaneous, 6, 104–6,
260; relevance, 23, 109–10, 121,
130, 237, 259, 260; length of, in
Committee of the Whole, 27, 28,
119, 135–7, 144, 258; length of,
in House (exceptions), 27n; number of, in Committee of the
Whole (suggested limitations), 27,
136, 137, 144; order of speakers,
103–4, 169, 176, 258; quotations,
106–8; repetition, 108–9, 259, 260;
speaking twice, 167; length of
(suggested limitations), 214, 255,
256, 258
Sproule, T. S., 15n, 62, 62n, 64, 65,
68n, 69
"Spying strangers." *See* Privilege, exclusion of strangers
Standing Committee on Agriculture
and Colonization, 194–5, 197–8,
203n
Standing Committee on Banking and
Commerce, 19, 248
Standing Committee on Contingencies,
195
Standing Committee on Debates, 198
Standing Committee on Estimates, 144,
170, 195, 202n, 216, 228, 257–8;
establishment of, 217–21; powers
of, 221; procedure in, 221–3; func-
tions of, 221, 222
Standing Committee on Expiring Laws,
195n
Standing Committee on External
Affairs, 195, 225–6
Standing Committee on Forests, Water-
ways and Waterpower, 195
Standing Committee on Immigration
and Colonization, 194
Standing Committee on Industrial and
International Relations, 195
Standing Committee on Industrial Rela-
tions, 195, 225n
Standing Committee on Marine and
Fisheries, 195, 198, 208, 225n
Standing Committee on Mines, Forests
and Waters, 195, 208, 225n
Standing Committee on Mines and
Minerals, 195

Standing Committee on Miscellaneous
Private Bills, 19, 98n, 202, 243,
248, 257
Standing Committee on Privileges and
Elections, 40, 41–2, 48, 50, 80,
84, 191
Standing Committee on Public Accounts, 36n, 45, 199n, 204n, 205,
226–7, 228, 257–8
Standing Committee on Railways,
Canals and Telegraph Lines, 19,
196, 223n, 225n, 246, 248
Standing Committee on Standing
Orders, 19, 218, 245, 246, 247,
249, 250–1
Standing Committee on Veterans
Affairs, 195, 200, 225n
Standing committees: size of, 14, 25,
195–7, 209, 257; change in rules
relating to, 19, 26; defined, 194;
powers of, 194; appointment,
194–5; names of (1867), 194–5;
names of (1962), 195n; quorums
of, 195–7, 209; party representation on, 197; sectional representation on, 197–8, 210, 256–7; chairmen of, 198–9, 227, 249, 257;
functions of, 208–9; possible reforms, 209–10; Government bills
sent to, 233, 257; private bills
sent to, 247, 257; reports on private bills, 249
estimates sent to. *See*: Estimates, sent
to committee; Standing Commit-
tee on Estimates
See also: Witnesses; and individual
committees by name
Standing orders: defined, 8; method of
amendment, 15; development,
21–8
amendments to, caused by third
parties, 25, 26, 213–14
amendments to, recommended by:
standing committees, 19, 218, 244,
246, 250–1; Government, 19–20,
123, 131n, 212; back-bench members, 20, 25, 26, 138–9, 185, 195,
196–7, 217–19; Speaker, 20, 27,
94, 136, 137, 150, 175, 220, 256;
Clerk of the House, 94, 138, 150,
168, 175, 186
amendments to, recommended by
committee: *of 1876*, 15, 17, 22,
96; *of 1887*, 18, 19; *of 1903*

INDEX OF RULES AND
STANDING ORDERS CITED